Hippocrene U.S.A. Guide to

BLACK AMERICA

*A Directory of Historic and Cultural Sites
Relating to Black America*

Marcella Thum

HIPPOCRENE BOOKS
New York

The author wishes to thank the many librarians, archivists, curators, historians—and friends—for their assistance in collecting the material for this book. And a special thanks to my sister, Gladys Thum, for her never-ending moral support.

My gratitude is great, but the errors in the book—hopefully few—are my own.

Copyright © 1991 by Marcella Thum

All rights reserved.

For information, address:
HIPPOCRENE BOOKS, INC.
171 Madison Ave.
New York, NY 10016

Library of Congress Cataloging-in-Publication Data available.

ISBN 0-87052-045-8

Printed in the United States of America

Hippocrene U.S.A. Guide to

BLACK
AMERICA

CONTENTS

INTRODUCTION

For many years there have been missing pages in history books about America. These were the pages that told of the part that black Americans played in the development of our country. Today, historians are filling in those missing pages, but information about historic and cultural sites of significance to black America is still lacking from guidebooks of the United States.

Visitors to Washington, D.C., rush from the Lincoln Memorial to the Washington Monument, most of them unaware that only a few miles from the Washington Monument is a National Historic Site dedicated to another great American— Cedar Hill, the home of Frederick Douglass, justifiably called the George Washington of black America. Tourists to historic Boston visit the Old Granary Burying Ground, where three signers of the Declaration of Independence are buried. How many of them know that in the same cemetery is also buried Crispus Attucks, a black man and the first man to be killed in the Boston Massacre.

How many visitors to the Art Institute of Chicago realize that not far away is the DuSable Museum of African-American history? Or that there are many other unique black museums, such as the Black American West Museum in Denver, Museum of African-American Art in Los Angeles, Great Blacks in Wax Museum in Baltimore and the George Washington Carver Museum at Tuskegee.

Admittedly, during the days of slavery and the long, hard years afterward, black men and women had neither the wealth nor leisure to look back upon their own heritage and culture and try to preserve what they could for their children and their children's children. Unfortunately, many black landmarks have long been erased by time. Often only a plaque remains to mark the spot where an historic event in American history took place in which Afro-Americans were involved.

Times do change, however. The Smithsonian Institution is planning a National African-American Museum on the Mall in Washington, D.C. And in recent years, a growing number of museums have been formed—or already established landmarks and art and history museums have been refurbished—honoring African Americans, their African heritage, and the vital role they played in the shaping of this nation. Some of the museums are small, run by a dedicated group of volunteers; others, like the Museum of African American History in Detroit and the National Museum of African Art in Washington, have large, professional staffs and are housed in modern facilities.

This guidebook, though, is not just a listing of black history and art museums and museums with good African-American heritage exhibits. Included are naval ships and battlefields where African-Americans fought in America's wars, military museums with exhibitions on the role of the black soldier, Western forts where the black Buffalo Soldiers were stationed, and towns established and run by black citizens.

The tragic story of slavery is retold at plantations, such as Carter's Grove in Virginia, where costumed guides interpret how slaves actually lived and worked, and still existing Underground Railroad Stations used in America's first concerted effort to help fugitive slaves escape to freedom. The struggle for civil rights, the memorials and monuments to such martyred leaders as Dr. Martin Luther King, Jr., the historic civil rights march from Selma to Montgomery, Alabama, are also highlighted in the guidebook, along with a select list of black colleges and churches.

Not only places connected with great black leaders like Douglass and King, George Washington Carver and Booker T. Washington, are listed, but sites connected with less known black men and women like musicians W. C. Handy and Scott Joplin, black voodoo queen Marie Laveau, the black explorer York, trail blazer James Beckwourth, writer Paul Dunbar, abolitionists Sojourner Truth and Harriet Tubman, scientist Benjamin Banneker, educator Mary McLeod Bethune, and sports figures Jackie Robinson and Joe Louis are included among the many, many others who are part of the black experience in America.

Information on Afro-American heritage tours of a city, where available, is also provided. For those travelers wanting to research further into their heritage, a select list of archives and libraries with good black American research collections is given.

The sites are arranged alphabetically by state along with location, a brief description, hours of operation, and cost of admission, if any.

Since hours and days of the year during which exhibits are open, as well as admission charges, are subject to change, it is always best to phone or write ahead to check these details. If arrangements are made in advance, special tours often can be provided for small groups.

Finally, although visits to these landmarks should be of special interest to black Americans, they would be of equal, if not more, benefit to all Americans. For only by learning as much as possible about each other, sharing the mutual experiences and heritage of all our many peoples, can America one day be truly indivisible, with liberty and justice for all.

ALABAMA

BIRMINGHAM

ALABAMA SPORTS HALL OF FAME, Birmingham-Jefferson Civic Center, 1 Civic Center Plaza, highlights careers of some of Alabama's great black sports figures such as Joe Louis, Jesse Owens, Hank Aaron, Willie Mays, and John Stallworth, among others. Athletes in the Sports Hall of Fame are showcased in many sight-and-sound exhibits, honoring the role they played in Alabama's sports history. There are also films of great sports moments and memorabilia from the athletes, themselves.
Wed.–Sat. and holidays 10–5, Tues. and Sun. 1–5. Closed Dec. 25 and Jan. 1. Adults $1.50, students and seniors 75 cents, under 6 free.
BIRMINGHAM MUSEUM OF ART, 2000 8th Avenue N, includes primitive, pre-Columbian, Asian as well as African and Indian art and artifacts.
Tues.–Sat. 10–5, also Thurs. 5–9, Sun. 1–6. Closed Dec. 25 and Jan. 1. Free.
KELLY-INGRAM PARK, 5th Avenue N at 16th Street, is closely associated with the civil rights movement in Birmingham. The park served as the assembly point for many major marches, demonstrations, rallies and prayer services. It was from a Birmingham jail that Dr. King wrote his famous letter. A statue of Dr. Martin Luther King, Jr., stands in the

park, across the street from the SIXTEENTH STREET BAP-
TIST CHURCH (northwest corner of 6th Avenue and 16th
Street N). On September 15, 1963, during the racial unrest, a
fatal bomb explosion at the church, killing four little girls,
became a turning point in the civil rights protest in Birmingham. The church is open by appointment only.

The future home of the City's Civil Rights Museum will be
across from the park.

CARLTON

HAL'S LAKE, off Clarke County Road 19, was named
during the mid-1800s for a courageous ex-slave who aided
runaway slaves from Mississippi. Runaways took refuge at the
lake before traveling north.

MT. NEBO BAPTIST CHURCH AND CEMETERY,
near Hal's Lake off Clarke County Road 19. Also called
Effigy Cemetery, this unique cemetery has several grave
markers that bear the likeness of the person buried beneath
them. A black artist, Isaac Nettles, cast the death masks and
made the markers in the late 1800s. Ironically his own grave is
not even noted with a simple slab.

DECATUR

MORGAN COUNTY COURTHOUSE, formerly Old
Decatur Courthouse, at the corner of Ferry and Cain streets,
was the scene of the famous retrial of the Scottsboro Boys in
1933. This case brought about the landmark Supreme Court
decision that a defendant has the right to be judged by a panel
of his peers, with the result that black Americans could no
longer be excluded from jury service.

FLORENCE

W. C. HANDY HOME AND MUSEUM are at 620 West College Street. The log cabin in which W. C. Handy, "the Father of the Blues," was born November 16, 1873, has been restored as it might have appeared when Handy lived there with his mother and minister father.

Behind the restored home is a museum containing many mementos of W. C. Handy's life, including sheet music, photographs, souvenirs and the actual piano on which he composed the "St. Louis Blues." His famous golden trumpet may also be seen.

Tues.–Sat. 9 noon and 1–4. Closed Jan. 1, July 4, Thanksgiving and December 23–25. Adults $1, under 18, 25 cents.

ST. PAUL A. M. E. ZION CHURCH on Cherokee Street, was founded in 1860. Both W. C. Handy's grandfather and father served as pastors here. An original stained glass window, given to the church by Handy's father, can still be seen.

GULF SHORES

FORT MORGAN is located at Fort Morgan State Park, 21 miles west of Gulf Shores on AL 180 at the entrance to Mobile Bay. FORT GAINES is directly opposite, on E. Bienville Boulevard, on Dauphin Island and may be reached by bridge on AL 163, or ferry. Both forts were the sites of an important Civil War naval battle in which black sailors were engaged.

Fort Morgan and Fort Gaines guarded the strategic Confederate seaport of Mobile. In August 1864 a Federal fleet, led by Admiral Farragut of "Damn the torpedos, full speed ahead" fame, attempted to pass the forts and came under heavy attack. Among the black infantry, naval, and artillery men under his command was John Lawson, who served on board the Admiral's flagship, the *Hartford.*

When an enemy shell from a Confederate ironclad exploded in the midst of a six-man gun crew Lawson, though wounded, refused to go below. He remained at his station until the battle was won and the forts were surrendered. By the end of the war five black sailors had been awarded the Congressional Medal of Honor. John Lawson was one of them.

One-fourth of the sailors in the Union navy were African-Americans, serving as firemen, landsmen, seamen and all ranks short of petty officers.

Today, both Fort Morgan and Fort Gaines have been restored much as they were during the Civil War with gun emplacements and other relics, and each houses a museum containing old photographs, uniforms and naval battle displays.

The forts are open daily 9–5, closed Jan. 1, Thanksgiving and Dec. 25. Adults $2, seniors and ages 6–15 $1. There is a ferry that runs from Fort Morgan to Dauphin Island.

HUNTSVILLE

ST. BARTLEY PRIMITIVE BAPTIST CHURCH, 3020 Belafonte Avenue, N.W. was organized in the late 1820s by the Reverend William Harris. It is one of the oldest African-American church buildings in Alabama.

LEESBURG

CEDAR HILL METHODIST CHURCH, off U.S. 411 and AL 68, is the Mother Church of Methodism, founded in 1830 by a slave named Moses Hampton. The hill upon which the church stands formerly belonged to the Cherokee Indians who allowed Hampton and a band of settlers from the Carolinas to camp on the land.

MOBILE

U.S.S. *ALABAMA* BATTLESHIP PARK is located 1½ miles east of the town on I-10, Battleship Parkway exit. The U.S.S. *Alabama* and the submarine U.S.S. *Drum* participated in many World War II battles in the Pacific. The black W-Division served aboard the *Alabama,* mainly as stewards and cooks, although during engagements they had the dangerous job of handling the powder that was hoisted up to the big guns.

Segregation in the armed forces continued into World War II although black sailors faced less discrimination in the merchant marine, where they served on the small, crowded Liberty ships. Eighteen of these ships were named for black heroes. A small contingent of blacks also were accepted as pilots in the air force. Segregation in the armed forces was officially ended by President Truman . . . at least on paper . . . by Executive Order 9981 in 1948.

Visitors may tour the battleship *Alabama* and the submarine *Drum* as well as a B-52 bomber and World War II fighter planes.

The park is open daily 8 to sunset, closed Dec. 25. Ticket office closes 1 hour before sunset. Adults $5, ages 6–11 $2.50.

THE FINE ARTS MUSEUM OF THE SOUTH, in Langan Park on Museum Drive, has a good collection of African art.

Tues.–Sun. 10–5. Closed Mardi Gras Day, July 4, Thanksgiving and Dec. 25. Free.

MAGNOLIA CEMETERY, at Ann and Virginia streets, is a national cemetery containing the remains of Union soldiers killed during the attack on Fort Blakeley in 1865, during the capture of Mobile. Among them are the black soldiers of

General Hawkins' First Division. By the end of the Civil War 186,000 black soldiers had fought in more than fifty-two major military engagements and hundreds of minor skirmishes.

Also buried in Magnolia Cemetery is Bettie Hunter (1852–1879), who was born a slave but became an affluent businesswoman. The beautiful, Italian-style home in which she lived at 504 St. Francis Street, is not open to the public.

SLAVE MARKET SITE, at the corner of St. Louis and Royal streets, is where slaves were displayed and sold. It received the last cargo of slaves brought to the United States aboard the slaveship *Clotilde* in 1859.

STATE STREET A. M. E. ZION CHURCH, 502 State Street, was built in 1854. One of the largest churches constructed for a black congregation prior to the Civil War, it is the oldest Methodist church in Mobile.

ST. LOUIS STREET MISSIONARY BAPTIST CHURCH, 108 North Dearborn, was one of only four black congregations established in Alabama before 1865. The present building was completed in 1872.

MONTGOMERY

ALABAMA DEPARTMENT OF ARCHIVES AND HISTORY at 624 Washington Avenue, State Capitol Complex, exhibits a unique collection of portraits honoring famous Alabamians, including noted black citizens.

Mon.–Fri. 8–5, weekends 9–4:30. Closed on major holidays. Free.

ALABAMA STATE UNIVERSITY, LEVI WATKINS LEARNING ARTS CENTER, has a special archives which includes the letters and papers of Dr. E. D. Nixon, a leader in the Montgomery bus boycott. Other black history items are also displayed in the center.

Mon.–Wed. 8–6, Thurs.–Fri. 8–9, Sat. 8–6, Sun. 1–6. Free.

CIVIL RIGHTS MEMORIAL is located at the corner of Washington and Hull streets on the grounds of the Southern Poverty Law Center. The nation's first memorial to martyrs of the civil rights movement was dedicated November 5, 1989. The impressive round black granite table beneath a cascading fountain was designed by Vietnam Memorial artist Maya Lin. Important events of the civil rights movement, as well as the names of 40 people who died in the struggle for racial equality from 1955 to 1968, are inscribed on the stone.

DEXTER AVENUE KING MEMORIAL BAPTIST CHURCH at 454 Dexter Avenue was organized in 1878 and held its meetings in a building once used as a slave-trading pen, giving it the name of the Slave Pen Church. Black churches have always played an important role in social reform and the fight for civil rights. Several churches in Montgomery were involved in the civil rights movement, but it was from the pulpit of the present Dexter Avenue building that Dr. Martin Luther King, Jr., a very new pastor of the church, preached his philosophy of passive resistance and nonviolence during the Montgomery bus boycott of 1954.

A unique mural in the church depicts major events in Dr. King's life and leaders in the fight for black civil rights. A historic marker on the church grounds highlights events of the struggle.

Mon.–Fri. 8:30–noon and 1–4:30, weekends by appointment. Free.

COURT SQUARE, 1 Court Square, was used before the Civil War for slave, cotton and land auctions. On December 1, 1955, Rosa Parks boarded a Montgomery City bus directly across the street from the fountain in the square. She sat in the seating reserved for white patrons and was arrested, thus starting a citywide bus boycott by the black citizens of Montgomery.

During the Selma to Montgomery civil rights march in 1965, demonstrators passed Court Square on their way to demonstrations at the capitol. The ALABAMA STATE CAP-

ITOL, 1 Dexter Drive, was built in 1851. The first capitol of the Confederacy, the building has interior staircases which are the work of Horace King, a noted black bridge builder.

A brochure of the sites along the historic civil rights march from Selma to Montgomery may be obtained from the Alabama Bureau of Tourism, 532 South Perry Street, Montgomery, Al 36104.

OLD ALABAMA TOWN HISTORIC DISTRICT, 310 North Hull Street. Not all slaves worked on plantations. Many worked in the city. Old Alabama Town is a restored neighborhood, showing visitors what life was like in these homes in the 1850s. Among the houses open to the public is the ORDEMAN-SHAW townhouse with slave quarters above the kitchen. The simple but sturdy furniture was constructed by the slaves themselves. THE FIRST COLORED PRESBYTERIAN CHURCH in the Old Town District was built in 1890 when the black and white Presbyterians of Montgomery separated. It is one of the few black churches that has been restored to its original state.

Mon.–Sat. 9:30–3:30, Sun. 1:30–3:30. Closed Jan. 1, Thanksgiving and Dec. 25. Tours begin with an audio-visual presentation at Lucas Tavern and cover nine more historic buildings. Tape tours: adults $5, ages 6–18 $2.

OLD SHIP A. M. E. ZION CHURCH, 483 Holcombe, was built in 1834 and in 1852 was given to its black members who rolled it on logs to its present location. Old Ship was the first black church in Montgomery.

ROOTS AND WINGS, 1345 Carter Hill Road, houses an art gallery, theater and book store which showcases black painting and graphic arts. Lectures and films are scheduled throughout the year and the works of famous African-American writers are displayed.

Mon.–Sat. 10–6. Closed Sun. and major holidays. Free admission to art gallery and book store.

WORLD HERITAGE MUSEUM, 119 West Jeff Davis Avenue, exhibits special black-related events in the area as

well as photographs and history of the civil rights movement in Montgomery.
Open by appointment.

OAKVILLE

JESSE OWENS MONUMENT, off AL 157, is dedicated to the memory of black Olympic athlete Jesse Owens (1913–1980). After breaking three world track records at college athletic meets, he set so many track records at the 1936 Olympics in Berlin, Germany, that he destroyed Hitler's claim of the "Aryan superiority" of his German athletes.

PLATEAU, EAST MOBILE

CUD-JOE LEWIS MEMORIAL, 506 Bay Ridge Road, stands in front of the Union Baptist Church. The *Clotilde,* the last slave ship to arrive, illegally, in the United States (import of slaves was forbidden after 1808) reached Mobile, Alabama, in 1859. The 130 black men, women and children aboard had been stolen from a Tarkar village in West Africa. Because the ship's captain was unable to sell his captives, they were finally freed when the Civil War started. Unlike other slaves who were sold separately and seldom saw people from their own native village again, the Tarkars managed to stay together. Under the leadership of Ka Zoola (Cud-Joe Lewis), they formed a village called Africa Town. They retained their African customs, kept their Tarkar names, and spoke the Tarkar language among themselves. Many of their descendants remain in Plateau today.
PLATEAU CEMETERY, across from the Union Baptist Church, is the final resting place of Cud-Joe Lewis, along with others aboard the *Clotilde.*

PRICHARD

AFRICA TOWN, U.S.A. STATE PARK, northeast of
Mobile, in the process of being developed, will be the first
park in the United States acknowledging African-American
history and, in particular, the last slave ship, *Clotilde*, to arrive
in the country.

SELMA

BROWN CHAPEL A. M. E. CHURCH, 410 Martin
Luther King Street, founded in 1867, served as headquarters
for black protestors during the civil rights movement. On
March 7, 1965, 525 demonstrators, seeking to overturn
Southern voting barriers, left Brown Chapel and marched
along U.S. 80 from Selma to Montgomery, the state's capital.
They were stopped by police officers at the EDMUND PET-
TUS BRIDGE, which spans the Alabama River, intersection
of Broad Street and Water Avenue. The violent confrontation
at the bridge injured 87 marchers and outraged the nation.
Two weeks later the marchers, joined by the Reverend Martin
Luther King, Jr., and armed with a federal court order, completed their journey. The Selma to Montgomery march led to
the passage of the 1965 Voting Rights Act. A monument to
Dr. Martin Luther King, Jr., stands in front of Brown Chapel.
The chapel is open by appointment only.
OLD CITY HALL, Franklin Street, served as the jail in
which Dr. King and the civil rights protesters were imprisoned in 1965. The nearby WILSON BUILDING is decorated with striking murals of black life.
OLD DEPOT MUSEUM, foot of Water Avenue, runs the
gamut from Civil War to civil rights, including mementos of
Dr. Martin Luther King, Jr., the Nobel Peace Prize winner,
and the much earlier black leader Benjamin Sterling Turner, an
ex-slave who became Selma's first black Congressman during

Reconstruction. A monument to Turner may be seen in the OLD LIVE OAK CEMETERY, AL 22, West Dallas Avenue, where many former slaves and prominent Selma residents are buried.

Mon.–Fri. 10–12 and 2–4. Free.

Brochures of the Black Heritage Tour through Selma can be obtained at the Selma/Dallas County Chamber of Commerce, 513 Lauderdale Street.

TALLADEGA

TALLADEGA COLLEGE, 627 West Battle Street, established in 1867, was the first college opened in Alabama to all persons, without regard to race. THE SAVERY LIBRARY on campus houses the famous Amistad Murals of the Cinque mutiny, painted by black artist Hale Woodruff.

In 1839 fifty-three kidnapped Africans were chained aboard the *Amistad,* a Spanish slave ship headed for Cuba. Led by Cinque, son of a Mendi chief, they broke their chains, overthrew their captors and took over the ship. Finally captured by a U.S. Navy brig, Cinque and his men were taken to New Haven, Connecticut, to stand trial. Lewis Tappan, a man who hated slavery, formed a committee to raise money to defend the Amistad Africans. Spain demanded that the United States return the Africans and the case finally reached the Supreme Court. John Quincy Adams, who had been the sixth president of the United States, defended the Amistad mutineers and won. Cinque and the others were returned to their homes in Africa a year later.

The three-panel murals on display in Savery Library catch the drama of the battle aboard the slave ship and the sharp psychological tension of the courtroom scene. All but four of the faces were painted from portraits done from contemporary sketches.

Savery Library is open to visitors during the regular school year. Closed summers but can be seen by appointment Mon.– Fri. 9–4. Free.

TUSCUMBIA

ALABAMA MUSIC HALL OF FAME, AL 72W, pays tribute to Alabama's musically talented natives. Visitors can walk through a giant 1950s style jukebox, and check out jazz to rock, country to pops. Composers, songwriters, singers are all honored in the Hall of Fame Room which includes such notables as Nat King Cole and W. C. Handy.
Mon.–Sat. 10–6, Sun. 1–5. Adults $6, seniors and students $5, children 6–12 $3, under 6 free.

TUSKEGEE

TUSKEGEE INSTITUTE NATIONAL HISTORIC SITE, 1212 Old Montgomery Road. The historic site includes THE OAKS (Booker T. Washington's home), THE GEORGE WASHINGTON CARVER MUSEUM and the TUSKEGEE UNIVERSITY CAMPUS with more than twenty-seven landmarks associated with Carver and Washington.
On July 4, 1881, twenty-five-year-old Booker T. Washington and thirty young men and women gathered in a one-room shanty to open Alabama's first normal school for the training of black teachers. The original brick buildings, including The Oaks, were built and designed by the students themselves, and the school eventually became the Tuskegee Institute, now Tuskegee University. Washington was a strong believer in learning by doing and in the importance of vocational education—beliefs which brought him into conflict with other black leaders, such as William E. B. DuBois, who believed that black students should be educated beyond voca-

tional subjects. Nevertheless, under Washington's leadership, Tuskegee Institute became one of the outstanding black colleges in the country.

THE OAKS, Washington's home on campus, is now a museum. The restored rooms look much as they did when Washington lived in the house.

Tours scheduled at 9, 10, and 11 and 2, 3, and 4 daily. Closed major holidays. Free.

If Booker T. Washington had accomplished nothing else in his lifetime, his bringing a black scientist by the name of George Washington Carver to Tuskegee would have given him a place in history books. Born a slave 1860-1864, his exact birth date unknown, at Diamond Grove, Missouri (the site is now a National Historic Monument), Carver was thirty years old before he graduated from Iowa State College. In 1896, Washington brought him to Tuskegee to start an Agriculture Department, where he remained for over sixty years. Carver did more than teach students. He developed practical ways for farmers in Alabama to improve their soil and income by switching from cotton to other crops like soybeans, sweet potatoes and peanuts. He also invented an amazing number of valuable products that could be made from these crops—300 byproducts from peanuts alone—and he became one of the most famous scientists of his day. George Washington Carver and Booker T. Washington are both buried in the UNIVERSITY CEMETERY at Tuskegee.

The GEORGE WASHINGTON CARVER MUSEUM on the Tuskegee campus has a replica of Carver's early laboratory, personal mementos of his life, and exhibits of the results of his research. A biographical film is shown. The museum also contains an art gallery with examples of African art and sculpture. Maps for a walking tour of the historic Tuskegee campus may be obtained at the visitor center of the museum.

Daily 9–5. Closed Jan. 1, Thanksgiving and Dec. 25. Free.

THE DANIEL "CHAPPIE" JAMES CENTER FOR AEROSPACE SCIENCE on the Tuskegee University campus houses the university's Department of Army and Aerospace Sciences as well as a memorial hall for General Daniel "Chappie" James, who became the country's first black four-star general.

Mon.–Fri. 9–noon and 1–4, weekends by appointment. Free.

MOTON FIELD/TUSKEGEE ARMY AIR FIELD, located at Tuskegee Municipal Airport off Chappie James Drive, has been called the "Home of Black Aviation." C. Alfred Anderson inspired the founding of the School of Aviation at Tuskegee University and trained 966 blacks who became military aviators. The pilots in the original 99th Squadron performed so well they were joined by the 100th, 301st, and 302nd black fighter squadrons.

TUSKEGEE UNIVERSITY LIBRARY has the Booker T. Washington Collection of archival material and many books and artifacts by and about black Americans.

Mon.–Thurs. 8 a.m.–10 p.m., Fri. 8–4:30, Sat. 12–4, Sun. 2–10. Free.

For brochure "Alabama's Black Heritage" and other travel information about Alabama, contact:

Alabama Bureau of Tourism and Travel
532 S. Perry Street
Montgomery, AL 36104
1-800-ALABAMA

ARIZONA

CAMP VERDE

FORT VERDE STATE HISTORIC PARK is near the center of the town off I-17. In April 1885 a company of black troopers from the 10th Cavalry were sent from Texas to Fort Verde, which served as a base in General Crook's campaign against Geronimo and the Chiricahua Apaches. The last battle in north central Arizona between Apaches and cavalrymen took place in 1886 at Battle Ground Ridge, thirty five miles east of Fort Verde.

There are four restored structures from the old fort and an interpretative center/museum with Indian, pioneer and military artifacts from the Indian Wars.

Daily 8–5. Closed Dec. 25. Adults $1, under 18 free.

PHOENIX

ARIZONA HALL OF FAME MUSEUM, 1101 West Washington, honors people who have made significant contributions to Arizona in changing exhibits. The first black woman to be inducted into the Arizona Women's Hall of Fame was Vernell Myers Coleman, in 1990. For more than forty years, Mrs. Coleman worked to improve living conditions not only in the housing project in which she lived, but for the poor and elderly throughout Phoenix. One of her

most noteworthy accomplishments was reviving the June-
teenth celebration in Phoenix, commemorating June 19, 1865,
when black slaves in Arizona and Texas first learned that they
had been freed by the Emancipation Proclamation.
   Mon.–Fri. 8–5. Closed holidays. Free.
   ARIZONA STATE CAPITOL MUSEUM, 1700 W. Washington. The 1938 addition to the Arizona state capitol, on the
third floor of the research library, contains eight colorful
murals of the history of Arizona, painted by Jay Datus. One
depicts the black guide Estevan, the first man other than
Indians to explore the territory that is now New Mexico and
Arizona.
   Daily 8–5. Closed holdiays. Free.
   HEARD MUSEUM, 22 E. Monte Vista Road, specializes
in the cultural history of the American southwest and also has
exhibits of African art and artifacts.
   Mon.–Sat. 10–5. Sun. 1–5. Adults $3, over 65 $2.50, children and students $1.

SIERRA VISTA

   CORONADO NATIONAL MEMORIAL, on Mon-
tezuma Canyon Road, which joins AZ 92 about 20 miles west
of Bisbee, 22 miles south of Sierra Vista. Francisco Vasquez de
Coronado led the first European military reconnaissance expedition into the American Southwest in 1540. However,
Estevan the Black (also known as Estevanico) and Father
Marcos de Niza had already explored the region the year
before. Estevan acted as de Niza's guide and his mapping and
discoveries assured the success of Coronado's later expedition.
   Interpretative exhibits, viewing platform and visitor center
open daily 8–5. Closed Jan. 1, Thanksgiving and Dec. 25.
Free.
   FORT HUACHUCA MILITARY BASE is at the mouth

of Huachuca Canyon in the city of Sierra Vista and may also be reached from Huachuca City. The fort is 70 miles southeast of Tucson, following I-10. Take Fort Huachuca exit at AZ 90 to main gate. The historic fort was founded in 1877 and is the nation's oldest active cavalry post.

Black troops from the fort played a major role in the capture of Geronimo, the Apache leader, in 1886. The black 10th Cavalry served at the fort for twenty years and joined General Pershing in his punitive expedition into Mexico in pursuit of Pancho Villa. During World War II, the all-black 92nd Division trained here before being sent overseas.

FORT HUACHUCA MUSEUM occupies two buildings at Boyd and Grierson avenues in the Old Post, which is just to the west of present-day Fort Huachuca. The Old Post retains many of its original buildings and the museum has an outstanding collection of uniforms, weapons, saddlery and memorabilia from the times when the U.S. Cavalry . . . and the Buffalo Soldiers, as the Indians called black troopers . . . ruled the West. There is a statue to these early black troopers at the main gate.

Museum open daily 8–5. Closed federal holidays. Free.

TOMBSTONE

TOMBSTONE, on U.S. 80, first gained fame as a silver-mining town, but it is best known today as the site of the battle of the O.K. Corral, between the Earps and the Clantons. Black, as well as white, prospectors came west to try their luck at gold and silver mining and Tombstone, in its heyday, was a lusty, brawling town.

One of its sheriffs was John Slaughter, and one of his cowhands was John Swain, who had been born a slave and came west after the Civil War. Despite several near brushes with death in defense of his mining claim, John Swain lived to

a ripe old age and was buried with honor in the BOOTHILL
GRAVEYARD (Row 11).

Today, the town of Tombstone is a National Historic Landmark and many of its buildings have been restored, including
the Bird Cage Theater, O.K. Corral, and the Boothill Graveyard. The SILVER NUGGET MUSEUM, Allen and 6th
streets, contains fascinating exhibits about the history of
Tombstone.

Museum open daily 9–5. Closed Dec. 25. Adults $1, under
18 free.

WHITERIVER

FORT APACHE is four miles south of Whiteriver on the
Fort Apache Reservation. Black soldiers were housed at this
post under the command of General George Crook, during
the Indian Wars. Black troopers also left from this fort to join
the expedition against Pancho Villa in Mexico. Fort Apache is
now the site of the Theodore Roosevelt Indian School and
Apache Culture Center Museum. The museum also has uniforms, weapons and other military artifacts from Fort Apache.

Mon.–Fri. 8–5. Donations.

WILLCOX

FORT BOWIE NATIONAL HISTORIC SITE is an iso-
lated fort 22 miles south of Willcox, which is located on I-10.
Take secondary road AZ 186 from I-10 to a graded road
leading east into Apache Pass. The last 1½ miles must be
traveled on foot. Two of the eight cavalry regiments stationed
at this fort were black. The museum at the adobe ruins of this
old fort tells the story of a handful of black and white cav-

alrymen fighting to control a vast territory and defeat the determined Geronimo and his band of Apaches. Military and Indian artifacts may be seen at the museum.

Daily 8–5. Free.

For further information about Arizona, contact:

Arizona Office of Tourism
1100 W. Washington
Phoenix, AZ 85007
602-542-8687

ARKANSAS

CAMDEN

POISON SPRING STATE PARK, (BATTLE OF POISON SPRING) 10 miles west of Camden on AK 76, is the site of a Civil War battle in 1864, part of the Union army's Red River campaign in Arkansas. During the battle, Confederate forces overran a Union wagon supply train manned by the 1st Kansas Colored Regiment, then killed the captured and wounded black soldiers.

The 1st Kansas Colored Regiment had been the first black unit to see action in the Civil War at Island Mounds, Missouri. By the time the war ended, they ranked twenty-first among Federal regiments in percentage of total enrollment killed in action.

There is an historic marker at the site of the battle and a Confederate cemetery containing the graves of more than two hundred soldiers killed in the fight.

HELENA

PHILLIPS COUNTY MUSEUM is two blocks east of U.S. 49 (business) at Porter and Pecan streets. The Mississippi River port of Helena was besieged by Confederates in July 1863 in an attempt to relieve pressure on Vicksburg. Black soldiers of the 2nd Infantry Regiment of African Descent fought side by side with whites as they defended the city. As was often the case during the Civil War, more soldiers lost their lives to disease than to battle wounds.

Several historic monuments around town mark the battlesites. A Confederate cemetery occupies the heights of Crowley's Ridge overlooking the Mississippi River.

The PHILLIPS COUNTY MUSEUM devotes a large exhibit area to the Battle of Helena and the Civil War days in the town.

Tours Mon.–Fri. 1:30–4:30, Sat. 10–noon and 1–4. Closed holidays. Free.

LITTLE ROCK

LITTLE ROCK CENTRAL HIGH SCHOOL, 1500 Park Street, became the focus of nation-wide attention in the fall of 1957 when nine black students attempted to enroll in the previously all white school. The Supreme Court decision of 1954 outlawed racial segregation in public schools. However, it took President Eisenhower's use of troops at Little Rock to protect the students attempting to enter the school and enforce the court's order to desegregate "with all deliberate speed."

SHERIDAN

JENKINS' FERRY STATE PARK, (Battle of Jenkins' Ferry) 13 miles south of Sheridan on AK 46 (Leola Highway) was the site of battle in the Union army's Red River campaign in the spring of 1864. Retreating from Camden after the battle at Poison Spring, Union troops fought off an attack by Confederates as they crossed the flooded Saline River at Jenkins' Ferry. Their wounded and captured comrades had been killed by the Confederates at the earlier encounter and now the 1st and 2nd Kansas Colored regiments overran a Confederate battery shouting "Remember Poison Spring," and inflicted 150 casualties on the enemy.

More information about this battle may be obtained at the GRANT COUNTY MUSEUM, 409 W. Center Street, Sheridan.

Tues.–Sat. 9–noon and 1–5. Closed major holidays. Free.

PINE BLUFF

ISAAC HATHAWAY FINE ARTS CENTER at the University of Arkansas at Pine Bluff has a permanent exhibit entitled "Persistence of the Spirit." Through a series of panels, text, photographs and memorabilia, the exhibit chronicles the rich experience of black Arkansans from pioneer days prior to 1803 through 1986. Themes touch upon slavery, the impact of black labor, and the skill and creativity of black men and women in agriculture, politics, education, labor, business and religion. For three hundred years, black Arkansans have engaged with their world and helped to shape it. Against heavy odds, they have persisted.

"Persistence of the Spirit" is located in the West Gallery of the Fine Arts Center. A video is available by appointment which examines black history in Arkansas chronologically and suggests that blacks came to the state as early as 1541, in the company of Spanish explorer Hernando DeSoto.

Gallery open Mon.–Fri. 8:30–4:30, weekends by appointment. Free.

For further information about Arkansas, contact:

Arkansas Dept. of Parks and Tourism
1 Capitol Mall
Little Rock, AK 72201
1-800-628-8725

CALIFORNIA

BECKWOURTH

BECKWOURTH PASS In the 1840s, when wagon trains crossed the Sierra Nevada to reach the California gold fields, the wagons had to be taken apart and hoisted laboriously over the perpendicular cliffs of the towering mountains. That was until flamboyant black mountain man and explorer James Beckwourth discovered a pass through the Sierra Nevada in April of 1850. He led the first wagon train of settlers through it. After him, thousands of pioneers and gold seekers, trudging along beside their ox-drawn wagons, took his route into California. The pass is still used by modern-day motorists and may be found on CA 70, the spectacular Feather River Highway, just east of the junction with U.S. 395, several miles north of Lake Tahoe, California. A memorial to Jim Beckwourth was erected at the summit of the pass and a town 15 miles west on CA 70 is named after him.

JAMES BECKWOURTH'S CABIN is located on Rocky Point Road, south of CA 70, midway between the towns of Beckwourth and Portola. Beckwourth built the combination home and trading post in the Sierra Valley in 1852. There, emigrants traveling west could buy much needed food and fresh horses. Perhaps Beckwourth's most famous visitors were General Fremont and Kit Carson. Beckwourth drew a map on the floor of his cabin which helped guide the pathfinder west to California.

The cabin was also where Beckwourth dictated his memoirs which were later published. Like all mountain men, Beckwourth loved to exaggerate, yet his life was amazing enough without embellishment. A run-away slave from St. Louis, he went west with one of the first fur trapping expeditions, was captured by and lived with the Crow Indians, then he explored further west across the mountains, operating a trading post on the Arkansas River, among other places. He fought in the California revolt of 1845, owned a ranch near Taos, New Mexico, and found gold in California. He died among the Crow Indians and was given a chief's burial. The exterior of his cabin has been renovated.

PLUMAS COUNTY MUSEUM, 500 Jackson Street, in Quincy which is on CA 70, 35 miles west of Portola. Among its relics of pioneer times, this museum has a few rare artifacts connected with James Beckwourth, an original daguerrotype of the mountain man, his bullet mold made of stone, and his stirrups.

Mon.–Fri. 8–5, weekends 10–4, May–Oct. Rest of year Mon.–Fri. 8–5. Free.

CLAREMONT

CLARK HUMANITIES MUSEUM at Scripps College, 1030 N. Columbia Avenue, has an excellent African art collection, including the Wagner collection of African sculpture.

Mon.–Fri. 9–noon and 1–5. Closed holidays and summers. Free.

EARLIMART

COLONEL ALLENSWORTH STATE HISTORIC PARK is located 8 miles west of Earlimart on CA 43 between Fresno and Bakersfield. Allen Allensworth was born a slave in Kentucky in 1842 and was sold "down river" for attempting to learn to read and write. During the Civil War, he served in the Union navy and later, after becoming a Baptist minister, served as the first black chaplain to the all black 24th Infantry. He retired with the rank of lieutenant colonel, the first black man to receive that honor. He moved with his family to California in 1908 and with several friends established the town of Allensworth in the San Joaquin Valley, hoping that black residents could be self-sufficient there and free of the racial prejudice they faced elsewhere.

Although the town prospered as a small farming community, a critical water shortage forced settlers to leave. The town might have vanished completely, but in 1970 a bill was passed proposing that Allensworth, the only town in California founded, financed and governed by blacks, be preserved as a historical state park.

Buildings have been restored to reflect the early days of Allensworth, including the school, general store, a library, and several homes. The visitor center gives a video presentation of the history of the colonel and his town. Camping and picnicking are permitted. The visitor center and museum are open daily 10–3. Closed Jan. 1, Thanksgiving and Dec. 25. Day use free.

HOLLYWOOD, GREATER LOS ANGELES

MANN'S CHINESE THEATRE (formerly Grauman's) is at 6925 Hollywood Boulevard. This world-famous theater's cement courtyard features hand and footprints of more than one hundred and sixty motion picture stars. In 1967 Sidney Poitier became the first black actor to achieve this mark of respect.

In the early days of Hollywood movies, black actors and actresses maintained the stereotype of the ignorant, shiftless black man or the faithful "Mammy." Today their roles have

become more realistic, such as the proud, competent and compassionate man, whom Sidney Poitier played in the *The Lilies of the Field*, winning the coveted Oscar for best actor in 1965.
Courtyard open daily. Free.

LOS ANGELES

CALIFORNIA AFRO-AMERICAN MUSEUM at 600 State Drive, Exposition Park, has both permanent and traveling collections of art and artifacts relating to Afro-American life. The museum, designed by a black architect, also houses galleries, films, a research library, and a theater.
Daily 10-5. Closed Jan. 1, Memorial Day, Thanksgiving and Dec. 25. Free.
DUNBAR HOTEL CULTURAL AND HISTORY MUSEUM, 4225 South Central Avenue, is located in the first hotel owned by blacks in Los Angeles. When completely renovated, the first floor will be a museum consisting of art, artifacts, and memorabilia of the Afro-American jazz greats who appeared at the Dunbar in the 1920s.
East Los Angeles College, VINCENT PRICE GALLERY, at Monterey Park, has the actor's African art collection.
Open during school hours. Free.
EL PUEBLO DE LOS ANGELES HISTORIC PARK is in the heart of downtown Los Angeles, bounded by Alameda, Arcadia, Spring and Macy streets. The Spanish village of Los Angeles was founded here in 1781 by forty-four persons, twenty-six of whom were of African ancestry. A black man was mayor of Los Angeles in the 1770s. More than two hundred years passed before another black man, Thomas Bradley, took that office in 1973. Another black resident, Pio Pico, was governor of California in the 1840s.
Today the founding site of Los Angeles has been restored and contains historic buildings surrounding a plaza, cultural

exhibits and shops. One of the restored homes PICO HOUSE at 424-436 N. Main Street, was owned by Pio Pico, the last governor of California under the Mexican flag.

Free guided walking tours Tues.–Sat. at 10, 11, noon and 1, (except Thanksgiving and Dec. 25) from the visitor center in the Sepulveda House, 622 N. Main Street.

Park open daily 10–10 in summer, 10–7:30 in winter. Visitor center open Mon.–Fri. 10–3, weekends 10–4:30. Closed holidays. Free.

Golden State Mutual Life Insurance Company, 1999 West Adams, established in 1965 a showplace within their building for their AFRO-AMERICAN ART COLLECTION, both historic and contemporary. On the walls of the lobby are two famous murals by Hale Woodruff and Charles Alston. They depict the roles that black Americans, such as Estevan the explorer, James Beckwourth the mountain man, William Leidesdorff the first black millionaire in California, Mary Ellen Pleasant an early civil rights activist, and unknown black gold miners, pony express riders, and Buffalo Soldiers, played in the exploration and settlement of California. Also on display are drawings, paintings and sculptures by black artists of the Harlem Renaissance, such as Charles White's remarkable ink-and-wash portrait of Harriet Tubman.

Tours of the art collection may be arranged through the Public Relations Dept. of Golden State. Mon.–Thurs. 9–4, Fri. 9–11 a.m. Free.

LOS ANGELES COUNTY MUSEUM OF ART, 5905 Wilshire Boulevard, has the renowned Paul Tishman collection of African sculpture, as well as paintings by famous black American artists, such as Henry Ossawa Tanner.

Tues.–Fri. 10–5, weekends 10–6. Closed Jan. 1, Thanksgiving and Dec. 25. Adults $3, seniors and students $1.50, ages 5–12, 75 cents. Free on second Tues. of each month.

LOS ANGELES COUNTY NATURAL HISTORY MUSEUM, 900 Exposition Boulevard, has among its many ex-

hibits a diorama showing the first forty-four settlers to come to Los Angeles, including twenty-six African Americans.
Tues.–Sun. 10–5. Free
MUSEUM OF AFRICAN AMERICAN ART, 4005 Crenshaw Boulevard, third floor, consists of an archives/library and museum of traditional sculpture for southeast and west Africa, including soapstone sculpture of the Shona people. There are also works by contemporary black artists from the United States, the West Indies, and South America. The collection includes audio-visual media and original historic documents.
Thurs. 12–8, Fri.–Sat. 11–6, Sun. 12–5. Free.

OAKLAND

EBONY MUSEUM OF ART, INC., 1034 14th Street, has an extensive collection of over five thousand antiquities from Africa, paintings by African Americans, and exhibits on black history.
Tues.–Sat. 11–6, and by appointment. Adults $5, children $2.
NORTHERN CALIFORNIA CENTER FOR AFRO-AMERICAN HISTORY AND LIFE, 5606 San Pablo, has books, photographs, documents, and artifacts covering the history of black Californians. There are guided tours, lectures, films, and changing exhibits.
Tues. 12:30–7, Wed.–Fri. 12:30–5:30, Sat. 11–4. Closed holidays. Free.
OAKLAND MUSEUM at 10th and Oak streets has almost one hundred and fifty works in its collection by black American artists and sculptors, including lithographs by Grafton T. Brown, one of the earliest black artists in California.
The contributions of black Americans to the settlement and growth of California are also well represented by exhibits in the Cowell Hall of California History depicting the stories of

Alvin Coffey, a successful black gold miner; Col. Allensworth, who founded a town in California; Captain William T. Shorey, the only black whaling captain on the Pacific Coast; and many others.

Guided tours are available. Open Wed.–Sat. 10–5, Sun. noon–7. Closed legal holidays. Free.

REDDING

SHASTA STATE HISTORIC PARK is 6 miles west of Redding on CA 299. It was to this gold town that black gold miner Alvin Aaron Coffey came to earn enough money to buy freedom for himself and his family. His first master had brought Coffey from Missouri to California in 1849 and promised him his freedom for one thousand dollars but then reneged on his word. Back in Missouri, his second master allowed Coffey to return to California to once again try to dig enough gold to buy his freedom. After three years in the mines at Shasta, Coffey earned the seven thousand dollars he needed to set his entire family free. In later years Coffey became a respected farmer at Red Bluff (he is buried at the OAK HILL CEMETERY there) and the only black man in the Society of California Pioneers.

Coffey, however, was not the only black gold miner in '49. The first black miner to "round the Horn" to California was Waller Jackson who dug gold at Downieville. Other sites where blacks dug for gold included Placerville, Grass Valley, Negro Bar, and Mormon Hall. At Mokelumne Hill, when a black miner asked white prospectors where to dig, they pointed to what they thought was a barren hillside in town. However, the happy black miner returned with a sack of gold.

At HORNITOS GOLD MINING CAMP, 14 miles off CA 49 North, Moses Rodgers, another slave who bought his freedom, made his fortune not from gold but from quartz. He owned a group of mines near Quartzburg and became a well-known mining engineer in California.

Today historic gold mining camps may still be seen along CA 49 (from Oakhurst to Yuba Pass) about three hours' drive from San Francisco. The best way to tour the region is from south to north. There are gold rush museums at Auburn, Angels Camp, Mariposa, Grass Valley, Placerville, Mokelumne Canyon and Sonora.

The GOLD RUSH MUSEUM at Shasta State Historic Park, where Coffey worked the mines, is located in an old courthouse.

Daily 10–5, March–Oct.; Thurs.–Mon., rest of year. Closed Jan. 1, Thanksgiving and Dec. 25. Adults $1, ages 6–17, 50 cents.

SACRAMENTO

CALIFORNIA VIETNAM VETERANS' MEMORIAL, 15th and L. streets, east end of State Capitol Park. Built entirely with donations, the twenty-two black granite panels memorialize more than five thousand Californians, dead and missing in the Vietnam War. The full-relief bronze figures depict the human reality of daily life during the Vietnam conflict. Vietnam was America's first war fought with a fully integrated military force, and as the conflict was brought home on television screens, the black soldier became "highly visible" for the first time.

ST. ANDREW'S AFRICAN METHODIST EPISCOPAL CHURCH, at 2131 Eighth Street, organized in 1850, was the first A. M. E. church on the Pacific coast. The first public school for blacks, Indians and Orientals was held in the basement of the church. The present attractive building was built in 1951.

In 1852 the second A. M. E. church west of the Mississippi was opened at 916 Laguna Street, San Francisco.

SAN FRANCISCO

BARRY'S TOURS AND CRUISES, 610 Webster Street, Suite 8, conducts Black History Tours of San Francisco.

MISSION SAN FRANCISCO DE ASIS (Mission Dolores) is at 16th and Dolores streets. Priests at Spanish missions scattered across California were among the earliest settlers in the state. At San Carlos Mission (near Monterey) Ignacio Ramirez, a slave who had bought his freedom, was given the first Christian burial by the Catholic church in California in 1771. Father Junipero Serra officiated. At Mission Dolores may be found a memorial stone marking the grave of William Leidesdorff. Leidesdorff, of Danish-black parentage, was the first millionaire in California and maintained a lavish home in San Francisco. The city's first wharf, at Leisdesdorff and California streets, was named for him.

SAN FRANCISCO AFRICAN-AMERICAN HISTORICAL AND CULTURAL SOCIETY is located at Fort Mason Center, Bldg. C, Room 165, Buchanan Street and Marina Boulevard. This West Coast-based black museum consists of African-Haitian artifacts, art by Sargent Johnson and other Afro-American artists, as well as Civil War-era and other historical collections. Guided tours, films, gallery talks, concerts.
Wed.–Sun. 12–5. Closed holidays. Adults $1, children 50 cents.

SANTA CLARA

DE SAISSET MUSEUM on the Santa Clara university campus has an excellent African art exhibit in its collection. Tues.–Fri. 10–5, weekends 1–5. Closed holidays. Free.

WHITTIER

PIO PICO STATE HISTORIC PARK, 6003 S. Pioneer
Boulevard, contains the restored home of Pio Pico, the black
governor of California in the 1840s. Unfortunately, the thir-
teen-room house, built in the 1850s, is closed temporarily due
to earthquake damage.
   Park opens Wed.–Sun. 9–5. Closed Jan. 1, Thanksgiving,
and Dec. 25. Free.

For further information about California, contact:

California Office of Tourism
PO Box 9278, T98
Van Nuys, CA 91409
1-800-862-2543

COLORADO

BRECKENRIDGE

BARNEY FORD HILL, just southeast of the city limits, is named after black miner Barney Ford, a fugitive slave who came to Colorado in 1860 in search of gold. With his friend Henry O. Wagoner, Ford filed a gold claim on a hill outside of Breckenridge. The seam was supposedly so rich that jealous white miners jumped the claim and forced Ford and Wagoner to leave. Ironically, despite years of searching, no gold was ever found in Barney Ford's Hill, as it is still known today. Barney Ford and his friend fared much better than the claim jumpers. They started several successful businesses in Denver, including the Inter-Ocean Hotel, barbershops and restaurants. Barney Ford also lobbied in Washington, D.C., to make sure that when Colorado entered the Union, her black citizens would have the right to vote.

CENTRAL CITY

CENTRAL CITY OPERA HOUSE on Eureka Street was the pride of the town, which in its hey-day was one of the wealthiest gold mining camps in Colorado. Black women as well as men came to Central City to seek their fortune. One of these women was Clara Brown, who found her fortune not in gold but in running a laundry. She used her wealth to bring thirty-eight of her relatives west.

Believed to be the first black resident of the territory of Colorado, Clara Brown was a member of the Colorado Pioneers Association. At her death, the Aunt Clara Brown Chair was dedicated and placed in the Central City Opera House, along with other hickory chairs carved with pioneer names. The Opera House, with its crystal chandeliers and murals, still holds performances.

Tours daily 11:30–4, May–June and Aug.–Oct. Tickets $3.

COLORADO SPRINGS

PRO RODEO HALL OF FAME, 101 Pro Rodeo Drive, west of I-25, exit 147, covers the history of rodeo and honors its champions with art, audio-visual programs and memorabilia. In Heritage Hall, which traces the evolution of the modern rodeo, may be found an exhibit on Bill Pickett. One of the earliest of black rodeo riders, Bill Pickett developed a unique form of steer wrestling that involved biting the lip of the steer before wrestling it to the ground. Bill Pickett can also be found in the Hall of Champions which displays trophies and tack belonging to the greats of professional rodeo. In his day Pickett was an international rodeo rider and was called "the greatest sweat and dirt cowhand that ever lived, bar none."

Daily, 9–5 Memorial Day–Labor Day, rest of year 9–4:30. Closed holidays. Adults $4, seniors $3.75, ages 5–12 $1.25.

U.S. AIR FORCE ACADEMY, 12 miles north on I-25, opened in 1954 and prepares students for careers as officers. Near the Cadet Chapel may be found a statue honoring the Tuskegee Airmen, the first black air force pilots who were trained at Tuskegee Institute (now Tuskegee University) and flew as fighter pilots in World War II. Sixty-six of these pilots were killed in aerial combat and another thirty-two were shot down and captured as prisoners of war. Black airmen returned home with 150 Distinguished Flying Crosses.

A self-guiding tour map of the grounds is supplied at the visitor center. Daily, 9–6 June–Aug.; rest of year 9–5. Free.

CRAIG

THORNBURGH BATTLEFIELD SITE is 17 miles south of Craig on CO 13, then left 11 miles to a side road and right 0.6 mile to the site. A granite shaft has been erected where Major Thornburgh and 160 troopers were pinned down by a war party of Ute Indians in 1879. Over fifty-six men were killed or wounded before messengers managed to sound the alarm and a troop of the all black 9th Cavalry under Captain Francis Dodge slipped in among Thornburgh's men during the night. With the help of these Buffalo Soldiers, the Indians were held off for three more days until reinforcements arrived and drove them away.

One of the 9th Cavalrymen, Sergeant Henry Johnson won the Medal of Honor for risking his life during this engagement while caring for the wounded. In the thirty years that the Buffalo Soldiers served on the frontier, fourteen noncommissioned officers won the Congressional Medal of Honor for their courage under fire.

DENVER

BLACK AMERICAN WEST MUSEUM AND HERITAGE CENTER is located at 3091 California Street in Denver's Five Points historic district. This one-of-a-kind museum was founded by Paul Stewart, who spent years researching the little-known role of black Americans in frontier days. After the Civil War, thousands of blacks headed west as prospectors, stagecoach drivers and fur trappers, as well as cowhands. One-fourth of the men who rode behind the great herds of cattle during the western drives of 1866–1895 were black.

The museum houses thousands of artifacts of the early black pioneers, as well as photographs and taped interviews. The first gallery showcases blacks in the West during the nineteenth century and the second displays memorabilia of blacks who contributed to early Denver history. The mementos range from the rodeo artifacts of Bill Pickett, the first black man to be elected to the National Cowboy Hall of Fame, to saddles, branding irons and cowboy buffalo coats. There is even a photograph of Mary Fields, a gun-toting pioneer in Cascade, Montana, who was the second woman ever to drive a U.S. mail coach. The museum also provides guided tours and traveling exhibits.

Wed.–Fri. 10–2, Sat. 12–5, Sun. 2–5. Adults $2, seniors $1.50, 12–17, 75 cents, children 50 cents.

DENVER ART MUSEUM, at 100 W. 14th Avenue, has works from nearly every culture and period in history including excellent pieces of African art and sculpture.

Tues.–Sat. 10–5, Sun. 12–5. Closed holidays. Adults $3, over 65 and students $1.50, under 6 free.

COLORADO HISTORY MUSEUM, 13th and Broadway, next to the Civic Center, has exhibits and dioramas on Colorado history, fur trade, pioneer days, the gold rush and more. There is an exhibit on African-American history.

Mon.–Sat. 10–4:30, Sun. 12–4:30. Closed Thanksgiving and Dec. 25. Adults $2.50, seniors and ages 6–16 $1.

FORT GARLAND

OLD FORT GARLAND MUSEUM is on the south edge of town at U.S. 160 and CO 159. Most of the 9th Cavalry that was transferred from Texas in 1875–1876 were stationed in New Mexico, but one company of Buffalo Soldiers ended up at Fort Garland. The fort was primarily a supply point and served as a deterrent to Indian hostilities. Abandoned in 1883, it has been restored as a military museum.

Mon.–Sat. 10–5, Sun. 1–5, Memorial Day weekend through Labor Day; rest of year by appointment. Adults $2, over 65 and ages 6–16 $1.

PUEBLO

EL PUEBLO MUSEUM, at 905 S. Prairie Avenue, has a full-size reproduction of Old Fort Pueblo. Also known as the Gantt-Blackwell Fort, it was built in the autumn of 1842 by fur traders near an important fording point over the Arkansas River. James Beckwourth, the black fur trader who was active in beaver trapping along the Arkansas River, is among the traders credited with its founding. The fort became such a thriving community that Beckwourth dubbed it Pueblo, meaning town. Mountain men, trappers, traders, Indians and immigrants passed through this crossroads post until 1854 when a raiding band of Ute Indians destroyed the fort.

The replica of the fort is complete with adobe walls, sentry posts, living quarters, blacksmith shop and stable.

Tues.–Fri. 10–5, Sat. 10–2, Memorial Day through Labor Day; rest of year Wed.–Sat. 11–3. Adults $2, 65 and ages 6–16 $1.

WRAY

BEECHER ISLAND BATTLE MARKER, on CO 53, marks the site where Colonel Forsyth and fifty soldiers were trapped and held under siege for eight days by several hundred Indians. Without medical supplies and food, and with very little water, the command was rescued by the all black 10th Cavalry, garrisoned at Fort Wallace, who rode a remark-

able eighty-five miles in forty-eight hours. The site is marked
by a cement monument and five gravestones.

For further information about Colorado, contact:

The Colorado Tourism Board
1625 Broadway
Denver, CO 80202
1-800-433-2656

CONNECTICUT

BRIDGEPORT

HOUSATONIC MUSEUM OF ART, Housatonic Community College, 510 Barnum Avenue (I-95 exit 28) has an expanding collection of African and Asian art and artifacts, along with contemporary Hispanic art and pieces by contemporary white and black Connecticut artists.
Mon.–Thurs. 8 a.m.–9. p.m., Fri. 8–4. Free.

CANTERBURY

PRUDENCE CRANDALL HOUSE MUSEUM is at the junction of CT 14 and CT 169. An active Underground Railroad ran through Connecticut before the Civil War, leading escaped slaves to freedom. Nevertheless, when Prudence Crandall admitted Sarah Harris, a young black girl, to her Private Academy for Girls in 1832, the white students were withdrawn by their parents. Prudence Crandall decided then to reopen her school and instruct "young ladies and misses of color," thus establishing the first black female academy in New England. Students came from many states to her school.
When a Black Law was passed by the Connecticut General Assembly, making it illegal to instruct black students who were not residents of the state, Prudence was arrested, imprisoned and brought to trial. Although she was released, her

students were harassed and finally the building, itself, was attacked by a mob. Concerned about the safety of her pupils, Prudence regretfully closed her school and left Canterbury, although she continued teaching throughout her long life. Years later, in atonement for the wrong done her, Prudence was voted a small yearly pension by the state lawmakers.

Today the PRUDENCE CRANDALL SCHOOL has turned into a museum with permanent and changing exhibits on Prudence Crandall, and the black experience in pre-Civil War Connecticut. A research library is open to the public for in-house study.

Wed.-Sun. 10–4:30, Jan. 15 through Dec. 15. Closed Thanksgiving. Adults $2, seniors and children $1.

FARMINGTON

Not all captured black people submitted to slavery without a fight. Some fifty-five slave mutinies at sea were recorded for the years 1699–1845. One occurred in 1839 when fifty-three slaves under the leadership of Cinque, the son of a Mendi chief, took over the Spanish slave ship *Amistad*. Captured by a U.S. Navy brig, Cinque and his men were taken to New Haven, Connecticut, to stand trial. The case finally reached the Supreme Court where the Africans were defended by John Quincy Adams who won their acquittal.

Joseph Cinque and his rebel slaves lived in Farmington from 1839 to 1841, before and after their trial. There they attended the FIRST CHURCH OF CHRIST, CONGREGA-TIONAL, at 75 Main Street, and were taught English in a small church school. After their acquittal, local citizens supplied them with money to return to Africa.

Unfortunately, during their stay in Farmington, one of the African rebels, named Foone, drowned while swimming. He is buried in the FARMINGTON CEMETERY and a marble headstone erected by the townspeople marks his grave.

Church open Mon.–Fri. 8–4, tours by request. Free.

GROTON

FORT GRISWOLD STATE PARK, Monument Street and Park Avenue (I-95 exit 85) is the site of the 1781 massacre by British troops under Benedict Arnold, who attacked the garrison men, leaving eighty-five Americans dead.

One of the defenders of the fort was a black man, Jordan Freeman, who killed a British major. Another black soldier, Lambert Latham, killed a treacherous Tory officer who bayoneted the American commander after he surrendered. Both Freeman and Latham died in the massacre.

GROTON MONUMENT, on the hilltop near Fort Griswold, is dedicated to the victims of the massacre and bears a tablet with their names. The tablet also shows Jordan Freeman killing British Major Montgomery. Many emplacements remain and there are historical displays in the museum.

Park open year round. Monument and museum are open daily 9–5, Memorial Day–Labor Day; Labor Day–Columbus Day, weekends only. Free.

HARTFORD

HARRIET BEECHER STOWE HOUSE is at 73 Forest Street, adjacent to the Mark Twain House. Harriet Beecher Stowe was inspired to write *Uncle Tom's Cabin* to "show what an accursed thing slavery is." The book, which told of slave life in Kentucky from the viewpoint of the slaves, was published in 1852 and quickly became a best-seller, as well as a very popular stage play. Thousands of people began to sympathize with, and join, the abolitionists. Few slaves, however, accepted their mistreatment with the Christian martyrdom of Uncle Tom. Perhaps a more realistic character is the escaped slave in the book, George Harris, who was perfectly willing to fight and die to protect his wife and son.

The restored Stowe house contains many furnishings and mementos of the author.

Tues.–Sat. 9:30–4, Sun. noon–4; Mondays also June through Columbus Day and December. Adults $6.50, ages 6–12, $2.75. Admission covers Stowe and Mark Twain house.

MYSTIC

MYSTIC SEAPORT MUSEUM is along the Mystic River on CT 27, ¾ miles south of I-95 exit 90. There are seventeen acres of historic homes, shops and buildings, as well as a wooden whaling ship, which may be toured by visitors in this nationally acclaimed "living" museum. More than one hundred other ships and boats are on display along with ship models, scrimshaw, figureheads and other artifacts from the mid-nineteenth century seaport.

Blacks were actively involved in the whaling industry, and both manned and built ships. It was a black metalsmith, Lewis Temple, who invented a more efficient whaling harpoon, called a "toggle harpoon." A future exhibit is planned at the museum which will focus on the role of African-Americans and other minorities and their experience at sea.

The complete complex, including the museum, is open 9–5 early April–late Oct., 9–4 rest of year. Limited hours on holidays. Adults $12.50, ages 5–18 $6.25, children under 5 free.

NEW HAVEN

CONNECTICUT AFRO-AMERICAN HISTORICAL SOCIETY, 444 Orchard Street, is a research center and museum dedicated to collecting, preserving and circulating exhibits on the significance of Afro-Americans in the building of

Connecticut and America. Displays include The Black Man and the Sea; Black Women in America, past and present; Blacks in the Old West; Black Scientists.

Mon. 11:30–1:30 and by appointment. Free.

MUSEUM OF THE NEW HAVEN HISTORICAL SOCIETY, 114 Whitney Avenue near Trumbell Street, has a portrait of Joseph Cinque who led the *Amistad* mutineers. The portrait was painted for Robert Purvis, a prominent black abolitionist in the nineteenth century. New Haven is approximately thirty miles from Farmington, where Cinque and the other mutineers lived for two years. Other research material available at the museum's library concerns the role that blacks have played in the history of Connecticut and of America.

Tues.–Fri. 10–5, Sat.–Sun. 2–5. Closed holidays. Museum free, library $2.

Sterling Memorial Library, Yale University, has the JAMES WELDON JOHNSON MEMORIAL COLLECTION OF NEGRO ARTS AND LETTERS, one of the most important black research collections in the country. James Weldon Johnson was not only a prominent black author, he was a lawyer, civil rights leader, diplomat and successful song writer. His popular "Lift every voice and sing" became a national anthem for black people.

The collection is so huge that it is only possible to name a few of the more important items, such as the original manuscripts from authors of the Harlem Renaissance, a complete collection of spirituals and blues, as well as original musical scores by outstanding black composers like Henry Burleigh.

As with other scholarly collections, the research material is not available to the general public. However, there are constantly changing exhibit areas within the library.

Open during regular academic year. Closed during August and university recesses. Free.

UNITED CHURCH-ON-THE-GREEN, Temple and Elm streets, is where Henry Ward Beecher preached to Captain Line's antislavery company of eighty men as they were starting out for Kansas in 1855. New Haven was a haven for escaped slaves before the Civil War. TEMPLE STREET CHURCH, with its black pastor, was one of several Underground Railroad stations.

Tues.–Thurs. 9:30–4:30.

NORWICH

SLATER MEMORIAL MUSEUM AND ART GALLERY, off CT 2 at 108 Crescent Street, has an excellent collection of African art.

Mon.–Fri. 9–4, weekends 1–4, Sept.–June; Tues.–Sun. 1–4 rest of year. Closed holidays. Free.

STRATFORD

CAPTAIN DAVID JUDSON HOUSE, 967 Academy Hill, has slave quarters in its cellar. Slave holding in the North was less prevalent than the South, and slave quarters rarely remain to be seen today. In many cases household slaves in the North did not occupy a separate building but lived in the family house, as in the Judson house. The inventory of the Judson estate in 1775 listed seven slaves, valued at 267 pounds. The house has been restored and furnished as it was in colonial days, with a collection of farm and craft tools in what was once slave quarters.

Wed., Sat. and Sun. 11–4, April 15–Oct. 31; and by appointment. Adults $2, children and seniors $1.50.

WASHINGTON

JUDEA CEMETERY has the grave of Jeff Liberty, a slave who volunteered to serve in the Revolutionary War and joined the black Connecticut Regiment. Slaves who fought in the war were given their freedom, as was Jeff Liberty. His grave marker reads: "In remembrance of Jeff Liberty and his colored patriots."

For further information about Connecticut, contact:

State of Connecticut Dept. of Economic Development
865 Brook St.
Rocky Hill, CT 06067-3405
1-800-CTB-OUND

DELAWARE

DOVER

JOHN DICKINSON PLANTATION, boyhood home of the colonial patriot, is 6 miles south of Dover on U.S. 113, then ½ mile east on Kitts-Hummock Road. Known as the "Penman of the American Revolution," Dickinson owned slaves but believed in their gradual formal emancipation. In 1777 he freed all his slaves on the condition that they serve him for a period of twenty-one years in exchange for food, clothing, shelter and remuneration. In 1785 he freed all his slaves unconditionally. After they received their freedom, many continued to reside in log dwellings on Dickinson's farm. Today the plantation has been restored to its early eighteenth-century appearance and visitors can see how slaves and freed blacks lived and worked in the house and fields.

Tues.–Sat. 10–4:30, Sun. 1:30–4:30. Guided tours. Closed holidays. Free.

RICHARD ALLEN MARKER at Lockerman and Federal streets was dedicated in 1990 to the founder of the Free African Society. Richard Allen was a Delaware slave who bought his freedom and that of his wife and moved to Pennsylvania. Rather than worship in a segregated church, he started the Mother Bethel A. M. E. Church in 1794 in Philadelphia. Allen became the first bishop of the A. M. E. church in 1816 and spoke out strongly against sending free blacks to colonize settlements in Africa, saying, "We were stolen from our mother country and brought here. We have tilled the ground and made fortunes for thousands . . . This land which we have watered with our tears and blood is now our mother country."

WOODBURN MANSION, at King's Highway and Pennsylvania Avenue, is today the Governor's Mansion, but was at one time used as an Underground Railroad station. Delaware was a border state and Dover residents were divided on the slavery issue as were the rest of Delaware's citizens. Nevertheless, many prominent families in Dover helped runaway slaves. A marker at the mansion tells of its history.

Scheduled tours of the Governor's Mansion may be arranged by groups. 2:30–4:30 Saturdays. Free.

WILMINGTON

AFRO-AMERICAN HISTORICAL SOCIETY OF DELAWARE, 512 East 4th Street, sponsors activities and exhibits relating to black history and culture. Check with them for information about currently scheduled events.

Mon.–Fri. 1–5. Free. (302-652-1313)

DELAWARE MUSEUM OF NATURAL HISTORY, 5 miles northwest on DE 52 (greater Wilmington). Exhibits include information on the natural history of Africa, with the Hall of Mammals displaying a variety of lifelike African wildlife.

Mon.–Sat. 9:30–4:30, Sun. noon–5. Closed holidays. Adults $3.50, seniors $2.50, children $2.

CRADLE OF AFRICAN-AMERICAN POLITICAL LEADERSHIP MONUMENT, C St. and New Castle Avenue, honors black political leaders of the twentieth century.

FORT CHRISTINA PARK, at the foot of 7th Street, is where the Swedes first landed in 1638, the first permanent settlement in the Delaware Valley. The next year Delaware's first black man, Black Anthony, slave to Governor Johann Printz, arrived at Wilmington. A marker at Fort Christina Park tells of Black Anthony.

Historic log house within the park is open Mon.–Sat. 8:30–4:30, Sun. 1:30–4:30. Free.

MOTHER AFRICAN UNION METHODIST PROTESTANT CHURCH, 812 North Franklin Street, was established in 1813 by Peter Spencer, a freed black. THE PETER SPENCER PLAZA, French Street between 8th and 9th streets, was named for the minister who also began the AUGUST QUARTERLY FESTIVAL. The festival dates back to the 1700s when slaves were let free one day every year. Today the celebration continues in August with church revivals, craft fairs and food.

Also in the plaza there is a MONUMENT TO THE UNDERGROUND RAILROAD and to the courage and resourcefulness of Railroad conductors like Harriet Tubman and Thomas Garrett, a Wilmington businessman. Before the Civil War, a busy Underground Railroad ran a regular north-bound route through Delaware. Almost three thousand slaves were spirited away to free soil by the underground movement.

OLD TOWN HALL MUSEUM, 512 Market Street Mall, has on display a silver service given by the colored people of Wilmington to a local abolitionist Thomas Garrett, in recognition of his work with the Underground Railroad. There is also a draft wheel used during the Civil War to choose men to serve in the Union army. The last set of draft tickets pulled were for black men, listed as "colored" or "slave," but the war ended before they could be called up. Other exhibits give information on the black community and the part it played in the Delaware of the 1890s.

Tues.–Fri. noon–4, Sat. 10–4. Closed major holidays. Donations.

For further information about Delaware, contact:

Delaware Tourism Office
99 Kings Hightway, P.O. Box 1401
Dover, DE 19903
1-800-441-8846

DISTRICT OF COLUMBIA

THE ANACOSTIA MUSEUM, Museum of Afro-American History and Culture, is located at 1901 Fort Place, S.E. in Fort Stanton Park. The B-4 metrobus stops in front of the museum, in the historic Anacostia section of southeast Washington.

A branch of the Smithsonian Institution, the Anacostia began as a neighborhood museum and has become one of the outstanding African-American collections in the country. There are constantly changing exhibitions on Afro-American life, history and culture. Past exhibits have included "Black Women: Achievements against the Odds" and "Out of Africa: From West African Kingdoms to Colonizations." An exhibition on the Harlem Renaissance told the story of the period in the 1920s when black artists, writers and musicians expressed their racial pride through their work.

The museum also has a research center and offers traveling exhibits, lectures, films and workshops on Black America.

Daily 10–5. Closed Dec. 25. Guided tours are offered Mondays through Fridays at 10 and 11 and 1. Group sizes should be limited to 35. Free.

ARLINGTON NATIONAL CEMETERY, directly across the Potomac River from Washington (actually in Virginia) was established in 1864 on the confiscated estate of Robert E. Lee.

Medgar Evers, a leader in the civil rights movement in Mississippi, is buried at Arlington. He was slain outside his home in Jackson, Mississippi, on June 12, 1963, and now he's with many other Americans who fought and died to preserve the highest ideals of this country.

Three of the best-known grave sites are the Tomb of the Unknown Soldier and the graves of President John F. Kennedy and his brother Robert. On the day that Medgar Evers was buried, President Kennedy forwarded to Congress a bill guaranteeing equal rights in public accommodations, thus giving the attorney general the power to sue for enforcement of the fourteenth and fifteenth amendments. The attorney general at the time was Robert Kennedy.

Daily 8–7, April–Sept., rest of year 8–5. A temporary pass to visit gravesites of friends or relatives may be obtained at the visitor center on Eisenhower Drive. Otherwise, tourmobiles that leave from the visitor center provide the only motorized transportation through the cemetery. A narrated tour covering all major points of interest is $2.50 for adults, ages 3–11 $1.25.

ASSOCIATION FOR THE STUDY OF AFRO-AMERICAN LIFE AND HISTORY, 1407 14th Street, N.W. Over the years blacks have been missing from the pages of America's history books. It was this association, founded in 1915, that began to promote black historical research which would fill those pages and explore the role that black people have played in America's history and in civilization. Today its large library and archives contains books, periodicals and manuscripts on black history and culture. The association publishes the *Journal of Negro History* and other publications relating to Afro-American life and history. The library and archives are open for scholarly researchers only.

The association also maintains the CARTER G. WOODSON home at 1538 9th Street, N.W. (not presently open to the public). Dr. Woodson founded the association and was one of the first black historians to research and write about the contributions which black citizens have made to the nation. Dr. Woodson also helped establish Negro History Week in 1926, now observed each February.

BENJAMIN BANNEKER CIRCLE AND FOUNTAIN is located at the Mall end of L'Enfant Promenade and Maine Avenue. During the colonial era, Benjamin Banneker was as famous a black scientist as George Washington Carver. An unschooled Maryland farmer, he made the first striking clock of wood in America. He taught himself mathematics and astronomy and assisted Andrew Ellicott in surveying and planning the new city of Washington, D.C. Banneker also published in 1792, an almanac which proved so useful that he became known as the Afro-American Astronomer.

BETHUNE MUSEUM AND ARCHIVES, at 1318 Vermont Avenue, N.W., a fully restored nineteenth century townhouse, was the last home of the noted black educator, Mary McLeod Bethune. Starting with only her "faith and a dollar and half," she founded in 1904 one of the outstanding black teacher-training colleges in the country at Daytona Beach, Florida. Mrs. Bethune was not only an educator and the founder of the National Council of Negro Women, she also became a highly respected advisor to four presidents and was a powerful force in the struggle for civil rights.

Five galleries within the house display photographs, manuscripts, paintings and artifacts covering the history and contributions of black women to America and the world. The archival collection documents the history of black women in the United States. Guided tours and access to the archives by appointment.

Tues.–Fri. 10–4:00, Sun. 12:30–4. Free.

MARY McLEOD BETHUNE MEMORIAL, a statue of the famous black educator, is located in Lincoln Park, East Capitol Street, N.E., between 11th and 13th streets. The statue shows Mrs. Bethune teaching two children. The statue was the first memorial honoring a black woman erected in a District of Columbia park.

BLACK HISTORY NATIONAL RECREATION TRAIL in Washington, D.C., is part of the National Trails System and tells the story of the black community in the nation's capital. For a free descriptive booklet of this trail and some of the sites which may be visited along the way, write the National Park Service, National Capital Region, 1100 Ohio Drive, S.W., Washington, D.C. 20242.

DECATUR HOUSE, 748 Jackson Place, N.W., the first private residence on Lafayette Square was built in 1819 for naval hero Commodore Decatur. In the 1830s the house passed into the hands of hotel owner and notorious slave trader John Gadsby. Slaves, destined to be sold in the back courtyard of the house, were kept chained in the attic while fashionable balls were hosted in the drawing room.

In the 1870s the house was sold and remodeled in the Victorian style. Today the elegant residence has Federal and Victorian furnishings.

Tours every half-hour, Tues.–Fri. 10–2, weekends noon–4. Adults $3, seniors and ages 6–18 $1.50.

THE EMANCIPATION PROCLAMATION at the Library of Congress, across the street from the capitol, off Independence Avenue, S.E., is the earliest of the three drafts that Lincoln read to his cabinet on July 22, 1862, and may be seen on permanent exhibit at the Library of Congress. Although the Emancipation Proclamation only freed slaves in territories not held by federal troops, there is no doubt that the document led to the end of slavery in the United States.

Exhibit areas open Mon.–Fri. 8:30 a.m.–9:30 p.m., weekends 8:30–6. Free.

EMANCIPATION STATUE, Lincoln Park, East Capitol Street between 11th and 13th Street, N.E. The statue of Abraham Lincoln holding the Emancipation Proclamation, along with a statue of a liberated slave breaking his shackles, was unveiled in 1876. Frederick Douglass read the proclamation aloud at the dedication ceremony. The memorial was almost completely paid for by funds donated by freed black men and women, and black soldiers who fought in the Union army during the Civil War.

EVANS-TIBBS COLLECTION OF AFRICAN-AMERICAN ART, 1910 Vermont Avenue, N.W., is housed in the home of Lillian Evans Tibbs, America's first black opera singer to gain international recognition, although her race barred her from singing at the Metropolitan Opera in New York. In the 1920s her home in D.C. was a gathering place for black artists and intellectuals and her patronage of African-American artists formed the nucleus of the art collection which has been expanded by her descendants.

Artists represented here include Richard Barthe, Romare Beardon, Jacob Lawrence, Charles White, Hughie Lee Smith, Charles Alston, and many more.

Wed.–Sun. 2–5 and by appointment. Free.

FORD'S THEATRE, 511 10th Street, N.W., is where President Abraham Lincoln was fatally shot by the actor John Wilkes Booth on April 14, 1865. The theater has been restored to its appearance on the night that Lincoln was assassinated. On the lower level is the Lincoln Museum which contains unusual mementos from Lincoln's life. Plays are once more being presented in the theater and the museum sometimes closes for rehearsals.

Daily 9:30–4:30. Museum free, charge for performances.

The house where Lincoln died is the PETERSEN HOUSE, 516 10th Street, N.W., across the street from Ford's Theatre. Lincoln was carried here after he was shot and the house has been restored to its 1860s appearance and is open to the public.

Daily 9–5. Closed Dec. 25. Free.

FREDERICK DOUGLASS NATIONAL HISTORIC SITE (Cedar Hill) is at 1411 W Street, S.E., overlooking the Anacostia Historic District. The Douglass home can best be reached from D.C. by crossing the 11th Street Bridge. Go south on Martin Luther King, Jr. Avenue to W Street. Turn left and continue four blocks to the visitor center parking lot. The home is near the Anacostia Museum.

As George Washington led the fledgling country of America toward freedom for white men, Frederick Douglass, ex-slave and self-taught speaker, author and journalist, led America toward freedom for all men, black and white. After the Civil War, he continued fighting not just for the welfare of the newly freed black men but for women's rights and world peace. During the last years of his life he lived in a nine-acre hillside estate, called Cedar Hill. The home is decorated just as it was when Douglass lived there. The visitor center has exhibits and a film on Douglass' life.

Daily 9–5, April–Sept., rest of year 8:30–4:30. Free.

THE CEDAR HILL TOUR, which includes the home of Frederick Douglass, Capitol Hill, Lincoln Park and the U.S. Navy Yard, departs from Arlington National Cemetery and the Washington Monument daily at 10 and 1, June 15–Labor Day. Reservations should be made about an hour before departure at ticket booths at Arlington National Cemetery or the Washington Monument.

Adults $5, ages 3–11 $2.50.

GEORGETOWN UNIVERSITY, 37th and O streets, N.W. Father Patrick Francis Healy, the son of a slave mother and wealthy Irish father, became the first black president of an American Catholic university in 1874. His brother, Father James Healy, was the first black Catholic bishop in America. Under Father Patrick's leadership, this historic university was greatly expanded. The administration building is named in honor of Father Healy, who is buried in the Jesuit cemetery on campus.

A selection of some historic black churches in the District of Columbia and Georgetown:

EBENEZER UNITED METHODIST CHURCH, 4th

and D streets, S.E., was originally founded in 1805 by white and black members. As was the custom, black members were required to sit in the balcony of the building. In 1827 the black members withdrew and built their own church, called Little Ebenezer. Immediately after the Civil War the first public school for blacks in D.C. was held in this church. The present church was built in 1897.

FIFTEENTH STREET PRESBYTERIAN CHURCH, 15th and R streets, N.W., was launched in 1841 by an ex-slave schoolmaster, John F. Cook. The church had many outstanding leaders, including the Reverend Henry Highland Garnet, a powerful antislavery speaker, and the Reverend Francis J. Grimke. The Reverend Grimke and his attorney brother, Archibald, sons of a white father and slave mother, were prominent crusaders against racial discrimination in D.C. for sixty years. Archibald's daughter, Angeline, was a noted poet and teacher at Dunbar High School in D.C., in its time one of the few outstanding black high schools in the country. The first black high school in America was begun in the basement of the Fifteenth Street church in 1870. The present church was erected in 1979.

METROPOLITAN A. M. E. CHURCH, 1518 M Street, N.W., was begun in 1822 when segregated blacks broke away from a white church to form the first A. M. E. church of this denomination in the District of Columbia. The present massive red-brick building was built in 1886 by black artisans and has been called the national cathedral of the African Methodist Episcopal movement. In 1895 the funeral of Frederick Douglass was held in this church, attended by 2,500 mourners. The church has hosted speeches by Frederick Douglass and American presidents, as well as serving as the concert hall of the Washington Philharmonic Orchestra.

Nearby, at 17th and M streets, is the CHARLES SUMNER SCHOOL, an early school for black students which now houses a small museum.

Open weekdays 9–4. Sunday morning services at 8 and 11.

MT. ZION UNITED METHODIST CHURCH, 1334
29th Street, N.W., (Georgetown) was begun in 1816 and is
considered the oldest black congregation in D.C. Before
Washington became the national capital, Georgetown was a
thriving port whose slaves and free black citizens worshipped
at this church.

A short walk from the church, behind 2515-2531 Q Street,
N.W., are MT. ZION CEMETERY and FEMALE UNION
BAND CEMETERY, the oldest predominantly black burying grounds in Washington. Legend has it that Mt. Zion
Church was a station on the Underground Railroad before
the Civil War, and that escaped slaves were hidden in a burial
vault in Mt. Zion Cemetery. Neglected in recent years, the
cemeteries are presently being restored, and the surviving
gravestones are being plotted and recorded.

ST. LUKES EPISCOPAL CHURCH, 15th and Church
streets, N.W., was one of the early black churches in D.C. Its
founder, in 1879, was the noted orator and black leader, the
Reverend Alexander Crummell. Crummell was an articulate
spokesman for black liberation in the United States and Africa
and founded the American Negro Academy, a group of black
intellectuals and scholars.

HOWARD UNIVERSITY, 2400 6th Street, N.W., LeDroit
Park, was founded in 1867, and was the largest institution of
higher learning established for black freedmen in the immediate post-Civil War period. The college was named for General
Oliver Otis Howard, commissioner of the Freedmen's Bureau
and a staunch supporter of the school. Today, Howard is one
of the most prestigious black universities in the nation. Its
faculty has included such distinguished black scholars as Dr.
Charles Drew, who pioneered in blood plasma preservation,
and Ralph Bunche, who won the Noble Prize for Peace for
1950.

Visitors are welcome on campus and may enter at 2400
Sixth Street. On the south side of the main quadrangle is the

Founders Library with the MOORLAND-SPINGARN RE-
SEARCH CENTER, housing one million sources, the country's most comprehensive collection of literature relating to
blacks in the Americas and Africa. There are also black history exhibits. Mon.–Fri. 9:30–4:30. Library archives open
for research only.

THE JAMES V. HERRING GALLERY OF ART, College
of Fine Arts (located behind the Ira Aldridge Theater) at
Howard University has one of the finest collections of African art and works by contemporary black artists in the
country, including paintings, prints, drawings and graphics,
mid-nineteenth century to present. The African collection
was begun by Alain Locke, the black author and historian,
who gave his personal holdings to the gallery.

Mon.–Fri. 9–4:30. Free.

LINCOLN MEMORIAL in Potomac Park is directly on a
line with the capitol and the Washington Monument. This
magnificent memorial, with the colossal seated statue of
Abraham Lincoln, is visited by thousands of people daily. On
Easter Sunday, 1939, 75,000 visitors gathered there to hear a
concert by black contralto Marian Anderson who, because of
her race, had been denied permission to sing at Constitution
Hall.

Perhaps the largest crowd gathered on August 28, 1963,
when more than 200,000 Americans of all races, colors and
creeds marched on Washington, D.C., to stage a civil rights
protest on the steps of the Lincoln Memorial. The most
compelling words of the day were spoken by Dr. Martin
Luther King in his famous "I have a dream" speech.

LINCOLN PARK, East Capitol Street, N.E., between
11th and 13th Street, has the Emancipation Statue and the
statue of educator Mary McLeod Bethune.

MARTIN LUTHER KING, JR., MEMORIAL LI-
BRARY, 901 G. Street, N.W., has in its lobby a mural showing the life of Dr. Martin Luther King, Jr., as well as the
history of the civil rights movement.

THE PHILLIPS COLLECTION, 1600–1612 21st Street, N.W., at Q Street, has a distinguished collection of European and American paintings, including thirty of black artist Jacob Lawrence's sixty panels on the *Migration of the Negro*. Jacob Lawrence's family accompanied the first migration of black people from the rural South to the big northern cities. A self-trained artist active during the Harlem Renaissance, Lawrence used episodes of black life and history as themes for his works.

Tues.–Sat. 10–5, Sun. 2–7. Closed holidays. Tours Wed. and Sat. at 2. Suggested donation $5, seniors and students $2.50.

The following are Smithsonian museums. Unless noted otherwise, they are located along both sides of the Mall, which stretches between the capitol and the Washington Monument. All are closed on Dec. 25, a few on Jan. 1 also. Some have extended summer hours. All offer some sort of tour.

ARCHIVES OF AMERICAN ART, 8th and F streets, N.W., D.C. 20560, has in its collection the personal papers of more than fifty African-American painters, sculptors, and print makers, from the late nineteenth century to the present. Also included are more than seventy tape-recorded interviews with noted black artists. Microfilmed material is available for loan from the Washington, D.C., headquarters and regional offices around the country. Contact Washington, D.C., office for information.

NATIONAL AIR AND SPACE MUSEUM, at 6th Street and Independence Avenue, S.W., one of the world's most popular museums, has exciting exhibits on the history of the development of air and space technology. The more than 20 galleries include the "Black Wings" exhibit which reflects the participation and contributions of blacks to aviation. Displays range from the first days of powered flight to the present, from the beginnings of black military aviation at Tuskegee Institute up through black involvement in the nation's space program today.

One of the earliest black military pilots was Eugene Bullard who, although born in America, fought with the French Foreign Legion in World War I and later flew with the Lafayette Flying Corps. The French poetically dubbed him the "Black Swallow of Death."

Among many other attractions, visitors to the museum can stroll through the huge Skylab space station or contrast Jules Verne's imaginary space capsule with the studio model of the U.S.S. *Enterprise* used in the "Star Trek" television series. Films and multimedia shows are also available.

Daily 10-5:30, extended hours in summer. Free guided tours at 10:15 and 1. Museum free, charge for planetarium and theater.

NATIONAL GALLERY OF ART, off the Mall, consists of two buildings at 4th Street and Constitution Avenue, N.W. The gallery owns one of the world's finest collections of western European art as well as American art from colonial to contemporary times. The gallery also has early art by African-American painters, including five rare portraits by Joshua Johnston. Equally rare is the small collection of watercolors of slave handicrafts, part of the gallery's Index of American Design. Slaves were often skilled in wood carving, spinning, weaving, carpentry, even the making of dolls for the plantation children. Index may be seen by appointment only.

Mon.–Sat. 10–5, Sun. noon–9. Free. Tours available.

NATIONAL MUSEUM OF AFRICAN ART, 950 Independence Avenue, S.W., is the only museum in the United States dedicated exclusively to the collection, exhibition, and study of the traditional arts of sub-Saharan Africa. African art is interwoven with daily life in ways quite different from most Western art. Religious beliefs are expressed in the masks and figures created for ceremonial purposes and in the practical objects used in everyday life.

The African continent has more than one-tenth of the world's population and approximately 900 distinct cultures. Although more than 25 million Americans trace their heritage to Africa, not a great deal is understood about these cultures and traditions. The National Museum of African Art hopes to serve as a bridge between the unknown and the known through educational programs, tours, lectures and special events.

Daily 10–5:30. Tours available. Free.

NATIONAL MUSEUM OF AMERICAN HISTORY is on Constitution Avenue between 12th and 14th streets, N.W. This museum covers every facet of American life, from the ruby slippers worn by Judy Garland in *The Wizard of Oz* to George Washington's false teeth! On the second floor devoted to social and political history may be found an exhibit of particular interest to Afro-American tourists, "Field to Factory, Afro-American migration, 1915–1940." During this crucial period hundreds of thousands of black Americans left the South to go north. The exhibit re-creates through photographs, artifacts, and life-like scenes the environment in which the migrants lived, a tenant farmhouse in Maryland, a row house in Philadelphia, even the coach of a train which took the migrants north.

There are numerous other displays that reflect the experiences of black as well as white Americans. The museum also offers public interpretative programs.

Daily 10–5:30. Extended hours in summer. Tours. Free.

NATIONAL MUSEUM OF NATURAL HISTORY is at 10th Street and Constitution Avenue, N.W. The museum has more than 80 million objects in its collections on people and their natural surroundings. One of the most interesting collections is the African Hall which has exhibits on traditional lifestyles which still may be found in rural Africa. Visitors can step inside a round house from southwestern Africa and join the Himba people who are visiting in the home. Or you can push a button at the Music of Africa showcase and hear drums, zithers and other instruments while at the same time slide projections show them being played.

An exhibit of textiles and clothing explains how class distinctions in Africa were often indicated by the quality of the fabric worn by a man or woman. The expert knowledge of weaving that black people brought with them from Africa was put to good use on the largely self-sufficient plantations of America where wool, flax and cotton were grown and spun into cloth by the women slaves.

Daily 10–5:30, extended hours in summer. Free. Guided tours are available.

NATIONAL PORTRAIT GALLERY and the NATIONAL MUSEUM OF AMERICAN ART are located off the Mall, housed in the Old Patent Office Building between 7th, 9th, G and F streets, N.W.

The National Portrait Gallery is entered from F Street. When the Harmon Foundation which had supported and collected works by black artists was discontinued in 1967, a great many of its paintings, including forty portraits of famous black Americans, were given to the National Portrait Gallery.

Also among its holdings is a special collection of portraits of writers and artists of the Harlem Renaissance period, including such well-known black authors as Countee Cullen, Jean Toomer, Langston Hughes and James Weldon Johnson. There are also portraits of singers Paul Robeson and Marian Anderson, historian W. E. B. DuBois and composer Harry T. Burleigh.

Daily 10–5:30. Free.

NATIONAL MUSEUM OF AMERICAN ART is entered from G Street. This museum has more than 1,400 works by African-American artists, ranging from the early nineteenth century to the present. There is a special gallery of works by nineteenth century African-American artists.

Daily 10–5:30. Walk-in tours weekdays at noon and 2 p.m.
Sundays. Gallery talks, workshops, films and musical performances. Free.

The TIDAL BASIN BRIDGE spans the Tidal Basin located
near the Thomas Jefferson Memorial. A monument to be
envied, it is one of the many engineering projects of Archie A.
Alexander, a black architect and engineer. Although discouraged from entering the field of engineering, Mr. Alexander persisted and finally headed his own construction firm.
From this bridge in the spring, visitors can look out over a
mass of cherry blossoms blooming beside the water. The
Cherry Blossom Festival in Washington, D.C., usually takes
place in early April.

VIETNAM VETERANS MEMORIAL, near the Lincoln
Memorial between the Reflecting Pool and Constitution Avenue, is dedicated to the men and women of the U.S. armed
forces who served in Vietnam. The polished black granite
walls of this monument are inscribed with the names of the
dead, listed chronologically by date of casualty. Almost
275,000 blacks served in Vietnam from 1965 to 1974 and 5,681
died in the war, which was one of the most controversial
conflicts in America's history.

Daily 24 hours. Free.

For further information about the District of Columbia,
contact:

Washington Visitor Information Center
1455 Pennsylvania Avenue, N.W.
Washington, D.C. 20004
202-789-7038

Smithsonian Information Center
Smithsonian Institution
Washington, D.C. 20560
202-357-2700

FLORIDA

BUSHNELL

DADE BATTLEFIELD STATE HISTORIC SITE, ½ mile west on county road 476, was the site of one of the bloodiest battles of the Seminole Wars. In December 1835, Major Francis Dade and a troop of soldiers were ambushed by a group of Seminole Indians accompanied by escaped slaves from Georgia and the Carolinas. By the time the attack ended, Dade and his company, except for three men who managed to escape, were all dead.

The Dade Massacre touched off the Second Seminole War in Florida. The war dragged on for seven years and was the most costly Indian war in American history. By 1838, 1,400 blacks were living with the Seminoles, some of them as slaves of the Indians, although it was a far more lenient slavery than they had known with their previous masters. Black men fought side-by-side with the Indians using guerrilla tactics, engaging in small skirmishes then vanishing into the swamps and everglades. One escaped slave, Abraham, served as advisor to the Seminole leader. The war ended when white Americans forced the Seminoles and their black slaves to remove to Oklahoma. Descendants of inter-marriages between Seminoles and blacks were later hired by the U.S. Army in 1870. Known as Seminole Negro Indian Scouts, they formed the most decorated military unit ever placed in the field.

The Dade battlefield site contains a museum, monuments and reproductions of the log breastworks used in the battle.

Grounds open daily 8–sunset, museum open daily 9–5. $1 per vehicle.

DAYTONA BEACH

BETHUNE-COOKMAN COLLEGE, 640 Second Avenue, was founded in 1904 by black educator Mary McLeod Bethune. One of 17 children, Mrs. Bethune spent her youth picking cotton. After struggling to achieve her own education, she was determined to start a school for the black railroad laborers' children who were without schools. Her first school was a shack near the city dump. It grew into one of the first colleges in the United States for African-American women. Later Mrs. Bethune founded the National Council of Negro Women and became an advisor to presidents. (A statue honoring Mrs. Bethune may be seen in Lincoln Park in Washington, D.C.) Her home on campus, a white frame, two story house, is open to the public. Eleanor Roosevelt occupied the guest room on numerous occasions.

Mon.–Fri. 8–5. Free.

CARL SWISHER LIBRARY is located on the campus of Bethune-Cookman College at 640 Second Avenue. A part of the collection consists of artifacts, documents, books and archival material on Mrs. Bethune as well as information on Afro-American history and Florida black history.

Mon.–Thurs. 8 a.m.–10 p.m., Fri. 8–5, Sat. 9–1, Sun. 3–11 p.m. Free.

EATONVILLE

The town of Eatonville, just north of Ocala, was incorporated in 1888 and may be the oldest black-run community in the nation. The town remains virtually all black today. Its most famous citizen was the acclaimed black novelist Zora Neale Hurston, who died in poverty but whose books, such as *Their Eyes Were Watching God,* are still read today. Recently the town held its first Zora Neale Hurston Festival of the Arts, celebrating the author's life and works.

FORT GEORGE ISLAND

KINGSLEY PLANTATION STATE HISTORIC SITE is located about 25 miles northeast of Jacksonville on Fort George Island. The island may be reached from the beaches on FL A1A and by ferry from Mayport. The Dames Point Bridge provides access to the island via FL 105. On the island, the plantation is on the north bank of the St. John River, 3 miles north of the St. John River ferry off FL A1A.

Florida was only lightly settled during the days of slavery. However, there were cotton and tobacco plantations in northern Florida. One such, on Fort George island, was owned by slave trader Zephaniah Kingsley. Although the importation of slaves had been prohibited by law in America in 1808, Florida was Spanish-owned when Kingsley moved to Fort George Island in 1817. On the Kingsley plantation African men and women were taught to be craftsmen and farmers, then smuggled into Georgia, where they were sold for 50 percent more than the regular market price.

Kingsley's African wife, Anna Jai, lived in a separate house on the estate and assisted him in running the prosperous plantation. Kingsley's paradoxical attitude toward slavery was revealed in his will, where he advised his wife and children "to remove themselves to some land of liberty where the conditions of society are governed by some laws less absurd than that of color."

Kingsley plantation has been restored. The remains of the original slave quarters, as well as the plantation homes and a small museum, may be visited. The island of Fort George, in addition to its historic interest (the Spanish established a blockhouse on the island in the 16th century) is also a wildlife sanctuary with well-marked nature trails.

Daily 8–5. Tours Thurs.–Mon. at 9:30, 11, 1:30 and 3. Adults $1, under 6 free.

FORT LAUDERDALE

MUSEUM OF ART, 1 East Las Olas Boulevard, has a collection of American and European art from the late-nineteenth century to the present, including folk art from West Africa.

Tues. 11–9, Wed.–Sat. 10–5, Sun. noon–5. Closed holidays. Adults $3.25, seniors $2.75, students $1, under 12 free.

JACKSONVILLE

AMERICAN BEACH is 37 miles north of Jacksonville on Amelia Island, between Fernandina Beach and the Amelia Island Plantation, off of FL A1A. This oceanfront property was purchased by blacks in the 1920s and 1930s, when other beaches were segregated. American Beach is still a black beach today and is being restored.

LAKE CITY

FLORIDA SPORTS HALL OF FAME, 201 Hall of Fame Drive, off U.S. 90W, honors the achievements of more than 100 athletes who lived or played sports in Florida. Such famous black athletes as tennis player Althea Gibson, football player Bob Hayes, known as the "world's fastest human," and baseball great Andre Dawson, have been inducted into the hall. There are audio tapes of the athletes, footage of the big games and great plays, and computerized games where visitors can test their skills against the greats.

Mon.–Fri. 9–9, Sat. 9–9 p.m., Sun. 10–7 p.m. Adults $3, children $2.

MELBOURNE

BREVARD ART CENTER AND MUSEUM, 1463 Highland Avenue, has special exhibitions of work by contemporary regional and local white and black artists, and exhibitions of international art, including African art.

Tues.–Fri. 10–5, Sat. 10–4, Sun. noon–4. Closed major holidays. Adults $2, children $1. Free Thursday afternoons.

MIAMI

Miami is a city of many cultures, many with black roots. The black neighborhood in Coconut Grove was built in 1889 by Bahamian settlers and has shops, outdoor cafes, and fashion boutiques; Overtown is a black community that through the 1940s and 1950s was called "Little Broadway" because of its many jazz clubs featuring big name black entertainers; Opa-locka is known for its unique Moorish architecture; Little Haiti has shops painted in brilliant colors reminiscent of colorful homes in Haiti, and Liberty City, a black community begun in 1937, is the home of Miami's soul food specialists.

At Liberty City is the Miami-Dade Chamber of Commerce, 6255 N.W. 7th Avenue, (305) 751-8648, where you can secure a free *Guide to Black Miami* as well as information about the numerous black festivals that are held in the city.

BLACK ARCHIVES HISTORY AND RESEARCH FOUNDATION is located at the Joseph Caleb Community Center, 5400 N.W. 22nd Avenue, also in Liberty City. This was recently formed to study Afro-American history in

southern Florida. A part of the collection is posters of black
entertainers, such as Nat King Cole, Billie Holiday, and
others who played at the Knight Beat Club in Overtown.
Future plans include a Black Heritage Trail tour of southern
Florida along with exhibits on black Americans. Check for
special programs.

Mon.–Fri. 10–5. Donation.

BLACK HERITAGE MUSEUM, University of Miami,
Dept. of Minority Students, Dickinson Drive, Bldg. 37B
(Coral Gables) is another recently formed museum, library,
gallery and historical society. The collection consists of African art, masks, paintings and carvings of the eighteenth and
nineteenth centuries from Kenya, Ghana, South Africa, the
Ivory Coast and Haiti.

Mon.–Sat. 8:30–5. Free.

OLUSTEE

OLUSTEE BATTLEFIELD STATE HISTORIC SITE is
about 2-1/2 miles east on U.S. 90, 50 miles west of Jacksonville. The largest Civil War battle on Florida soil involved
10,000 men with 3,000 casualties in a four hour period.

Three of the nine Union regiments in this battle were black:
the 1st North Carolina Colored, the 54th Massachusetts Volunteers and the 8th U.S. Colored of Pennsylvania. The 8th
U.S. Colored troops, among the first to engage in the battle,
were mostly raw recruits who had not had even an hour's
practice in loading or firing their weapons. They lost more
than 300 men out of 550 and were retreating in confusion
when the 54th Massachusetts arrived on the scene. The 54th
managed to hold the area until dark, covering the retreat of
the rest of the corps, and were the last to leave the battle
scene.

Site open daily 9–5. Walking tour. Museum is open Thurs.–
Sun. 9–5. Free.

ORLANDO

ORLANDO MUSEUM OF ART, 2416 North Mills, is noted for its exhibits of 20th century American art and African tribal sculpture.
Tues.–Fri. 10–5, weekends, noon–5. Closed holidays. Free.

ST. AUGUSTINE

CASTILLO DE SAN MARCOS NATIONAL MONUMENT is at Castillo Drive and Avenue Menendez in downtown St. Augustine. Take U.S. 1 business and FL A1A. The Castillo de San Marcos was built by the Spanish in 1671 and is the oldest masonry fort in the United States. In the 1700s slaves who escaped from the Carolinas and Georgia and managed to make their way south to Florida could find refuge with the Spaniards. In 1738 the Spanish even set up a settlement for escaped slaves two miles north of St. Augustine, called Fort Moosa. The small group of black men and women at the fort joined with the Indians and Spaniards in fighting against their former masters. The fort is in the process of being excavated by archaeologists.

The Castillo de San Marcos has four massive bastions, and a moat on three sides. A stairway leads to the gun deck overlooking Old St. Augustine. Exhibits trace the history of the fort and there are cannon firings on weekends from mid-June through Labor Day. There is also an exhibit on black history and the role of free blacks in Spanish Florida.

Daily 9–5:15, Labor Day–Memorial Day, rest of year 9–5:45. Closed Dec. 25. Adults $1, seniors and under 13 free.

MISSION NOMBRE DE DIOS, 27 Ocean Avenue, has a diorama showing Pedro Menendez de Aviles with white settlers and their black slaves who landed at this site on Septem-

ber 8, 1565, and founded St. Augustine, the oldest city in the
United States.

SUMATRA

FORT GADSDEN STATE PARK, 6 miles southwest of
Sumatra, on FL 65. When the British abandoned a fort at this
site in 1814, it was taken over by Indians and runaway slaves
and renamed Fort Negro. Southern slaveholders angrily in-
sisted that the government should see that "their property"
was returned. In the summer of 1816, Fort Negro was attacked by American gunboats. After a four-day siege, a can-
nonball struck a powder magazine and the fort, with all its
black and Indian defenders, was destroyed. The destruction
of the fort helped to bring about the First Seminole War.

Today only a marker, remains of the earthworks, and a
network of trenches that once were part of the fort may still
be seen.

TALLAHASSEE

BLACK ARCHIVES RESEARCH CENTER AND MU-
SEUM is located in the Carnegie Library at the Florida
Agricultural and Mechanical University. The collection includes African and Afro-American exhibits and research material from the colonial period to date, along with information
on Florida Afro-Americans.

Mon.–Fri. 9–4, weekends by request. Free.

TAMPA

BUSCH GARDENS, THE DARK CONTINENT, 3000
Busch Boulevard, is on FL 580, 2 miles east of junction I-275

(exit 33). This African theme park and family entertainment center has one of the country's largest collections of African animals displayed in natural settings. An air-conditioned monorail whisks visitors through the Serengeti Plain where zebras, ostriches, giraffes and other animals roam. Other sections of the park include a marketplace in Morocco, the village of Stanleyville, an animal nursery in Nairobi, Congo River Rapids, Timbuktu, and many other areas that help visitors experience an exciting visit to turn-of-the-century Africa. There are also rides, live entertainment, restaurants, shops and games.

Daily 9:30–6, extended hours in summer and selected holidays. All inclusive admission $20.95, under 2 free.

TITUSVILLE

SPACEPORT U.S.A. is on FL 405, 11 miles east of I-95, just south of Titusville. Multimedia exhibits explain U.S. space programs using actual spacecraft and models, along with a film featuring shots taken by astronauts in space.

A two hour bus tour to the KENNEDY SPACE CENTER begins here, stopping at various sites depending on the space operations in progress at the time. Dr. Ronald McNair was the second African-American to orbit earth on a NASA mission. (Lt. Col. Guion Bluford, Jr., was the first in 1983). Tragically, Dr. McNair was one of seven crew members aboard the flawed shuttle Challenger, which exploded shortly after lift-off from Cape Kennedy and plunged into the waters off the Florida coast in January 1986.

SPACEPORT, U.S.A. open daily 9–sunset, closed Dec. 25 and during certain space shuttle launches. Free. Charge for admission to IMAX Theater. Tours of Kennedy Space Center daily 9:45 until 2 hours before sunset. Adults $4, ages 3–12 $1.75.

WOODVILLE

NATURAL BRIDGE BATTLEFIELD STATE HIS-
TORIC SITE is at Ochlockonee River State Park, 4 miles
south of Sopchoppy on U.S. 319. The 22nd and 99th U.S.
Colored Infantry Regiments, among others, sought to cap-
ture St. Marks and Tallahassee in this Civil War battle in
March 1865.

For further information about Florida, contact:

Florida Division of Tourism
126 West Van Buren St.
Tallahassee, FL 32399-2000
904-487-1462

Information about Black Miami:
Miami-Dade Chamber of Commerce
6255 N.W. 7th Ave.
Miami, FL 33150
305-751-8648

GEORGIA

ALBANY

ALBANY MUSEUM OF ART, at 311 Meadowlark Drive, has changing exhibitions of American and European art and a permanent collection of African and African-American art.

Tues.–Sun. noon–5. Closed holidays. Adults $2, students $1, children free.

AMERICUS

ANDERSONVILLE NATIONAL HISTORIC SITE is 10 miles north of Americus on GA 49. Black soldiers fighting in the Union army often faced more than prison if captured. Some were shot or resold into slavery. Those Union soldiers, black or white, who ended up in Southern prison camps found their lives barely endurable. (Northern prisoner-of-war camps were not much better.)

One of the most notorious of the Southern prisoner-of-war camps was Andersonville Prison. Built to house 10,000 prisoners, Andersonville at times held more than 32,000. The poverty stricken Confederacy could supply the prison with very little food, and 26 percent of the men imprisoned at Andersonville during the Civil War died from starvation, disease or exposure.

One such prisoner was Corporal James Henry Gooding of

the all-black 54th Massachusetts Volunteers who was wounded and taken prisoner at the Battle of Olustee, Florida. In September 1863 Corporal Gooding had written a letter to President Lincoln, protesting the fact that black soldiers received lower pay than white soldiers. In disgust, the black soldiers of the 54th had elected to take no pay at all. Therefore, Corporal Gooding died at Andersonville in 1864 without ever having been compensated for his military service.

A month after Gooding died, the United States Congress finally passed a bill authorizing equal pay for black soldiers.

Today the site of Andersonville Prison commemorates the Civil War prisoners as well as all American prisoners of war. More than 16,000 veterans, including those from Andersonville, are buried at the nearby National Cemetery. There are remains of original wells and escape tunnels, and a portion of the prison stockade has been rebuilt.

A visitor center offers walking tours and talks in the summer, and presents a slide show and displays artifacts relating to Andersonville. There is also a museum which houses exhibits dealing with prisoners of war from the Revolutionary through the Vietnam wars.

The site and museum are open daily 8:30–5. Free.

ATLANTA

APEX (African-American Panoramic Experience) MUSEUM is a collection of Afro-American life and heritage located at 135 Auburn Avenue, N.E. The museum is the focal point of Sweet Auburn Historic District which, in the 1900s, was called the richest Negro street in the world. There is a replica of the first black-owned drug store in Georgia and visitors can sit in Trolley Car #105 which serviced Auburn Avenue in 1905 and watch audio-visual presentations on the history of Auburn Avenue, "Sweet Auburn, Street of Pride," and "Soul Music." There is also an impressive collection of art and artifacts and rotating exhibits by local and national black artists, along with the Paul Jones Collection of African Art.

Tues.–Sat. 10–5, Wed. 10–6. Sundays 1–5 during summer and February. Call ahead for schedule of guided tours. Adults $2, children under 12 and seniors $1. (404–521-2739)

ATLANTA LIFE INSURANCE HEADQUARTERS at 100 Auburn Avenue, N.E., was one of the businesses begun by black entrepreneurs on Auburn Avenue. The company was founded in 1927 by Alonzo Herndon and has an exhibition on the company's history in its lobby. Another Auburn Avenue enterprise was WERD, the nation's first black-owned commercial radio station.

The exhibit at the headquarters of Atlanta Life Insurance can be visited Mon.–Thurs. 8–4:30. Free.

CLARK ATLANTA UNIVERSITY, James P. Brawley Drive at Fair Street, has one of the most beautiful campuses in the South. The university is a merger of Clark College, founded in 1869, and Atlanta University, founded in 1865, one of the first schools begun by the Freedmen's Bureau after the Civil War. Dr. John Hope, the brilliant educator, was president of Atlanta University in the 1920s. Today Clark Atlanta University is one of six predominantly black institutions that make up the Atlanta University Center.

TREVOR ARNETT LIBRARY is located on the Clark Atlanta University campus, 111 James P. Brawley Drive, S. W. The library has many rare items from slave days in its collection, including an autographed copy of a poem by Phyllis Wheatley. Also in the collection are many of the original manuscripts, correspondence and personal papers of leading black writers during the Harlem Renaissance, such as Countee Cullen, Claude McKay and Arna Bontemps. There is a more recent collection of materials on the black Muslim and civil rights movements.

Daily 9 a.m.–11 p.m. Free.

THE WADDELL ART GALLERY is located on the lower level of the Trevor Arnett Library. In 1942, when the noted black artist Hale Woodruff was on the faculty, Atlanta University began an annual exhibition of the works of black American artists. Today the Atlanta University gallery represents probably the largest and most important collection of works of contemporary black artists to be found anywhere in America. It has works by Elizabeth Catlett, Charles White, Ernest Crichlow, Henry Ossawa Tanner and John Biggers, among many others.

Tues.–Fri. 10–4. Free.

HAMMONDS HOUSE GALLERIES AND RE-SOURCE CENTER OF AFRICAN AMERICAN ART, 503 Peeples Street, S.W., is located in a beautiful nineteenth-century Victorian home which was the residence of the late art patron Dr. O. T. Hammonds. The gallery features his African and African-American art collections, which include sculptures and masks from Africa, paintings from Haiti, and a variety of art forms by leading African-Americans. Some of the outstanding pieces are the earliest datable painting of Robert S. Duncanson, works by Romare Bearden, and art which depicts sterotypical images of African Americans. There are constantly changing traveling exhibits, tours, lectures, cultural programs and a resource center on artists of African descent.

Tues.–Fri. 10–6, weekends 1–5. Donation.

HERNDON HOUSE, 587 University Place, N.W., adjacent to the Atlanta University Center, was the home of Alonzo Herndon, a former slave and founder of the Atlanta Life Insurance Company, one of the largest black life insurance companies in the country. The beaux arts classical mansion was built in 1910 and still displays the family's collection of antique furniture, glass, silver, decorative arts and photographs, as well as oral histories of the Herndon family, 1910 to the present.

Tues.–Sat. 10–4. Tours. Free.

MARTIN LUTHER KING, JR. NATIONAL HISTORIC SITE includes the birthplace, church and grave of Dr.

Martin Luther King, Jr. Begin tour at Information Center, 449 Auburn Avenue, N.E. Civil rights leader and Nobel Peace Prize winner Dr. King was a native Georgian and has been called America's "drum major for justice" because he awakened the conscience of the nation and altered the course of world history.

Dr. King was assassinated in Memphis, Tennessee, on April 4, 1968, and his funeral was held at Atlanta. Thousands of mourners followed the simple mule-drawn wagon that carried his coffin from Ebenezer Church through the city streets.

EBENEZER BAPTIST CHURCH, 407 Auburn Avenue, N.E. Dr. King was associate pastor of this church. It was from here that Dr. King organized chapters of the Southern Christian Leadership Conference which radiated out through the South, advocating nonviolent protest against racial injustice. After his funeral service at Ebenezer, the mule-drawn wagon carried Dr. King's body to Morehouse College, his alma mater, where the eulogies were delivered. More than 150,000 paid their last respects to a great and fearless American martyr.

BIRTHPLACE OF DR. KING, 501 Auburn Street. Guided tours of Dr. King's birthplace are available, along with walking tours of the Sweet Auburn Historic area.

Daily, 10–5 June–August, 10–3:30 rest of year, extended hours during King Week in January. Free.

MARTIN LUTHER KING, JR. CENTER FOR NON-VIOLENT SOCIAL CHANGE, 449 Auburn Avenue, the product of the tireless efforts of Dr. King's widow, Coretta Scott King, is housed in the Freedom Hall Complex. Dr. Martin Luther King, Jr.'s burial site is on the mall of the center. The inscription on the marble crypt is taken from an old slave spiritual: "Free at last. Free at last. Thank God Almighty, I'm free at last."

Surrounding the crypt are the Freedom Walkway, a reflecting pool, the Chapel of All Faiths, and the Archives Building with an exhibit area. The King Library and Archives has manuscripts, records, audio-visual material and oral histories of the civil rights movement from the 1950s and 1960s, and records of Dr. Martin Luther King, Jr., and the Southern Christian Leadership.

Daily Mon.–Fri. 9–5. Free.

MOREHOUSE COLLEGE, 830 Westview Drive, S.W., now part of the Atlanta University Center, was founded in 1867 for ex-slaves. The Martin Luther King International Chapel on campus has a statue of Dr. King.

MORRIS BROWN COLLEGE, 643 Martin Luther King, Jr., Drive, N.W., part of the Atlanta University Center, was founded in 1881 as a coeducational college for blacks. The Ruth Hall Hodges Art Gallery at the college maintains display cases of African and African-American artworks outside of the gallery. The Gallery itself is open for special exhibits.

Mon.–Fri. 9–12. Free.

SPELMAN COLLEGE, 350 Spelman Lane, S.W., part of the Atlanta University Center, was founded in 1881. The buildings on this beautiful campus are considered historic landmarks.

STONE MOUNTAIN PARK, just east of I-285, via U.S. 78, is a recreational park of 3,200 acres and has the massive Confederate Memorial Carvings on the mountain itself. Within the park is the Antebellum Plantation, a collection of early nineteenth-century homes and work places moved here from throughout the state. The buildings include a traditional main house, overseer's house, and slave cabins, along with other outbuildings, authentically furnished to give visitors an idea of what plantation life was like in antebellum Georgia.

The two slave houses shown were obviously those used by the favored house slaves, with furnishings which were handmade by the slaves or cast-offs from the Big House. Field slaves generally lived in much more primitive housing closer to the fields where they worked.

Recreation offered within the park ranges from a golf

course and an ice skating rink to a lake front beach. There are also a riverboat cruise, scenic railroad, Swiss skylift, and wildlife trails.

Park open daily 6 a.m.–midnight. The Antebellum Plantation is open daily 10–9 in summer, 10–5:30 rest of year. Closed Dec. 24–25. Admission to plantation; adults $2.50, ages 4–11 $1.50. Admission cost to other attractions varies.

AUGUSTA

SPRINGFIELD BAPTIST CHURCH, 114 12th Street, one of the earliest black Baptist churches in Georgia, was started by the Reverends Jessie Peters and George Liele in 1787. Because of his work with the church, George Liele was forced to leave the country. He settled in Jamaica.

EATONTON

UNCLE REMUS MUSEUM, 3 blocks south on U.S. 441, in Turner Park, honors Joel Chandler Harris, who made world-famous the African-American folktale in his Uncle Remus stories. All the articles and furnishings in the log cabin museum are authentic to the time when Uncle Remus lived and are mentioned in the stories. There are wood carvings and paintings of Harris' characters.

Br'er Rabbit, the most famous of all the characters in the Uncle Remus stories, is portrayed by a statue in front of the courthouse in the center of Eatonton.

Cabin open Mon.–Sat. 10–noon and 1–5, Sun. 2–5, May–Sept. Closed Tues. rest of year. Adults 50 cents, students 25 cents.

Eatonton is also the hometown of noted black author Alice Walker, whose book *The Color Purple* won both the Pulitzer

Prize and the National Book Award in 1983. Plans are underway for a monument to Walker to be placed in the courthouse
square.

MACON

THE HARRIET TUBMAN HISTORICAL AND
CULTURAL MUSEUM, 340 Walnut Street, named after the
famous black conductor on the Underground Railroad, displays a mural by Wilfred Stroud depicting the history of
blacks from Africa through slavery, to the present. There is a
section of the museum dedicated to portraits of Harriet Tubman. Exhibits also chronicle black achievements in diffrent
fields and display works of black artists from across the
southeast, as well as African arts and crafts. A library of black
history, performances, arts and other cultural programs are
offered by the museum.
Mon.–Fri. 10–5, weekends 2–6. Closed major holidays.
Free.

SAVANNAH

FIRST AFRICAN BAPTIST CHURCH, 23 Montgomery
Street, was founded in 1777 at Brompton Plantation outside
of Savannah. Its current home at Franklin Square, built in
1832, was the first Baptist church built of brick in North
America. There is a legend that holes in the floorboards of the
church gave air to escaped Africans who hid in an earthen
tunnel beneath the building.
FIRST BRYAN BAPTIST CHURCH, 559 West Bryan
Street, was founded by Andrew Bryan in 1793. Bryan continued the Reverend George Liele's work when Liele was
forced to flee the country in the early 19th century. At the end
of the Revolutionary War, opposition to black churches rose
in the South for fear that they preached opposition to slavery.

Bryan was imprisoned, but after his release he continued his missionary work. There is a monument to the Reverend George Liele, the first American black Baptist missionary, at the church.

KING-TISDELL COTTAGE, 514 East Huntingdon Street, is furnished with belongings of a turn-of-the-century, middle-class black family. There are bills of sale for slaves written in Arabic by plantation slaves (indicating that some blacks came from highly developed cultures in Africa), African weapons, a dugout canoe, baskets and carvings.

Daily 12–5. Closed holidays. Adults $1.50.

SAVANNAH'S NEGRO HERITAGE TOUR begins at the King-Tisdell Cottage and takes in 17 sites, including the historic Second Baptist Church; the home of Thomas Williams who bequeathed the first hospital for blacks in America; and the Green-Meldrim House, where Union general Sherman met with 20 black leaders in 1864 to issue the famous Field Order 16, granting "forty acres and a mule" to newly freed black citizens.

General Tecumseh Sherman took Savannah in December 1864 and sent a message to President Lincoln, offering him the city for Christmas. Sherman's troops were accompanied into the city by black laborers and nearly 10,000 "contrabands" (escaped slaves) who remained under Union army protection until the end of the war.

Negro Heritage Tours must be scheduled at least two to three days in advance and cost $8 per person, or $4 for those who provide their own transportation.

THE SECOND AFRICAN BAPTIST CHURCH at 123 Houston Street, Greene Square, was built in 1859. Its walls are four feet thick and slaves were educated secretly in the basement. General Sherman read the Emancipation Proclamation in front of the church, and Dr. Martin Luther King, Jr., preached his "I have a dream" sermon inside this building before giving his famous Washington, D.C., address at the Lincoln Memorial.

For further information about Georgia, contact:

Georgia Department of Tourism
PO Box 1776
Atlanta, GA 30301
1-800-847-4842

Savannah Negro Heritage Trail Tour
King-Tisdell Cottage
314 East Huntingdon St.
Savannah, GA 31401
912-234-8000
Call two to three days in advance.

IDAHO

BOISE

BOISE ART MUSEUM, 670 S. Julia Davis Drive, at the entrance to the Julia Davis Park, has a small collection of African and black American artwork. The African collection has decorative art and jewelry, ornaments, bowls and cloth from the Masai and Zulu cultures. The African American artwork section includes a silkscreen print by Jacob Lawrence entitled *The 1920s . . . the Migrants Arrive and Cast Their Ballots.*

Tues.–Fri. 10–5, weekends and holidays noon–5. Adults $2, seniors $1.

ST. PAUL MISSIONARY BAPTIST CHURCH, at 124 Broadway Avenue, begun in 1909, is one of the few churches in Idaho with a predominantly black congregation.

POCATELLO

FORT HALL REPLICA is 1½ miles south on U.S. 30/ U.S. 91 and business route I-15, in Upper Ross Park. From its massive wooden gates, the fort is a full-scale replica of the trading post that was a vital stop for all travelers heading west on the Oregon trail between 1834 and 1860. Just north of Pocatello off U.S. 91, the ruts made by the heavily laden

wagons on the Oregon Trail can be seen alongside the site of
the original Fort Hall.

Although it is not widely known, black emigrants, as well
as white, followed the Oregon Trail, seeking a better life in the
western territories. In the spring of 1844 George William
Bush, a wealthy black cattleman, took his family from Missouri and joined the Simmons' wagon train heading west to
Oregon. In 1850 George Washington, born in slavery but
adopted by a white family, traveled out to the Oregon territory with his foster parents. Both men eventually settled in
Washington, where they prospered and made respected lives
for themselves.

Within the log house museum at Fort Hall, visitors can
experience life as it was when the Oregon Trail was one of the
main trails west, as well as wander through restored shops
and see buffalo, elk, deer and antelope roaming in a field next
to the fort.

Daily 9–8, June 1–Sept. 15; Tues.–Sat. 10–2, April–May.
Adults $1, ages 13–18, 50 cents, ages 6–12, 25 cents.

SPALDING

NEZ PERCE NATIONAL HISTORICAL PARK, U.S.
95. The park's headquarters and visitor's center are in the
town of Spalding, 11 miles east of Lewiston. The park occupies 12,000 square miles of north-central Idaho and primarily reflects the history and culture of the Nez Perce Indians. However, within the park is the Lolo Trail over which
the Lewis and Clark expedition traveled in 1805 and 1806, as
well as campsites used by Lewis and Clark.

At the Canoe Camp site the Lewis and Clark expedition
rested for twelve days while the black servant and slave York,
and other members of the expedition, built canoes from hol-
lowed-out logs so that they could return to water for the final
leg of their trip to the Pacific. As with other Indian tribes they

had encountered, York's black skin was the center of attention among the Nez Perce. Perhaps tiring of all the attention, when one of the Indians moistened his finger to see if the black would rub off York pulled his knife and glared at the man. The legend of York persists among the Nez Perce, who called him "make big eyes much white in eyes and look fierce at chief."

SPALDING SITE VISITOR CENTER, on U.S. 95, contains Nez Perce cultural artifacts as well as mementos of the Lewis and Clark expedition. An introductory movie explains relations between the explorers and the Indians. A park folder and map is available for self-guided driving tours of the historical and scenic sites within the park.

Daily 8–6 Memorial Day weekend-Labor Day; 8–4:30 rest of year. Closed Jan. 1, Thanksgiving and Dec. 25. Free.

For further information about Idaho, contact:

Idaho Travel Council
700 W. State St., 2nd floor
Boise, ID 83720
1-800-635-7820

ILLINOIS

ALTON

LOVEJOY MONUMENT at 5th and Monument streets is dedicated to the abolitionist newspaper editor Elijah P. Lovejoy, who was killed in 1837, protecting his press from a proslavery mob. The mob then dumped into the Mississippi River the printing press on which Lovejoy had published the *Alton Observer,* an anti-slavery newspaper. Three other presses owned by Lovejoy had already been destroyed by proslavery mobs.

The winged statue of Victory on the Lovejoy Monument, the tallest monument in Illinois, symbolizes the triumph of the cause for which he fought and died—the freedom of black people and the freedom of the press. Around the granite columns are bronze panels that tell of his life.

THE GRAVE OF ELIJAH LOVEJOY is about 75 yards behind the monument, down a graveled lane. The remains of his press, salvaged from the Mississippi River, are on display in the lobby of the offices of *The Telegraph,* 111 E. Broadway, during business hours.

The last LINCOLN-DOUGLAS DEBATE took place in Alton in 1858. A marker has been placed at the site, now a small park on Broadway and Market streets. The Underground Railroad ran through Alton, and Confederate prisoners of war were housed in the town during the Civil War. Over 1,300 prisoners died of smallpox during the 1860s.

THE MUSEUM OF HISTORY AND ART at 121 East Broadway, contains an 1830s printing shop, including a press similar to the one used by Lovejoy, along with exhibits on the Lovejoy story. Black pioneers are also remembered at this museum in various exhibits about the black experience in America.

Thurs.–Sun. 1–4. Closed on holidays. Free.

CHICAGO

ART INSTITUTE OF CHICAGO, Michigan Avenue at Adams Street, owns a large collection of paintings and sculpture by early black American artists, such as Henry Ossawa Tanner, Richard Hunt, Marion Perkins, Archibald Motley and Roger Brown. Tanner was the first internationally known black American artist, achieving success in Europe with his religious paintings in the late-nineteenth century. Like most black artists of his day, he avoided black subject matter and racial problems in his work.

By the 1920s black artists were painting the black man and woman and their life as it actually was. In the 1950s and 1960s, the black artists became more militant and bitter in their outlook. This can be seen in Roger Brown's painting at the Art Institute, *D-Yard Attica* choosing a racial prison riot as the subject of his work. The museum also owns an excellent collection of African art.

Mon.–Fri. 10:30–4:30 (also Tues. until 8), Sat. 10–5, Sun. and holidays noon–5. Closed Dec. 25. Adults $5, students and seniors $2.50, free to all on Tues. Tours, gallery walks, lectures.

Carter G. Woodson Branch of the Chicago Public Library at 9525 S. Halsted, is the home of the VIVIAN HARSH COLLECTION OF AFRO-AMERICAN HISTORY AND LITERATURE. Named in honor of the first black woman to head a branch of the Chicago Public Library, this is one of the nation's largest depositories of information on black history and culture in America. The library itself is named after the black scholar, who has been called "the father of black history."

Mon. and Wed. 1–9, Tues. and Thurs. 11–7. Sat. 9–5. Closed Fri. Free.

CHICAGO DAILY DEFENDER, 2400 South Michigan Avenue, begun in 1905, is not the oldest black-owned newspaper in the country, but it is one of the most influential. During the first half of the 1900s, the *Chicago Daily Defender* was instrumental in encouraging thousands of southern blacks to migrate north.

Behind-the-scenes tour of the newspaper by appointment, only.

CHICAGO HISTORICAL SOCIETY MUSEUM in Lincoln Park at North Avenue and Clark Street, has among its treasures and exhibits many related to black Americans.

There is a small replica and a diorama of the Du Sable Trading Post, built in 1779 at the mouth of the Chicago River. Jean Baptiste Pointe Du Sable was of mixed African ancestry, a fur trader and the first settler in what is now Chicago. The trading post prospered and a community grew up around it. (The actual site of the Du Sable trading post is marked by a plaque in the Pioneer Court on the northeast approach to the Michigan Avenue Bridge in Chicago.)

Several interesting portraits of black Chicago citizens may also be seen in the museum. Two such are of John Jones and his wife, Mary, who worked in the abolitionist movement. Jones made his fortune in the tailoring business and was Chicago's first black political leader. His home and sometime tailor shop were used as a station on the Underground Railroad. Chicago, because of its location on Lake Michigan, was an important transit point for slaves escaping into Canada. (A plaque commemorating the role that Chicago played in the Underground Railroad may be seen at 9955 South Verley Avenue.)

In the museum's Civil War Gallery visitors can see a slide-show called "Years of Anguish and Glory," which includes photographs of black sailors, infantry and artillerymen who served in the Civil War.

Mon.–Sat. 9:30–4:30, Sun. noon–5. Closed Jan. 1, Thanksgiving and Dec. 25. Adults $1.50, ages 6–17 and over 65, 50 cents. Free to all on Monday.

DU SABLE MUSEUM OF AFRICAN AMERICAN HISTORY, 740 E. 56th Place (57th and Cottage Grove Avenue in Washington Park) was founded in the 1940s and is one of the oldest and finest black history museums in the country. Among the ongoing exhibitions are "DuSable the Man," paintings and sculpture honoring Chicago's founding father; "The Washington Years, 1983–1987," photographs of the late mayor Harold Washington; and "Up From Slavery," tracing African-American life from slavery to the first half of the twentieth century.

Although primarily a history museum, it also has an excellent historic and contemporary art collection from the 1940s through the 1960s. There are also examples of African art, such as wood carvings, drums, dolls and some ancient spirit masks. Much like contemporary Western art, African art is often symbolic and highly stylized rather than realistic.

The museum has a library, cultural programs, films, speakers, gala fests and children's programs. Guided tours by appointment. DuSable also occasionally sponsors black heritage tours of Chicago.

Mon.–Fri. 9–5, weekends noon–5. Closed holidays. Adults $2, seniors and students $1.00, children 12 and under 50 cents.

FIELD MUSEUM OF NATURAL HISTORY, Roosevelt Road at Lake Shore Drive (in Grant Park) covers 10 acres and has a great many fascinating natural history exhibits. One of the most interesting is the "Inside Ancient Egypt" exhibit and the life-like animal dioramas, including African mammals.

The museum also has an outstanding collection of nineteenth-century African sculpture, notably art of the Cameroons and Benene bronzes. The Benene bronzes were cast by the sophisticated "lost wax" method. Although in the nineteenth century African art was considered primitive, by the 1930s great museums had started building up collections. Art critics realized that the tribal carvings in wood and ivory were not savage or uncivilized, but a unique stylized art form with a powerful, original beauty.

Daily 9–5. Closed Jan. 1, Thanksgiving and Dec. 25. Adults $2, ages 6–17 $1, over 65, 50 cents. Free to all on Thursday.

THE G. A. R. MEMORIAL MUSEUM, second floor at the Chicago Public Library Cultural Center, 78 East Washington Street, contains displays relating to slavery, the abolition movement and the Civil War. One of its recent exhibits, "A Nation Divided, the War Between the States," explored the many aspects of the conflict using a wide variety of materials.

Mon.–Thurs. 9–7, Fri. 9–6, Sat. 9–5. Closed holidays. Free.

JOHNSON PUBLISHING COMPANY, 820 S. Michigan Avenue, is the headquarters of the largest black cultural corporation in the United States and houses the editorial offices of several popular black publications such as *Ebony* and *Jet*.

Tours by appointment.

MALCOLM X COLLEGE, 1900 West Van Buren, is a junior college that was renamed for the young black leader who died in 1965. Before and after his death, Malcolm X symbolized for many black people their never-ending quest for political, economic and social freedom. There is a small art gallery on campus displaying works of professional artists and students.

Open during regular school hours. Free.

MILTON L. OLIVE PARK, Ontario Street on the lakefront, was named in honor of Private First Class Milton L. Olive, a black soldier in the Vietnam War. In October 1965, while part of a platoon moving against the Vietcong, he saved the lives of his fellow soldiers by throwing himself upon a grenade which landed in their midst. For his heroism, Private Olive was posthumously awarded the Congressional Medal of Honor.

MUHAMMAD UNIVERSITY OF ISLAM headquarters is located at 7351 South Stony Island. One of the most controversial religions on the black American scene was begun in the 1920s by Wallace Fard Muhammad. Elijah Muhammad greatly expanded the Nation of Islam and today there are temples in almost every major city in America. As much a political and social movement as a religious one, it stresses the Mohammadan belief in Allah as the true God, and the separation of the black and white races. An offshoot of the religion are the schools where black Muslim children and adults receive instruction.

PROVIDENT HOSPITAL AND TRAINING SCHOOL at 51st Street and Vincennes Avenue, saw the first successful operation on the human heart, performed in 1893 by black physician Dr. Daniel Hale Williams. In 1891 Dr. Williams had founded the Provident Hospital as the first training school for black nurses, and the first hospital in America for the use of all physicians and patients, without regard to color.

SOUTHSIDE COMMUNITY ART CENTER at 3831 S. Michigan Avenue was opened in 1939. Five generations of black Chicago artists have been nurtured here. The gallery includes works by black artists, primarily from the Chicago area and dating back to the 1940s.

Tues.–Fri. 12–5, Sat. 9–5, Sun. 1–5. Free.

VICTORY MONUMENT at 35th Street and Martin Luther King, Jr. Drive, honors the black soldiers and sailors from Illinois who died in the line of duty during World War I. The all black 370th U.S. Infantry, 93rd Division, fought in the terrible battle of the Argonne Forest and then pursued the Germans into Belgium. By the end of the war, General Pershing had awarded the Distinguished Service Cross for acts of extraordinary heroism to twelve members of the 37th, and sixty-eight of them received the Croix de Guerre from a grateful French government. 370,000 black servicemen served in World War I.

VIETNAM MUSEUM, a storefront museum at 5002 North Broadway, has military, civilian and cultural exhibits featuring memorabilia from both sides of the Vietnam War, including anti-war materials. Black soldiers were heavily engaged in this conflict, which brought about one of the most turbulent eras in American history. There is a small research library.

Tues.–Fri. 1–5, weekends 11–5. Closed weekdays Jan.–Feb. Donation.

WALL OF RESPECT, at 43rd and Langley, is an outdoor mural created in the summer of 1967 by the Organization of Black American Culture. This dramatic representation of black heroes and leaders sparked the national renaissance in public art. Other outdoor murals on buildings, painted by black artists, may be seen around Chicago.

EAST ST. LOUIS

KATHERINE DUNHAM MUSEUM, 1005 Pennsylvania, may be reached via I-55, exit at 4th and Broadway, right on Broadway to 10th Street and left on 10th, going north to Pennsylvania. Internationally acclaimed as the leader of a dance troupe, Katherine Dunham used the dances of her African ancestry to refine and popularize black dance in the 1940s and 1950s. The museum displays artifacts from West Africa, where she researched her dances, and memorabilia from the world tours of the Katherine Dunham Dance Company.

Tues. and Thurs. 4–6, weekends 2–6. Free. Guided tours by appointment.

GALESBURG

The town of Galesburg, in which KNOX COLLEGE is located, was a principal station for the Underground Railroad in Illinois. Black refugees from Missouri knew they could find shelter in these homes as well as at the college itself.

It was at Knox College that Abraham Lincoln and Stephen Douglas held the famous debate in which Lincoln declared prophetically, "A house divided against itself cannot stand. I believe that this government cannot endure permanently half-slave and half-free." This is the only site associated with those historic debates that is still standing, and the Old Main Building at Knox College has been declared a Registered National Historic Landmark. Documents about the debate are on display inside.

Open during regular college semester. Free.

JUNCTION

OLD SLAVE HOUSE (HICKORY HILL), 9 miles west of Shawneetown, near the intersection of IL 13 and IL 1, was built in 1834. Legend has it that kidnapped slaves were kept on the third floor, which has narrow doorways leading into small rooms that were used as slave quarters. Another legend tells how slave workers at the nearby Equality Salt Wells lived in the house. Since slavery was illegal in Illinois, special legislation had to be arranged for the slaves at the salt diggings. The house has been restored with its original furnishings, and the cramped slave quarters on the third floor can also be seen.

Daily 9–5, April–Oct.; weekends only 9–5, in November. Adults $3.50, children $2.50.

PETERSBURG

LINCOLN'S NEW SALEM STATE PARK, 2 miles south on IL 97, is a reconstruction of the town of New Salem where Abraham Lincoln lived as a young man from 1831 to 1837. A museum exhibits artifacts associated with Lincoln and other residents of the town.

Daily 9–5 late April–late Oct., 8–4 rest of year. Closed Jan. 1, Thanksgiving and Dec. 25. Free.

PRINCETON

OWEN LOVEJOY HOMESTEAD, East Peru Street (IL 6), was the home of Owen Lovejoy, fiery anti-slavery preacher and the brother of abolitonist publisher Elijah Lovejoy, who was murdered in Alton for his beliefs. The Lovejoy home served as a station on the Underground Railroad. In 1843 Owen Lovejoy was indicted by a grand jury for harboring two slave women in his home but was acquitted at his trial. In 1863 Mr. Lovejoy, who had been elected to Congress, introduced the bill that led to President Lincoln's signing of the Emancipation Proclamation. The Lovejoy home has been restored and looks much as it did when the family sheltered escaped slaves there.

Thurs. and Sun. 1–4:30, May–Oct.; open also by appointment. Adults $2, students 50 cents.

SPRINGFIELD

LINCOLN HOME NATIONAL HISTORIC SITE at 8th and Jackson streets is only one of several sites in Springfield commemorating the Great Emancipator. Many black men and women considered John Brown their true emancipator because, although Lincoln had strong personal feelings against slavery, his political intentions in the beginning were not so much to abolish slavery as to prevent its spread. Finally realizing as he himself had said, that the Union could not endure "half-slave, half-free" Lincoln issued the Emancipation Proclamation on Jan. 1, 1863.

ABRAHAM LINCOLN'S HOME has been meticulously restored to look as it did when Lincoln, his wife, and their three sons lived there from 1844 until 1861. The home is at the center of a four-block historic site, which includes the Lincoln Depot Museum and the Lincoln-Herndon Law Office.

Home open daily 8:30–5. Closed Jan. 1, Thanksgiving and Dec. 25. Free but tickets must be acquired on the day of the tour at the Lincoln Home Visitor Center, 426 S. 7th Street, open 8:30–5.

LINCOLN DEPOT MUSEUM at 10th and Monroe streets is where Lincoln delivered his poignant farewell address when leaving Springfield in 1861 to assume the presidency. Exhibit areas and an audio-visual presentation recreate Lincoln's journey to his inauguration.

Daily 10–4, June–Aug. Free.

LINCOLN-HERNDON LAW OFFICES, 6th and Adams streets, is the only surviving structure in which Lincoln maintained a law office.

Daily 9–5. Closed Jan. 1, Thanksgiving and Dec. 25. Free.

LINCOLN'S TOMB STATE HISTORIC SITE is at Oak Ridge Cemetery, about two miles north of Springfield. Lincoln's assassination on April 14, 1865, caused horror and anger among the black Americans he had freed. At the head of the funeral procession to the Capitol was a regiment of black troops with arms reversed. When the funeral train brought Lincoln to his final resting place in Springfield, every black person in town watched the procession pass by.

Lincoln, his wife, and three of his four children are buried in this tomb. Lincoln's body, however, was moved to various locations within the tomb. Once it was moved to foil a gang of counterfeiters who attempted to steal the body with the idea of holding it for ransom! It was not placed in its present location until 1901.

Daily 9–5. Closed Jan. 1, Thanksgiving and Dec. 25.

During June, July and August, on Tuesdays at 7 p.m., the 114th Infantry Regiment performs retreat ceremonies in authentic Civil War uniforms at the tomb. Free.

For further information about Illinois, contact:

Illinois Tourist Information Center
310 S. Michigan, Suite 108
Chicago, IL 60604
312-793-2094

INDIANA

BEDFORD

Deep within Hoosier National Forest, located in south-central Indiana five miles east of Paoli, are the remains of a once thriving black community, known as LITTLE AFRICA or LICK CREEK. Founded by freed slaves around 1820, this secluded area is estimated to have been home to 200 black families. By the end of the 1800s, the community had myste-riously disappeared. All that remains today are lilacs and jonquils that bloom where homes once stood, worn tombstones in a cemetery, and a plaque at the site of the village church.

The remains of Little Africa can only be reached by hiking a considerable distance over a Forest Service road. Directions may be received at the Hoosier National Forest Headquar-ters, 811 Constitution Avenue, Bedford; open Mon.–Fri. 8–4:30.

BLOOMINGTON

INDIANA UNIVERSITY ART MUSEUM located on the Fine Arts Plaza of the Indiana University campus at Seventh Street, has an excellent African arts collection.
Tues.–Sat. 9–5, Sun. 1–5. Closed holidays. Free.

FOUNTAIN CITY

THE LEVI COFFIN HOUSE STATE HISTORIC SITE is located in Fountain City which is 9 miles north of Richmond on U.S. 27. Indiana was on one of the main routes of the Underground Railroad by which slaves escaped to freedom. The Quakers Levi and Catherine Coffin ran such a successful Underground Railroad station in their home that Mr. Coffin has unofficially been called the "President of the Underground Railroad." During the twenty years they lived in Fountain City, the Coffins, along with their fellow citizens, helped 2,000 escaped slaves reach safety.

The attic of the house was often used to hide the fleeing slaves, even the space between the strawtick and featherbed. If there were no immediate danger of recapture, an exhausted refugee might stay for weeks with the Coffin family, building up strength to resume the journey north.

The Coffin house has been completely refitted in furniture of the period when the house served as a station on the Underground Railroad.

Tours Tues.–Sun. 1–4, June 1–Sept. 14; weekends only 1–4, Sept. 15–Oct. 31. Closed July 4 and Nov.–April. Adults $1, ages 6–18, 50 cents.

INDIANPOLIS

CHILDREN'S MUSEUM is located at 3000 N. Meridian Street (U.S. 31), bordered by 30th and Illinois streets. The museum is easily accessible from I-65 and I-70. The largest "hands-on" museum for children in the world, here are five stories of natural and man-made wonders which will keep children and adults fascinated for hours.

On the fifth floor an exhibit area is devoted to "African-American Scientists and Inventors from A to Z," featuring more than twenty well-known and not so well-known black figures. It covers such invaluable contributions as the derivation of cortisone from soybeans and the design for the golf tee.

Summer hours are Mon.–Sat. 10–5, Sun. noon–5; between Labor Day and Memorial Day open Tues.–Sat. 10–5, Sun. noon to 5. Closed Thanksgiving, Dec. 25. and New Year's Day. Adults $4, seniors and children 2–17 $3, Children under two free.

INDIANAPOLIS MUSEUM OF ART, 1200 West 38th Street, includes among its internationally famous collections exhibits of early African art.

Tues.–Sun. 11–5. Closed Thanksgiving, Dec. 25. Jan. 1. Free.

INDIANA STATE MUSEUM, 202 N. Alabama Street, brings black history to life at Freetown Village, a unique living history museum within a museum. The time is 1870 and visitors to the village meet the "local residents," Mother Endura who raises herbs, the Rev. Samuel Strong and Mrs. Strong, schoolteacher Matilda Addison, and can listen to gossip from street peddler, Guinea "Blue" Farnsworth. On special occasions visitors can attend a wedding celebration or relax and enjoy food and fun at an informal dinner theater. Freetown Village also sponsors touring history plays and workshops.

Freetown Village is part of the Streets of Indiana Exhibition Hall in the Indiana State Museum. The museum is open Mon.–Sat. 9–4:45, Sun. noon to 4:45. Performance times at Freetown Village are Wed.–Fri. 10–3, weekends 12–4. Free.

INDIANA WORLD WAR MEMORIAL MUSEUM occupies a plaza between Meridian, Pennsylvania, St. Clair and New York streets. In the lower concourse are exhibits on the contributions of Hoosiers in the armed forces. One section of the exhibit area pays tribute to the "Military Heritage of Black Americans in National Defense."

Daily 8:30–4:30. Closed Jan. 1, Thanksgiving and Dec. 25. Free.

MADAME WALKER URBAN LIFE CENTER, 617 Indiana Avenue, is a restoration of the former headquarters for the cosmetic business of Madame C. J. Walker, one of the country's first black women millionaires. Madame Walker, the daughter of impoverished ex-slaves, developed a formula for hair and beauty products specifically for black women. Ultimately she established beauty schools in major cities throughout the United States and provided economic opportunity for thousands of black female employees who represented her company.

Today, the restored Walker Urban Life Center provides meeting rooms for organizations. The fourth floor is the site of the Madame C. J. Walker Memorial Room, housing displays on the life and work of Madame Walker, who died in 1919. The glorious Walker Theatre, its colorful art deco motifs a memorial to Africa, is also part of the center. Many jazz greats have performed there.

Tours of the center must be arranged two weeks in advance, 8:30–5. Tours may be combined with catered lunch or with Friday night "Jazz on the Avenue." Price varies with tour.

MAJOR TAYLOR VELODROME at 3649 Cold Spring Road, is named for Marshall W. Taylor, Indianapolis-born black champion bicyclist at the turn of the century. The velodrome has a special concrete surface banked at 28 degrees, and is open to the public daily from May to November.

RICHMOND

INDIANA FOOTBALL HALL OF FAME, 815 North A Street, has pictures, statistics, and memorabilia of Indiana players inducted into the Hall of Fame, including such black football greats as Lamar Lundy, Rosie Grier, and Orderea Mitchell, among others.

Mon.–Fri. 10–4, May–Oct.; rest of year Mon.–Fri. 10–2; weekends by appointment. Closed holidays. Admission $1.

For further information about Indiana, contact:

Indiana Department of Tourism
One North Capitol, Suite 700
Indianapolis, IN 46204-2288
317-232-8860

IOWA

AMES

IOWA STATE UNIVERSITY, Lincoln Way. George Washington Carver was the first African American to enroll at Iowa State University in 1891 and went on to earn his master of science degree in agriculture in 1896. Carver also became the first African American faculty member of ISU, before pursuing a distinguished career in teaching, research and service at Tuskegee Institute in Alabama.

A building on the Iowa State campus, housing classrooms and administrative offices, has been named Carver Hall and contains a statue of George Washington Carver by Christian Peterson.

Recently, Iowa State University held a year-long celebration of diversity called "The Legacy of George Washington Carver," emphasizing the importance of multicultural and minority issues.

THE BRUNNIER GALLERY AND MUSEUM, on the top floor of the Scheman Building in the Iowa State Center, has on display a decorative arts collection, traveling exhibits, including African and African-American art exhibits, and university and community related exhibits.

Tues.–Sun. 11–4. Closed holidays. Free.

BETTENDORF

THE CHILDREN'S MUSEUM, 533 Sixteenth Street, has exhibits pertaining to local ethnic groups, including African Americans, and their contributions to Iowa and to America.
Tues.–Sat. 10–4:30, Sun. 1–4:30. Closed holidays. Donations.

DAVENPORT

DAVENPORT MUSEUM OF ART, 1737 W. 12th Street, houses a permanent collection of Haitian art, in addition to American and European works.
Tues.–Sat. 10–4:30, Sun. 1–4:30. Closed holidays. Free.

DES MOINES

EDMUNDSON ART FOUNDATION INC., Des Moines Art Center, 4700 Grand Avenue, has a small but excellent collection of African sculpture.
Tues.–Sat. 11–5, Sun. noon–5. Free.
STATE CAPITOL, Grand Avenue between E. 9th and E. 12th streets, houses a valuable collection of paintings, statues and war flags. Among the flags from the Civil War is that of the 1st Regiment Iowa Colored Infantry. Iowa lost almost one-third of its black adult male population in the Civil War.
Mon.–Fri. 8–4:30, weekends 8–4. Tours available. Free.

GRINNELL

GRINNELL HISTORICAL MUSEUM is at 1125 Broad Street, near Grinnell College. Josiah Bushnell Grinnell came west and founded his namesake town after an anti-slavery sermon lost him his pastorate in Washington, D.C. Grinnell remained an active abolitionist and became a friend of John Brown, the militant abolitionist. Brown stayed at Grinnell's house in 1859 while leading a company of fugitive slaves through Iowa to Canada. Brown drilled his troops and made final plans for his famous raid on Harper's Ferry at Springfield, Iowa, a small Quaker town a few miles east of Cedar Rapids.

The museum contains articles relating to the history of the town and of Josiah Grinnell, including his elaborate cubbyholed desk, which is almost an office in itself.

Tues.–Sun. 2–4, June–Sept., rest of year Fri. 2–4. Donation.

IOWA CITY

UNIVERSITY OF IOWA MUSEUM OF ART, 5 blocks west on N. Riverside Drive (use exit 244 south off I–80), displays African art and rare jade works, along with paintings and sculpture.

Tues.–Sat. 10–5, Sun. noon–5. Closed holidays. Free.

SALEM

THE LEWELLING QUAKER HOUSE in the small Quaker town of Salem was once known as the main ticket office of the Underground Railroad. The stone house was built in 1840 by Henderson Lewelling as a refuge for fleeing slaves. A trap door led to a tunnel under the house where the fugitive slaves hid. In 1848 a slave owner appeared with a group of armed men, threatening the house and the town citizens. He returned home empty-handed, though later he sued the citizens for their part in the flight of his "chattels."

The Bee Hive was another building involved in helping escaped slaves. The floor of one room on the first floor could be lifted by a wheel and rope in the attic, opening a secret cellar hideaway.

Open Sun. 1–4, May–Oct. Adults $1, students 50 cents. Weekdays by appointment. Adults $2.50, students $1.

TABOR

TODD HOUSE MUSEUM on Park Street. Tabor is 10 miles south of Glenwood on U.S. 275. The Todd House was one of the stations on the Underground Railroad in Iowa and hosted the famous abolitionist John Brown between 1854 and 1856. Tours of the house by appointment only through the Tabor Historical Society, P.O. Box 417.

For further information about Iowa, contact:

Iowa Tourism Commission
200 E. Grand Ave.
Des Moines, IA 50309
1-800-345-4692

KANSAS

BALDWIN

ROBERT HALL PEARSON (BLACK JACK) PARK, three miles east of Baldwin City on KS 56, then south ¼ mile, is the site of the first battle over slavery in the United States. It was fought in 1856 between federal troops and free state militia under the command of John Brown. Open 24 hours.

BAXTER SPRINGS

THE BATTLE OF BAXTER SPRINGS MONUMENT. In October 1863, Union general Blunt's troops, on their way to Fort Smith, Kansas, were unexpectedly attacked by the infamous Quantrill raiders, wearing stolen Federal uniforms. At a nearby camp, 100 Union troops, two-thirds of whom were from the 2nd Kansas Colored Infantry Regiment, were also attacked as they were having dinner. The defenders had to run the gauntlet of enemy fire and get to their weapons before they were able to drive the attackers away. The white and black troops who died fighting off Quantrill's raiders are buried in the Baxter Springs National Cemetery. A monument has been erected there in their honor.

CHANUTE

MARTIN AND OSA JOHNSON SAFARI MUSEUM, 16 S. Grant Avenue, is a collection of African artifacts and photographs by Martin and Osa Johnson, world-famous African wildlife photographers. They were among the first, through their photographs and books, to introduce the American public to the largely unknown continent of Africa. The "African Tribal Culture Exhibit" at the museum depicts African village life with household and religious items representing more than forty West African tribes.

Open Mon.–Sat. 10–5, Sun. 1–5. Closed holidays. Adults $2.50, ages 13–18 $1.

DODGE CITY

One of the most famous of the wide-open frontier towns of the Old West was Dodge City. Cowboys, raring to let off steam after long, hard months on the trail, brought prosperity—and lawlessness—to this prairie boom town. Black troopers from nearby Fort Dodge (now the Kansas Veteran Home) helped preserve law in the town.

Black cowboys, as well as white, roamed the streets of Dodge. One out of every four cowboys in the West was a black man. Before the Civil War, slaves had been used on western ranches to wrangle horses and tend cattle. After the war, many of these ex-slaves remained on as cowhands, receiving equal treatment and equal pay on cattle drives.

Just as there were black cowhands, there were also black rustlers, gunslingers and cardsharps. Ben Hodges was a black cowboy who came to Dodge City in the spring of 1872. He lived by his wits, stealing horses, playing cards and bilking the gullible. In his last years, Ben Hodges became a respected old-timer. When he died in the same year as Wyatt Earp, the people of Dodge City donated money for his tombstone. His grave can be seen in the old Maple Grove Cemetery.

THE BOOT HILL MUSEUM COMPLEX on Front Street recreates the Dodge City of the 1870s, including the historic cemetery, the Fort Dodge jail, and the Long Branch Saloon. The Boot Hill Museum has exhibits on local black residents and cowboys.

Daily 8–8, May 26–Aug. 26; rest of year, Mon.–Sat. 9–5, Sun. 1–5. Closed Jan. 1, Thanksgiving and Dec. 25. Adults $4.25, students and seniors $3.75, under 10 free. Prices lower Aug. 26–May 26.

FORT RILEY MILITARY RESERVATION

UNITED STATES CAVALRY MUSEUM is located in Bldg. 205—corner Sheridan and Custer Avenue—at Fort Riley, which is near Junction City. Fort Riley (take exit 301 off I-70) was established in 1853 to protect traffic on the Santa Fe Trail from the Indians. For many years it was the headquarters of the famed 7th Cavalry and Lt. Colonel George Custer. Also stationed at Fort Riley were black troopers of the 9th and 10th Cavalry. The black troopers were called "Buffalo Soldiers" by the Indians as a mark of respect, for the buffalo was sacred to the Indian. Twenty percent of the soldiers who patrolled the Western frontier were black men.

The museum tells the history of the U.S. Cavalry and the Buffalo Soldiers with photographs and exhibits.

Mon.–Sat. 9–4:30, Sun. 12–4:30. Closed Jan. 1, Easter, Thanksgiving, and Dec. 25. Free.

FORT SCOTT

FORT SCOTT NATIONAL HISTORIC SITE is located on Old Fort Boulevard in the city of Fort Scott. Fort Scott was established in 1842 on the military road that connected army posts from Minnesota to Louisiana. After the Civil War, the fort was the home of the 1st and 2nd Kansas Colored Volunteer Infantry regiments. The 1st Kansas Regiment, one of the first black regiments to be mustered into the Union army in January 1863, took part in seven engagements during the Civil War and suffered more casualties than any other Kansas regiment.

Twenty of old Fort Scott's buildings have been restored and furnished, among them the hospital, officers' quarters, barracks, and a guardhouse. There is a visitor center and museum which tells the fort's history, including information on the 1st Kansas Colored Regiment. Living history and audio-visual programs are given from May through September.

Daily 8–6, June–Aug., rest of year 8–5. Closed Jan. 1, Thanksgiving, and Dec. 25. Adults $1, over 61 and under 16 free.

HAYS

FORT HAYS STATE HISTORIC SITE is on U.S. 183 Alt., 4 miles south of I-70 in Frontier Historical Park. The 9th and 10th Cavalary both served at Fort Hays. The black troopers of the 10th Cavalry were first bloodied in battle in August 1867 shortly after they arrived at the fort. While on patrol from Fort Hays, they were ambushed and had to shoot their way through encircling Cheyennes. In the face of overwhelming odds, the raw recruits held their own. On the frontier, though, disease proved a more deadly enemy than the hostile Indians.

Fort Hays, built in 1865, has been restored with its guardhouse, blockhouse, and officers' quarters, along with buildings containing exhibits on the military history of the fort.

Tues.–Sat. 9–5, Sun.–Mon. 1–5. Closed holidays. Donation.

LARNED

FORT LARNED NATIONAL HISTORIC SITE is 6 miles west of Larned, via KS 156. Established in 1859, Fort Larned was one of the most active posts on the frontier, particularly during the Indian Wars of 1868–1869 when the Cheyennes, Kiowas, Comanches and Arapahos raided from Kansas to Texas. Black troopers of Company A, 10th Cavalry, were stationed at the fort from April 1867 to January 1869. Today the buildings have been restored to their 1868 appearance, with a museum displaying cavalry and infantry equipment, mementos of fort life, and living history programs most weekends. The actions and movements of the 10th Cavalry are mentioned frequently.

Daily 8–6 summer, rest of year 8–5. Closed Jan. 1, Thanksgiving and Dec. 25. Adults $1, under 16 free.

LEAVENWORTH

Fort Leavenworth, at 7th Street and U.S. 73, is home for the FRONTIER ARMY MUSEUM at Gibbon and Reynolds avenues. Built in 1827, Fort Leavenworth is one of the oldest and most beautiful army posts in the United States. During the Civil War, the Independent Kansas Colored Battery, with black officers, was formed at this fort.

In July 1866, Congress authorized the establishment of black troops in the regular peacetime army. Fort Leavenworth became the headquarters for the 10th Cavalry, under the command of Colonel Benjamin Grierson of Civil War fame. The other black units established were the 9th Cavalry and the 24th and 25th Infantry regiments.

Although the equipment and horses given to the black troopers were often rejects from the more favored 7th Cavalry, the 9th and 10th Cavalry developed into the hardest-fighting and best-disciplined mounted forces on the Western frontier. By the end of the Indian wars, 14 black soldiers had won the Congressional Medal of Honor. The 10th Cavalry also served with distinction during the Spanish-American War.

The Frontier Army Museum covers the history of the frontier army and the Civil and Indian wars. There is a slide program on the history of the fort.

Mon.–Sat. 10–4, Sun. and holidays 12–4. Closed Jan. 1, Easter, Thanksgiving and Dec. 25. Free.

NESS CITY

GEORGE WASHINGTON CARVER MARKER. Turn off KS 96 about 18 miles west of Ness City, then 1½ miles south of KS 96 on Ness County Road 523. The marker notes the northeast corner of the homestead where George Washington Carver spent two years as a farmer before going to college in Iowa and on to fame as a teacher and scientist at Tuskegee.

NICODEMUS

THE EXODUSTERS. In the 1870s, black immigrants headed west to secure a better life for their children and escape the bigotry and persecution that followed the Reconstruction period after the Civil War. The first wave of immigrants, often called Exodusters, was organized by Benjamin "Pap" Singleton who lectured throughout the South, urging blacks to move west to Kansas and Oklahoma. Five black settlements were the product of this movement, including the town of Nicodemus, Kansas, founded in 1877. In the years to come, many black settlements disappeared as crops failed and residents moved from the farm to the city. Nicodemus, one of the last to remain, was declared a National Historic Landmark in 1974.

A historical marker in a roadside park located along U.S. 24, two miles west of the Rooks-Graham county line, commemorates the Exodusters.

OSAWATOMIE

JOHN BROWN MUSEUM is found in the John Brown Memorial park at 10th and Main. In the years before the Civil War, the state of Kansas was torn by guerrilla warfare between antislavery and proslavery groups. Among the more militant leaders in the antislavery group were abolitonist John Brown and his five sons. Brown not only fought in several border skirmishes near the town of Osawatomie but raided into Missouri, freeing eleven slaves and leading them to safety in Canada.

Today the John Brown Cabin serves as a museum and memorial to Brown's life in Kansas, its interior remaining much as it was when John Brown was alive. There was once a cellar where fugitive slaves were hidden.

Tues.–Sat. 10–5, Sun. 1–5. Closed legal holidays. Donation.

TOPEKA

KANSAS MUSEUM OF HISTORY, 6425 S.W. 6th Street, tells the story of Kansas and includes a replica of the type of sod house in which early white and black settlers lived. There are also exhibits of Kansas soldiers during the Civil War.

Mon.–Sat. 9–4:30, Sun. 12:30–4:30. Free.

SUMNER ELEMENTARY SCHOOL, 330 Southwest Western Avenue, was the school which refused to enroll Linda Brown because she was black. In the famous Supreme Court case that resulted, Brown vs. Board of Education of Topeka, the court concluded that "separate education facilities

are inherently unequal," striking down the legal basis for
segregation in the public schools.

WALLACE

FORT WALLACE MUSEUM is ½ mile east on U.S. 40 at
Safety Rest Area. In 1868, Major General George Forsyth and
his men were pinned down by a Cheyenne attack at Sandy
Creek for almost a week. Their food and medical supplies
gone, and almost half-mad from the heat, the men were
forced to eat their dead horses. A messenger finally made it
through to Fort Wallace. Captain Louis Carpenter and his
black 10th Cavalry troopers, stationed at the fort, covered
almost 100 miles in two days to rescue General Forsyth and
his men.

The museum displays articles used by early settlers and the
garrisoned troops.

Mon.–Sat. 9–5, Sun. 1–5, May 1–Labor Day; rest of year
Sat. 9–5, Sun. 1–5. Free.

WICHITA

FIRST NATIONAL BLACK HISTORICAL SOCIETY
OF KANSAS, 601 N. Water, is located in the old Calvary
Church. This museum and cultural center was established to
give recognition to black participation in early Wichita.
Blacks arrived in Wichita shortly after the Civil War and
settled in the 500 and 600 blocks of north Main Street. Their
contributions in the fields of sports, government, entertainment, medicine, education and the military are depicted in the
museum. Also exhibited are African artifacts, wood carvings,
jewelry and dress.

Mon., Wed. and Fri. 10–2, Sun. 2–6. Donation. Tours by
appointment.

For further information about Kansas, contact:

Kansas Dept. of Commerce
400 Southwest 8th St., 5th Floor
Topeka, KS 66603-3957
913-296-2009

KENTUCKY

BEREA

BEREA COLLEGE is a mile from the Berea exit off I-75, on Chestnut Street. It seemed an impossible task in 1855, in a slave state, to found a school for both black and white students, based on the biblical doctrine that "God hath made of one blood all nations of men." In 1859, armed men forced the small school to close its doors but in 1865 it was reopened. During the next fifty years, the college continued to promote co-education of race and the sexes when neither idea was popular. The student body was almost equally divided between black and white students.

Another untraditional program offered students a tuition-free education in return for work in the school's 140 departments. This was particularly helpful for students coming from the poverty-stricken Appalachian area. Berea College is noted for teaching Appalachian mountain crafts such as ceramics, woodcraft, weaving, needlecraft, wrought iron and broomcraft. (Within the town of Berea, tourists can visit the workshops of professional craftspeople and artists.)

In 1983 the college established the Black Cultural Center and Interracial Education Program, to promote interracial understanding and equality of all persona.

The Dorish Ulmann Galleries, Rogers Art Building, has displays of African art as well as that of other countries.

Gallery hours Mon.–Thurs. 8 a.m.–9 p.m., Fri. 8–5, Sun.
1–5. Closed Sat. and college holidays.

Visitors are welcome on the campus. Free student-guided
tours are given Mon.–Fri. at 9, 10, 1, and 3, and Sat. at 9 and
2. The tours leave from the Boone Tavern hotel lobby.

ELIZABETH TOWN

EMMA RENO CONNOR BLACK HISTORY GAL-
LERY, 602 Hawkins Drive, in Elizabeth Town, or E'Town,
KY 65, south of Louisville. The gallery features pictures and
historical data depicting black Americans whose achievements
have contributed to the life and culture of the country.

Showings usually on weekends, 12–5, or as posted or by
appointment. Free.

FRANKFORT

KENTUCKY HISTORY MUSEUM, adjacent to the Old
State Capitol, Broadway at St. Clair Mall, has exhibits on the
state's geology and history, including a section dealing with
the role played by black men and women.

Mon.–Sat. 9–4, Sun. 1–4. Closed major holidays. Free.

KENTUCKY VIETNAM VETERANS MEMORIAL,
Coffee Tree Road in front of the State Library building, is an
unusual 14-foot-high sundial that casts a shadow on each
veteran's name on the anniversary of his death. There are
1,084 names on the granite plaza.

HODGENVILLE

ABRAHAM LINCOLN BIRTHPLACE NATIONAL
HISTORIC SITE is three miles south on U.S. 31E and KY

61. The log cabin in which President Lincoln was born is enshrined here, along with a visitor center with exhibits about the Lincoln family and a movie on Lincoln's Kentucky years. It was at nearby Knob Creek, where the family later moved, that Lincoln first saw slave dealers driving slaves along the public road.

Daily 8–6:45 mid-June through Labor Day, 9–5:45 April 1 to mid-June and after Labor Day–Oct 31, rest of year 8–4:45. Closed Dec. 25. Free.

LEXINGTON

KENTUCKY HORSE PARK, 10 miles north of the town at 4089 Iron Works Pike, I-75 exit 120, is a unique 1,032-acre park located amidst Lexington's beautiful bluegrass horse farms. Blacks have always worked in racing stables and horse farms, from slave days. One of the greatest jockeys of all times was Isaac Murphy, a black man and the first jockey to win three Kentucky Derbies, in 1884, 1890 and 1891. This record was not broken until Eddie Arcaro won his fourth Derby in 1948. In 1882 Murphy won 49 out of his 51 starts at the Saratoga race track, and in all his career rode 628 winners in 1,412 races. At one time he owned his own racehorse, an unusual distinction for a black man of his day.

In 1967 Isaac Murphy's almost forgotten grave was moved to Kentucky Horse Park where it was placed not far from that of the great racing horse Man O' War. The park has horse-drawn, motorized and walking tours of its facilities. The International Museum of the Horse tells the history of all breeds of horses. A film is shown in the visitor center, and the Parade of Breeds Show takes place daily, April 1–Oct. 15.

Park open daily 9–5, April–Oct.; rest of year Weds.–Sun. 9–5. Closed Jan. 1, Nov. 22–23, Dec. 24–25 and 31. Adults $7.95, seniors $7.45, ages 7–12 $3.95.

LOUISVILLE

J. B. SPEED ART MUSEUM at 2035 S. 3rd Street, ¾ miles west of I-65 (Eastern Parkway exit), is adjacent to the University of Louisville campus. Along with modern and old master paintings and sculpture, furniture and other decorative arts, there is an African culture exhibit.

Tues.–Sat. 10–4, Sun. 1–5. Closed holidays. Adults $2, seniors $1, students free. Free to all on Sat.

KENTUCKY DERBY MUSEUM is located at the entrance of Churchill Downs, 700 Central Avenue, where the famous Kentucky Derby is run the first Saturday in May. In the first Kentucky Derby, run in 1875, all except one of the jockies were black men. The winning jockey that day was Jockey Lewis, a black man. The horse ran the race in 2 minutes, 37¾ seconds, setting a world record for a 3-year-old running one mile and a half. Black riders guided fifteen of the winning horses in the first twenty-eight Derbies. Black men were also stablehands, trainers and horsebreakers on many horse farms.

At the museum, visitors can see racing artifacts connected with Derby Day along with hands-on exhibits which allow visitors to relive Derbies of yesteryear, and a 360-degree multi-image show about the event. A walking tour of Churchill Downs is available, weather permitting.

Daily 9–5. Closed Oaks and Derby days and Dec. 25. Adults $3, seniors $2.50, ages 5–12 $1.50.

MAMMOTH CAVE NATIONAL PARK is located between Louisville and Nashville, off I-65 from exits 48 or 53. Mammoth Cave, within the park, contains more than 300 miles of underground passages on five levels and is one of the longest cave systems known. There are unverified legends that the cave was used as a refuge for slaves escaping on the Underground Railroad. It was also explored by whites. A slave, Stephen Bishop, guided visitors through the cave before the Civil War. The guide who followed him was also black,

Matt Bransford, who was the first of five generations of Bransford explorers and guides. Both men are buried in the Old Guides Cemetery within the park.

Cave tours of various lengths are offered year round, beginning at the visitor center. First tour during the summer months is at 8 a.m., last tour at 5:30. Prices and schedules are available at the visitor center.

RICHMOND

WHITE HALL STATE HISTORIC SITE, I-75 exit 95 on U.S. 25/421, built in 1799, was the home of Cassius Marcellus Clay, an outspoken supporter of black emancipation. Although his father owned slaves, young Clay became an opponent of slavery while he attended Yale University, and in 1845 published a militantly abolitionist newspaper. When a mob seized the press while Clay was away, he moved the newspaper to Ohio and later, Louisville. He turned down a Federal major-generalship early in the Civil War because Lincoln had not emancipated the slaves. A violent, volatile man, in his last years Clay barricaded himself at his home at White Hall.

Daily 9–5, April–Labor Day; Labor Day–Oct. Wed.–Sun. 9–5. Adults $3, ages 6–12 $2.

"LION OF WHITE HALL" is an outdoor dramatic presentation telling of Cassius Marcellus Clay's youth, his political career and his dangerous anti-slavery campaign. I-75 exit 95 at White Hall.

Fri.–Sat. 8 p.m. June 29–Aug. 4. Admission charge.

WASHINGTON

Kentucky was a big slave market before the Civil War. Lexington and Washington were two major centers of the trade. In many communities slaves were sold on the steps of a courthouse or in open-air auctions, where black men, women and children mounted blocks so that they could be better seen by the audience of prospective purchasers. One such auction block may be seen on the courthouse green in Washington, an 18th-century town that has retained many of its historic homes and sites. It was at Washington that Harriet Beecher Stowe watched slaves being bought and sold. The horror of the experience stayed with her and later she used the scene in her novel *Uncle Tom's Cabin*.

For further information about Kentucky, contact:

Kentucky Dept. of Travel Development
Capital Plaza Tower
Frankfort, KY 40601
1-800-225-8747

LOUISIANA

BATON ROUGE

PORT HUDSON STATE COMMEMORATIVE AREA
AND MUSEUM, U.S. 61, 14 miles north of Baton Rouge, is
the site of one of the longest sieges in American history, May
23–July 9, 1863. Port Hudson on the Mississippi River was
defended by 6,800 Confederate troops. The task of making an
almost suicidal attack against the heavily garrisoned fortress
was given to five black regiments. One of them had been
formed only three months before and none of them were
experienced in combat.

Six times, a thousand black soldiers of the 1st and 3d
Louisiana Regiments, free blacks recruited in New Orleans,
charged across an open field and were driven back by mortar
fire, cannister and grapeshot. There were 212 casualties, but
even in defeat the black soldier had proven his valor. Less than
two weeks later at Milliken's Bend, the remains of two white
companies and three black regiments took the brunt of a
charge by 1,500 Texans. The assault was marked by terrible
bloodshed but the men beat back the Rebels, holding their
ground against seasoned veterans. Before the end of the Civil
War, black soldiers had participated in at least 39 major battles
and 410 minor engagements.

Today, an observation tower looks over what remains of the
trenches and breastworks of the battlefield, and there are

outdoor exhibits, trails and guided tours. A museum offers information about the battle and an audio-visual program. Living history demonstrations in summer.

Museum open Wed.–Sun. 9–5; grounds open Wed.–Sun. 9–7 p.m. April 1–Sept. 30, and Wed.–Sun. 9–5 Oct. 1–Mar. 31. Closed Mon. and Tues. and Thanksgiving, Dec. 25 and New Year's Day. Adults 13 and up, $2, children 12 and under free.

DERRY

MAGNOLIA PLANTATION, LA 119, one mile north of Derry, was built in 1784 and burned during the Civil War. Rebuilt on the old foundations, the plantation is still a working farm which may be toured by visitors. The Creole-style plantation house has 27 rooms and a complex of outbuildings, which includes a chapel, overseer's house, barns, a blacksmith shop and a mule-drawn cotton press. Some of the old slave houses have survived, a row of brick cottages with tin roofs, built like tiny forts.

Afternoons 1–4 or by appointment. Adults $4, students $2, children $1.

KENNER

KENNER HISTORICAL MUSEUM, 1922 Third Street, is in the historic Rivertown district of Kenner, a town just west of New Orleans on the Mississippi River. Other museums in the historic district include the Louisiana Toy Train Museum, a science center and planetarium, the Wildlife and Fisheries Aquarium and the Saints Hall of Fame, which celebrates the New Orleans professional football team and its white and black players.

Throughout much of its history, Kenner had a large black

population and the Kenner Historical Museum has a black history room.

Historical museum open by reservation only (504-468-7274). Other museums Tues.–Sat. 9–5, Sun. 1–5. Adults $1.50 (Saints Hall of Fame $2) seniors $1, children 50 cents.

MANSFIELD

MANSFIELD BATTLE COMMEMORATIVE AREA is 4 miles southeast of Mansfield on LA 175, 3 miles southeast of junction with U.S. 84. In 1864 Union general Nathaniel P. Banks was put in charge of the Red River campaign and sent into Louisiana. His troops included four regiments of black infantry. After a great loss of life on both sides, General Banks' advance was halted at the battle of Mansfield in April 1864. The next day at Pleasant Hill Federal troops, including the four black regiments, repulsed a Confederate attack before withdrawing to the south.

The Mansfield Commemorative Area Museum has historical exhibits, a slide show and relics from the battle. There is also a self-guiding walking tour of the battlefield.

Wed.–Sun. 8–4:30. Closed Jan. 1, Thanksgiving and Dec. 25. Adults $2, ages 6–12 $1.

MELROSE

MELROSE PLANTATION is 2 miles east of LA 1, via LA 493. The town of Melrose is 15 miles south of Natchitoches. Along the Cane River area of Louisiana in the 1800s there grew up a settlement of Afro-Creole planters. A deeply religious people with a great pride of race, they built their own plantations and often owned slaves themselves. One such plantation was Melrose. The original plantation house called

"Yucca," was built in 1796 for Marie Therese Coincoin, a freed slave and matriarch of the Metoyer family. In 1800 "Africa House," the only African-style structure standing in the United States today, was built. The Big House was built in 1833 and from here the Metoyer family controlled more than 50 slaves on their 2,000-acre plantation.

By the time of the Civil War, the plantation had been sold to a white family, but many of the Metoyer possessions and furniture may still be seen in the house. After the turn of the century Melrose became a center for artists and writers.

Daily noon–4. Closed major holidays and Fri. preceding special events, such as the Melrose Arts and Crafts Show held the second weekend in June, and Fall Tour the second weekend in Oct. Adults $4, ages 13–18 $2, ages 6–11 $1.

NEW ORLEANS

AMISTAD RESEARCH CENTER at Tilton Hall, Tulane University, 6823 St. Charles Street, is the largest American ethnic historical archives in the world, with documents ranging from the late-1700s to the present. More than 90 percent of the documents are on black-white relations. Also within the center are 110 African art objects and 250 Afro-American art works.

Daily 8:30–5. Free.

BLACK HERITAGE TOUR of New Orleans and vicinity is one of the tours conducted by LE OBs Tours, 4635 Touro Street. Group rates available. Daily 9 a.m.–9 p.m.

CHALMETTE NATIONAL HISTORICAL PARK is located on LA 46, 6 miles downriver from the New Orleans French Quarter. Chalmette was the site of the battle of New Orleans on Jan. 8, 1815, the greatest land victory of the War of 1812, but actually fought after the war had officially ended. The English hoped to attack and capture New Orleans, but when they reached Chalmette plantation, General Andrew

Jackson and 4,000 members of the militia formed a defensive line. The British soldiers came head-on against the Americans. The expert rifle and artillery fire from Jackson's militia, recruited from free blacks, Creoles, Indians, Kentucky backwoodsmen and even pirates, killed or wounded 2,000 of the British toops within thirty minutes.

Interestingly enough, black soldiers fought on both sides of this battle. The British had black troops, the 1st and 2nd West Indian Infantry Regiments, and General Jackson had several hundred black soldiers organized as the Louisiana Battalion of Free Men of Color.

The visitor center has exhibits about the battle and an audio-visual program. Interpretative talks and self-guiding auto tours of the battlefield are available.

Daily 8–5, extended hours in summer. Closed Jan. 1, Mardi Gras and Dec. 25. Free.

DILLARD UNIVERSITY, 2601 Gentilly Boulevard, has roots going back to 1869 and the Congregational and Methodist Episcopal Church. Located in a residential section of New Orleans, Dillard has handsome buildings and lovely landscaped lawns. The university was named for James Dillard who played an important role in black education in the nineteenth century. The Alexander Library has an important collection of materials on black American history, particularly black people in New Orleans before the Civil War, and black musicians and composers.

Library and campus open during regular academic schedule.

GRAVE OF MARIE LAVEAU, VOODOO QUEEN is in St. Louis Cemetery Number 2, Square No. 3, North Claiborne Avenue and Bienville Street. The cemeteries of New Orleans are unique in that burials are above ground, in lavish vaults. Cemetery Number 2 was laid out in two squares. Square Number 3 was set aside for the burial of black Catholics.

Noted black men and women of the 1900s are buried in this

cemetery including Marie Laveau, a black woman who was well-known throughout New Orleans in the 1800s for her "voodoo" powers. Although discouraged by slaveholders, African religious rituals persisted in New Orleans, and worshippers would meet far back in a swamp near the lake end of Bayou St. John. Marie was famed in the French Quarter and Congo Square for her powers to heal the sick, cure the lovelorn, and put a hex or *gris-gris* on a person's enemies. In her old age, Marie Laveau returned to the Catholic church and gave her money to the poor in the prisons of New Orleans and the St. Louis Cathedral.

Visits to this cemetery are conducted by the National Park Service (504-589-2636).

HERMANN-GRIMA HISTORIC HOUSE, 820 Saint Louis Street, is a restored 1821 Creole mansion with a stable, courtyards, and slave quarters. Tours of the house blend the life style of the nineteenth-century Creole family with seasonal Creole cooking demonstrations. The Creoles of Louisiana were of French and Spanish stock and had a liberal Latin-American attitude regarding slavery. Also, the Catholic church, which considered that blacks had souls just as whites, encouraged slaves to become Christians and allowed them to marry.

Mon.–Sat. 10–3:30. Creole cooking demonstrations every Thurs. Oct.–May. Adults $3, seniors and ages 8–18 $2.

JACKSON SQUARE, in the heart of the French Quarter, is one of the most photographed squares in the country. It was named in honor of Andrew Jackson, the hero of the battle of New Orleans at Chalmette. Black soldiers fought on both sides of this battle. Surrounding Jackson Square are beautiful buildings decorated with wrought and cast ironwork, much of which was constructed by black artisans.

LOUIS ARMSTRONG PARK, North Rampart and St. Ann Street, memorializes jazz musician Louis "Satchmo" Armstrong, who brought the music of New Orleans to the world. The statue of Armstrong in the park is by noted black sculptor Elizabeth Catlett. Many festivals and concerts are held here. At Congo Square in Armstrong Park (in front of the municipal auditorium) slaves met on Sundays for traditional African song and dance in antebellum times.

MARTIN LUTHER KING, JR. STATUE is located at Martin Luther King Boulevard and South Clairborne Avenue. Ceremonies are held here each year to celebrate the birthday of Dr. Martin Luther King, Jr.

MUSEE CONTI MUSEUM OF WAX, 917 Conti Street, presents costumed, life-size wax figures in realistic settings, depicting New Orleans history from 1699 to the early 1900s. Figures include Marie Laveau, the "Voodoo Queen," and voodoo dancers performing in Congo Square, as well as scenes from the jazz days of New Orleans. Other scenes show a slave auction and the infamous home of Madame Lalaurie, who treated her slaves so cruelly that she was run out of the city. Her home at 1140 Royal Street is still known today as the Haunted House.

Daily 10–5:30. Closed Mardi Gras Day and Dec. 25. Adults $5, seniors $4.50, ages 4–17 $3.

NEW ORLEANS HISTORIC VOODOO MUSEUM, 724 Rue Dumaine. A tour of the museum starts with a history of Marie Laveau, the city's most famous voodoo queen. Visitors can wander among altars, African masks, carvings, instruments used in ritual music, and voodoo dolls. The museum also conducts some exotic tours, such as a voodoo walking tour of the French Quarter. More extensive tours take visitors into bayous, plantations, and Indian burial grounds, even a visit to a voodoo ceremony.

Tours range from 2½ to 10 hours, prices from $15 to $55. Museum open daily from 10 to dusk. Adults $4, seniors $3, children $2, free for children under 6.

NEW ORLEANS MUSEUM OF ART, Lelong Avenue in the City Park, which is at the north end of Esplanade Avenue. This museum has a strong African art collection.

Tues.–Sun. 10–5. Closed holidays. Adults $3, seniors and ages 3–17 $1.50.

PONTALBA BUILDINGS, The Lower Pontalba (1850

House) at 523 St. Ann Street, is part of the Louisiana State Museum. The Pontalba buildings were completed in 1851 and are some of the oldest apartment buildings in America. From kitchen to top-floor slave quarters, each room in the Lower Pontalba (1850 House) is furnished as it would have been in the 1850s.

Guided tours on the hour, Wed.–Sun. 10–3. Adults $3, students $1.50, under 12 free.

PRESERVATION HALL, 726 St. Peter Street in the French Quarter, is where visitors go to hear traditional jazz in its purest form. Each night a different band takes its turn performing. Some of the musicians are jazz veterans who come out of retirement to play again. Although many styles (spirituals, ragtime, blues) have an Afro-American source, jazz is undoubtedly the most popular and has had the greatest influence in the world of music.

No food or beverages are sold. Limited seating, some standing room. Usually visitors have to wait for show.

Daily 8:30 P.M.–12:30 A.M. Doors open at 8 P.M. Closed Mardi Gras. Admission $2.

U.S. MINT MUSEUM at 400 Esplanade Avenue, is part of the Louisiana State Museum. It actually operated as a U.S. mint until 1909. Today in the restored building, on the second floor, are the JAZZ and CARNIVAL MUSEUMS.

The Jazz Museum traces the development of New Orleans music since 1700 and contains many black musicians' instruments, including Louis Armstrong's first trumpet, as well as photographs, documents and rare musical recordings.

The Carnival Museum displays the largest single Louisiana Mardi Gras collection. The first organized black Krewe, Zulu, to take part in the Mardi Gras appeared in 1909.

Wed.–Sun. 10–6. Closed holidays. Adults $3, seniors $1.50, under 13 free.

XAVIER UNIVERSITY, 7325 Palmetto Street, is the only predominantly black Roman Catholic university in the western hemisphere, and was founded in 1915.

ST. FRANCISVILLE

COTTAGE PLANTATION, U.S. 61, 6 miles north of St. Francisville, which is 50 miles south of Natchez, is one of the earliest and largest surviving sugar plantation complexes in Louisiana. There are many beautiful plantations that may be visited in this, as well as other southern states. Although the big houses have survived intact or been restored, many of the slave cabins have not. Slave labor built almost all the beautiful ante-bellum homes and slave labor kept the plantations running. Ironically, it was a Creole black man, Norbert Rillieux, who invented in 1843 a process of boiling the cane juice in vacuum pans to make sugar crystal. Thereupon, sugarcane, like cotton, became extremely profitable to grow, but also like cotton, required a large labor force. More and more slaves were imported or "sold south" to meet this demand.

The original outbuildings surviving at Cottage Plantation include a detached kitchen, schoolhouse, smokehouse, carriage house, milkhouse and a few of the slave quarters. Slaves working on the sugar plantations often died from cholera and malaria, as did many whites.

Today, a portion of the house is used as a hotel but tours may be arranged of the house and grounds. (504-635-3674)

For further information about Louisiana, contact:

Louisiana Office of Tourism
P.O. Box 94291
Baton Rouge, LA 70804-9291
1-800-334-8626

Greater New Orleans Black Tourism Network
1520 Sugar Bowl Dr.
New Orleans, LA 70130
504-523-5652

MAINE

BRUNSWICK

BOWDOIN COLLEGE, at Maine, Bath and College streets, established in 1794, was a hot bed of abolitionism before the Civil War. The first black graduate of Bowdoin was John Brown Russwurm, class of 1826. Russwurm started *Freedom's Journal,* the first newspaper edited by blacks, in 1827. At the time of his death in 1851, he was governor of the colony of Maryland in Liberia. General Oliver Otis Howard who founded Howard University, one of the first colleges for black students to open after the Civil War, was also a graduate of Bowdoin.

The Hawthorne-Longfellow library has in its collection the original manuscript of a poem by Phillis Wheatley, America's first black poet. There are also informal records of the Freedmen's Bureau formed after the Civil War to help the newly freed slaves along with papers of General Oliver Otis Howard.

The JOHN BROWN RUSSWURM AFRO-AMERICAN CENTER is housed in the Little-Mitchell House at 6-8 College Street. The center contains the offices of the Afro-American Studies Program, a library of African and Afro-American source materials and the Herman Dreer Reading Room, named in honor of a black graduate of the class of 1910. The historic Little-Mitchell house was a stop on the Underground Railroad.

Harriet Beecher Stowe began writing *Uncle Tom's Cabin* at her home on Federal Street in Brunswick while her husband taught at Bowdoin College. Stowe's inspiration for the book supposedly came from an anti-slavery sermon delivered at the FIRST PARISH CHURCH on Maine Street while she sat in the Stowe pew, number 23. The church's congregation included such notables as Henry Wadsworth Longfellow, Eleanor Roosevelt and Martin Luther King, Jr.

CASTINE

WILSON MUSEUM, on Perkins Street, has a small but good collection of prehistoric material from Africa, along with local Indian artifacts and colonial items.
Tues.–Sun. 2–5, May 27–Oct. 1. Free.

PORTLAND

CATHEDRAL OF THE IMMACULATE CON-CEPTION, 307 Congress Street, was the site of the consecration of the first black American bishop of the Roman Catholic Church, James Augustine Healy, on June 2, 1875. The mulatto son of a Georgia planter, Healy graduated from Holy Cross College in 1849 and was ordained in Paris in 1854. His brother, Patrick Francis Healy, became the first black president of an American Catholic university when he became rector of Georgetown University in 1874.

For further information about Maine, contact:

Maine Office of Tourism
Box 2300
Hallowell, ME 04347
1-800-533-9595

MARYLAND

ANNAPOLIS

BANNEKER-DOUGLASS MUSEUM OF AFRO-AMERICAN LIFE AND HISTORY, 84 Franklin Street, in Annapolis' historic district, is named after two outstanding black men in Afro-American history, scientist Benjamin Banneker, and abolitionist Frederick Douglass. The museum is located in what was formerly the Mount Moriah African Methodist Episcopal Church and exhibits focus on the Afro-American experience in Maryland. There are also changing shows by contemporary artists.

Tues.–Fri. 10–3, Sat.–Sun. 12–4. Donation.

MATTHEW HENSON PLAQUE may be seen at the Maryland State House on State Circle. The plaque honors the memory of the black explorer who was born in Charles County, Maryland. Matthew Henson accompanied Admiral Robert E. Peary on his polar expeditions and was actually the first man to reach the North Pole on April 6, 1909. Peary, barely able to walk, arrived there after Henson had taken a reading of his position and proudly planted the flag of the United States.

Guided tours and self-guiding tours of the historic State House daily 9–5. Closed Dec. 25. Visitor center closed Thanksgiving, Dec 25, and June 1. Free.

Another site in Maryland which honors Henson is the

MATTHEW HENSON STATE PARK at Aspen Hill which is 6 miles east of Rockville near the junction of MD 97 and MD 185.

BALTIMORE

BALTIMORE'S BLACK AMERICAN MUSEUM, 1769 Carswell Street, exhibits artwork associated with the civil rights movement from the 1960s and 1970s. All of its contemporary work was produced by Baltimore artists, black and white. There are also older pieces from African and other third-world countries. Tours of the three floors of galleries are conducted by artists. More than the typical staid art museum, the BAM offers an unusual glimpse into black art and culture as well as a commercial art service to the community.

Mon.–Thurs. 9–5, Fri. 7 P.M.–11 P.M. Free. Small charge for tours.

BALTIMORE MUSEUM OF ART, on Art Museum Drive near N. Charles and 31st streets, displays 18th-and 19th-century American and European paintings, sculpture and furniture, along with art from Africa. The Baltimore Museum of Art presented the first black American art show in the South in 1939.

Tues.–Fri. 10–4, Sat.–Sun. 11–6. Closed holidays. Adults $2, under 22 free. Free to all on Thurs.

CAB CALLOWAY JAZZ INSTITUTE is in the Parlett Moore Library at Coppin State College, 2500 West North Avenue. The collection includes photographs and other personal memorabilia of the great jazz musician Cab Calloway.

Mon.–Fri. 8–5. Free.

ENOCH PRICE FREE LIBRARY, 400 Cathedral Street, has an African-American collection of more than 5,000 photographs, magazine clippings and documents on African American history and culture.

Available for research during regular library hours. Free.

EUBIE BLAKE NATIONAL MUSEUM AND CULTURAL CENTER, 409 N. Charles Street, offers a panoramic display of Eubie Blake's life, from birth to death. The museum houses manuscripts, musical scores, photographs, paintings, and correspondence of the innovative black composer. James Hubert "Eubie" Blake collaborated in over 100 songs and produced one of the first black musical revues, *Shuffle Along* in 1921. Some of the songs from this show are still sung today.

Tues.–Fri. 12–6, weekends 12–5. Free.

GREAT BLACKS IN WAX MUSEUM, 1601 East North Avenue. America's first black wax historic museum features over 100 life-size, life-like wax figures of such historic black personalities as Harriet Tubman, George Washington Carver, and contemporary personalities like Rosa Parks and Malcolm X. Each wax figure is set in a scene depicting the struggles, achievements and contributions of African peoples worldwide. The displays are presented chronologically, highlighting ancient Africa, the Middle Passage, slavery, the Civil War, Reconstruction, the Harlem Renaissance, civil rights movement, and the present.

Tues.–Sat. 9–6, Sun. 12–6: Jan. 15–Oct. 15; rest of year Tues.–Sat 9–5, Sun. 12–5. Closed Mondays except during February. Adults $4.50, Seniors $4, Students 12–17 $3, Children 2–11 $2.50. Group rates.

MARYLAND HISTORICAL SOCIETY, 201 West Monument Street, maintains a museum of Maryland history, including period rooms, portraits by American artists, historic furniture, military uniforms and other costumes. The Society Library also has one of the best oral history collections in the state, covering the civil rights movement in Maryland.

Tues.–Fri. 11–4:30, Sat. 9–4:30 and Sun. (museum only) 1–5, Oct.–April. Closed holidays. Museum; adults $2.50, seniors $1, ages 4–12, 75 cents. Library $2.50. Museum and library free on Weds.

MORGAN STATE UNIVERSITY, Hillen Road and Cold
Spring Lane, was founded in 1867 for the training of black
Methodist ministers. Today, the university is a state-sup-
ported institution. The university has a collection of artifacts
relating to Benjamin Banneker and a Gallery of Art, which
includes the works of black American artists, along with
traditional African, Oceanic and European art.

The Soper Library at Morgan State University houses a
collection on African American history in the Beulah M.
Davis Special Collections Room. The collection is devoted to
materials by and about blacks. Also on campus is the Frederick Douglass Memorial Statue by black sculptor James Lewis.
The statue is 12 feet tall and its inscription reads simply,
"Frederick Douglass, 1817–1895, Humanitarian, Statesman."

Both the Gallery of Art and Soper Library open Mon.–Fri.
9–5. Free.

NAACP NATIONAL HEADQUARTERS is at 26 West
25th Street. After a race riot in Springfield, Illinois, on August 14, 1908, in which whites attacked and killed blacks, a
national conference was called in 1909 by both blacks and
whites to plan a civil rights organization. Called the National
Association for the Advancement of Colored People, the organization was born into a hostile world. From 1890 to 1910
the voting rights of blacks were curbed. Anger and violence
confronted African-Americans as they migrated from the
rural South to cities in the North, competing for jobs and
housing. Hostility came from within as well as outside the
black race. Booker T. Washington, the black educator, actively worked against the NAACP, believing that it was too
radical in its approach to civil rights.

Ironically, today there are some who consider the organization too conservative, although it continues its fight for full
rights for black citizens, often making its greatest impact in
court cases won by NAACP lawyers of both races.

The NAACP headquarters houses an archive which documents the organization's work over more than 70 years.

ST. FRANCIS XAVIER'S CATHOLIC CHURCH, 1007 North Caroline Street. As early as 1798 the Reverend Louis W. DuBourg was giving instruction in the Catholic faith to black men and women in Baltimore, but it wasn't until 1863 that the first church primarily for black Catholics in America was begun—St. Francis Xavier. From this parish, priests were sent to establish black missions in other cities.

The first black priest to be ordained in the United States, Father Charles Randolph Uncles, was a member of this parish.

BOWIE

BOWIE STATE UNIVERSITY is located 1 mile north of Bowie, off MD 197. The school was originally founded in 1867 for the training of black teachers but is now fully integrated. Bowie has in its library the Afro-American Newspaper Archives which contains photographs, files and clippings on the civil rights movement from the nation's largest African-American newspapers.

Open during regular academic hours.

CAMBRIDGE

HARRIET TUBMAN BIRTHPLACE MARKER. The Dorchester County Tourism Office, County Office Bldg. on Court Lane will help visitors find this marker which is located eight miles south of U.S. 50 on MD 397. Harriet Tubman was born a slave in a small cabin on the Brodas Plantation, southwest of the Bucktown post office, in Dorchester County, outside of Cambridge. Called the "Moses of Her People," Harriet led her parents and 300 slaves to freedom.

The tourism office can also put you in touch with the Harriet Tubman Association of Dorchester which hosts tours to the Harriet Tubman marker and several other places that Tubman and her family frequented in Maryland, such as the Bazzel M. E. Church. Once a year the association presents a video show about Tubman at the Dorchester County Library, and it observes Harriet Tubman Day on the third Sunday in June.

BETWEEN CATONSVILLE and ELLICOTT CITY

OELLA-BENJAMIN BANNEKER SITE, Westchester Avenue. Gilboa Chapel houses the Benjamin Banneker Memorial Obelisk, honoring the noted black American scientist and astronomer.

COLUMBIA

MARYLAND MUSEUM OF AFRICAN ART, 5430 Vantage Point Road, has a collection of traditional African art, including musical instruments, weapons, jewelry, masks, textiles, and household objects.

Tues.–Fri. 10–4, Sun. 12–4, Sat. by appointment for groups of 15 or more. Donation.

HOLLYWOOD

SOTTERLEY, 3 miles east on MD 245, is a carefully restored colonial mansion built about 1717 in tidewater Maryland. The outbuildings include formal gardens and the original slave quarters.

Daily 11–5, June–Sept. Adults $4, seniors $3, ages 6–16 $1.50.

MARSHALL'S CORNER, CHARLES COUNTY

AFRO-AMERICAN HERITAGE MUSEUM may be reached via MD 225 to Marshalls Corner Road to Bumpy Oak Road to Gwynne Road. Log cabin and various unique artifacts cover 200 years of Afro-American history in Maryland. Tours by appointment. (301-843-0371)

OXON HILL

OXON HILL LIBRARY, 6200 Oxon Hill Road, has The Sojourner Truth Collection, which includes a large number of African-American history and literature books and other cataloged items dating back to the slave years.
Open during regular library hours.

PRINCESS ANNE

UNIVERSITY OF MARYLAND EASTERN SHORE. The Frederick Douglass library on this campus has a large collection of newspaper clippings and other historical information about African Americans on Maryland's Eastern Shore.
Open during regular academic year.

For further information about Maryland, contact:

Maryland Office of Tourist Development
217 East Redwood St.
Baltimore, MD 21202
1-800-543-1036

MASSACHUSETTS

BOSTON

ABIEL SMITH SCHOOL, 46 Joy Street (corner of Smith Court on Beacon Hill), is the home of the Museum of Afro-American History. The Smith School, founded in 1834, was the first public school for black children in Boston. Today it is a museum containing a wide variety of materials and memorabilia on three centuries of African-American life in New England. A portion of the exhibit tells of the free blacks' role in the anti-slavery and Underground Railroad movement in New England. Although the conductors on the railroads were both white and black, free blacks played the most important role in conducting escaped slaves to safety. Abolitonism was always dominated by Afro-American freedmen and women.

The museum also has in its possession 4,000 volumes of Afro-American literature and history, focusing primarily on New England authors.

The museum conducts tours of the nearby African Meeting House, and brochures for the *Black Heritage Trail* may be picked up at the museum.

Tues.–Fri. 10–4. Free.

AFRICAN MEETING HOUSE, 8 Smith Court, is the oldest black church building still standing in the United States. When black preacher Thomas Paul faced discrimina-

tion in white churches, he and twenty members formed the
First African Baptist Church in 1805. The church building,
the African Meeting House, was completed the next year,
almost entirely using black labor. A school for black children
was started in the basement in 1808.

The meeting house was also the center of anti-slavery activities. The New England Anti-Slavery Society was founded
here in 1832. Abolitionist leaders like Frederick Douglass,
Harriet Tubman, Sojourner Truth, and William Lloyd Garrison spoke out from the pulpit, causing the building to be
referred to as the "Black Faneuil Hall." The African Meeting
House has been restored to look as it did in the nineteenth
century when it stood at the center of so many historic events.

The Museum of Afro-American History, located at Abiel
Smith School, 46 Joy Street, offers tours of the African Meeting House year-round, hourly, Mon.–Fri. 10–4. No tour at 1
p.m. Free.

BLACK HERITAGE TRAIL is a 1½ mile walking tour
that introduces visitors to the history and architecture of the
free African-American community of Beacon Hill in the
1800s. The trail weaves its way through the largest con-
centration of pre-Civil War African-American historic sites in
the United States.

The first Africans came to Boston in 1638 as slaves. By the
end of the American Revolution, though, there were more
free blacks than slaves living in the city and by the end of the
1700s, slavery had been outlawed in the Commonwealth.
Between 1800 and 1900 most Afro-Americans lived in the
West End of the city, on the north slope of Beacon Hill.

The Black Heritage Trail takes in the African Meeting
House and the Abiel Smith School, points out some of the
black historic homes on Beacon Hill, the Boston Massacre
Site, the Old Granary Burying Ground, the 54th Regiment
Monument, and other black-related sites.

Rangers from the National Park Service lead the guided
tours which begin at the Shaw/54th Regiment Monument at

the corner of Park and Beacon streets, across from the State House. The tour takes 1 to 2 hours. Brochures for the Black Heritage Trail may be picked up at the Abiel Smith School, 46 Joy Street, and the Boston Common Visitor Information Center.

Conducted tours Jan.–May by request only, with one day's advance notice; June–Aug. daily at 10, 12, and 2; Sept.–Dec. Mon.–Fri. at 10 and 2. Free.

BUNKER HILL MONUMENT is actually on Breed's Hill, Monument Square, in the Charlestown district, across the river from Boston. This famous Revolutionary War battle was fought in June 1775 under a broiling sun. The British, in full-dress uniform and heavy knapsacks, advanced up the hill against withering fire from the Americans who had fortified the summit.

Black American soldiers, such as Salem Poor, Grant Cooper, Prince Hall, Barzillai Lew, George Middleton, fought with white soldiers at Bunker Hill. Middleton led an all-black company called the "Bucks of America," and afterwards John Hancock presented them with a special silk company banner which may be seen at the Massachusetts Historical Society today. Caesar Brown and Prince Estabrook died at Bunker Hill in the battle which proved that the untried American soldier could stand up against the British regular.

The lodge at the base of the monument contains a three-dimensional model and dioramas of the battle.

Monument open daily 9–4:30; lodge 9–5. Free.

BUNKER HILL PAVILION, 55 Constitution Road, adjacent to the U.S.S. *Constitution* in Charlestown Navy Yard, off I-93 in Charlestown, has a multimedia re-creation of the Battle of Bunker Hill.

Daily 9:30–5 June–Aug., 9:30–4 April–May and Sept.–Nov. Closed Thanksgiving. Adults $3, over 62 and students $2, ages 5–16 $1.50.

COPP'S HILL BURYING GROUND, Hull and Snow-hill streets, uphill from Old North Church, is Boston's second-oldest cemetery, dating from 1659. The burying ground contains the bodies of Cotton Mather and other early Bostonians, including pre-Revolutionary War blacks. A monument to Prince Hall stands on the Snowhill Street side of the cemetery. Prince Hall founded the Masonic (African) lodge in 1787, the oldest black social organization in the United States. Prince Hall also helped to establish schools for black children and petitioned the Massachusetts legislature to abolish slavery.

CRISPUS ATTUCKS MONUMENT is on the Tremont Street side of Boston Common. The monument was erected in 1888 by the black and white citizens of Boston to honor the memory of the five Bostonians who were killed in March 1770 by British soldiers occupying Boston. Crispus Attucks, a former slave from Framingham, was the first to fall in what has become known as The Boston Massacre.

An illustration of the massacre showing Attucks lying in the foreground, can be seen at the base of the monument. Ironically, an engraving by Paul Revere of the Boston Massacre hanging in the National Gallery of Art, Washington, D.C., shows all five victims as white men. Attucks had become one of the invisible black heroes of America's history.

All five men killed that day are buried together in the Old Granary Burying Ground on Tremont Street, next to Park Street Church. The grave of Crispus Attucks and the other four victims is to the right of the entrance gate.

The actual site of the Boston Massacre is marked by a plaque in the center of the cobblestoned street in front of the Old State House on Washington Street, at the head of State Street.

FANEUIL HALL stands in Faneuil Hall Square, Merchants Row. The hall has been called the "Cradle of Liberty" because it was the scene of anti-British meetings before the Revolutionary War. The black abolitionist Frederick Douglass also spoke out against slavery at Faneuil Hall. The Boston Vigilance Committee, composed of black citizens, was formed at the hall in 1850 to assist fugitive slaves. Today the hall is a military museum with historical paintings of famous battles, including a picture of the shooting of Crispus Attucks.

The Faneuil Hall Marketplace includes the hall and the adjacent Quincy Market, which contains restaurants, boutiques and produce stands.

The hall is open Mon.–Fri. 10–4. Free.

HARRIET TUBMAN GALLERY AND RESOURCE CENTER, United South End Settlements, 566 Columbus Avenue, has a small research collection on Harriet Tubman. The black woman, relying only on her courage and quick wit, led countless fugitive slaves to freedom. Harriet Tubman then served as a spy and scout for Union forces during the Civil War. The center also has changing art exhibits by local white and black artists.

Mon.–Fri. 9–6. Free.

MUSEUM OF FINE ARTS, at Huntington Avenue and the Fenway, contains nearly 200 galleries of art, including a fine collection of African sculpture, as well as paintings by Afro-American artists. One drawing by Thomas Nast shows black soldiers of the 54th Massachusetts leading the march into Charleston, S.C., after its capture in February 1865.

Tues.–Sun. 10–5, Wed. to 10. Closed holidays. Adults $6, seniors $5, under 16 free. Free to all Sat. 10–noon.

MUSEUM OF THE NATIONAL CENTER OF AFRO-AMERICAN ARTISTS, 300 Walnut Avenue, off Columbus Avenue, is housed in a stone mansion located in the Roxbury section of Boston. The museum has over 4,000 pieces of African and Caribbean art, including musical instruments, paintings and sculpture, in addition to Afro-American prints and drawings. There are changing exhibits of works in various media by black American artists.

Tues.–Sun. 1–5, Sept. 1–June 30; Wed.–Sun. 1–6, July 1–Aug. 31. Closed holidays. Adults $1.50, students and seniors 50 cents.

OLD SOUTH MEETING HOUSE, 310 Washington Street, dedicated in 1730, was linked to the black community through one of its members, Judge Samuel Sewall. Sewall was one of the first men in Massachusetts to protest the African slave trade. Phillis Wheatley, the celebrated black slave poetess, was listed in the membership rolls for Old South in 1771, although it is doubtful whether a slave or a woman could have been a full member at that time. On display at the Old South Meeting House is a copy of George Washington's will in which he ordered that his slaves be freed after the death of Mrs. Washington.

A multimedia presentation explores three centuries of Boston's history.

Daily 9:30–5, April–Oct.; rest of year Mon.–Fri. 10–4, Sat.–Sun. 10–5. Closed holidays. Adults $1.75, over age 62 and students $1.25.

PARK STREET CHURCH, Park and Tremont streets, was the site of William Lloyd Garrison's first anti-slavery address in 1829.

Tues.–Sat. 9–4, July–Aug.; rest of year by appointment. Free.

ROBERT GOULD SHAW AND 54TH MASSACHUSETTS COLORED INFANTRY REGIMENT MONUMENT is on Beacon Street, facing the State House. Within thirty-six hours of the beginning of the Civil War, a mass meeting was held by black citizens of Boston at the Twelfth Baptist Church, pledging "to raise an army of 50,000 colored men."

However, it wasn't until 1863 that blacks were able to enlist in the Union army. In July 1863 the all-black 54th Massachusetts Colored Infantry Regiment, under the command of abolitonist Colonel Shaw, spearheaded the attack on Fort Wagner in South Carolina. They were new troops and in a forced march to reach the battle had received no rest and little food for two days. Colonel Shaw and about 90 men managed to claw their way to the parapet of the fort although they were caught in a withering crossfire from Confederate guns on nearby Sullivan's Island. Colonel Shaw was fatally wounded and nearly half of his black regiment of 600 volunteers were killed, wounded or captured. Colonel Shaw was buried in a common grave with his men.

Although the battle was a defeat for the Union forces, it signalled a victory for the black soldiers because it proved that black men would lay down their lives for freedom. Sergeant William Carney won the Congressional Medal of Honor for his heroism during the battle, becoming the first black soldier to receive this distinguished award.

Twenty years after the battle, the memorial honoring the 54th Massachusetts was commissioned by the city of Boston. When it was dedicated in 1897, the remaining veterans of the company, some still bearing their battle scars came and, as one man, stood to attention.

STATE HOUSE, on Beacon Street, is across the street from the Shaw Memorial. The archives of the Massachusetts State House include records detailing the history of the state's black citizens. Prince Hall's 1777 petition to abolish slavery is among them. The Hall of Flags contains the banner of the 54th Regiment, the flag saved at Fort Wagner by Sergeant William Carney who wrapped it around his body.

Mon.–Fri. 9–5. Free.

U.S.S. *CONSTITUTION* is berthed on the Charles River in the Charlestown Navy Yard, off I-93 in Charlestown. Launched in 1797, the warship fought against the pirates of Tripoli and in the War of 1812. Black sailors fought alongside white sailors aboard the *Constitution* during the Revolutionary War and the War of 1812. One black sailor was so proud of having served aboard "Old Ironsides" in the War of 1812 that he had the fact engraved on his tombstone.

The U.S.S. *Constitution* is still a commissioned navy ship as well as an historic shrine, and black sailors still serve on board today.

Guided tours daily 9:30–3:50. Free.

CAMBRIDGE

HOUGHTON LIBRARY at Harvard University is adjacent to the Widener Library, 221 Longfellow Hall, Appian Way. It houses mementos of the life of Phillis Wheatley, the black poetess (1753–1784), a few original manuscripts and some pieces of correspondence. Although born a slave, Phillis Wheatley was taught to read and write by her mistress and had a collection of her poetry published in London when she was only 20 years old. On a visit to England, she was presented with a folio copy of John Milton's *Paradise Lost,* a valuable manuscript now in the collection of the Houghton Library.

The library also has the original manuscript of an early poem by Wheatley in its extensive Afro-American Manuscript Collection, along with the personal papers of many abolitionist leaders.

Mon.–Fri. 9:30–4:45. Free. Some sections are closed to the general public.

THE PEABODY MUSEUM, housed in the Harvard University Museums of Natural History, entrance at 24 Oxford Street, has an excellent African art collection.

Mon.–Sat. 9–4:30, Sun. 1–4:30. Closed holidays. Adults $2, students and senior citizens $1.50. Free on Sat. 9–11 a.m.

OLD BURYING GROUND, Garden and Massachusetts Avenue, has graves of two black veterans of the Revolutionary War, Cato Stedman and Neptune Frost.

FRAMINGHAM

PETER SALEM'S GRAVESITE is located in the Old Burying Ground near Buckminster Square. Peter Salem is credited by some historians with shooting the British commander Major John Pitcairn at the Battle of Bunker Hill and a marker on his grave notes this tradition. Freed by his owners so that he could join the Continental Army, Salem also fought at Lexington and Concord.

GREAT BARRINGTON

W. E. B. DU BOIS MEMORIAL PARK. Born in Great Barrington in 1868, William E. B. Du Bois was one of the most influential, and controversial, black intellectuals of the first half of the twentieth century in America. His book *Souls of Black Folks* went against the teachings of the popular educator Booker T. Washington, because it argued that black people stood little chance to advance in America unless they fought for change. One of the founders of the NAACP, Du Bois had moved to Africa and was working on an encyclopedia of African history at the time of his death.

In 1969 a five-acre park was dedicated and named in honor of W. E. B. DuBois. Within the wooded park area there is a ten ton boulder upon which a bronze plaque has been placed in his memory.

LYNN

JAN ERNST MATZELIGER MONUMENT, standing on his grave in the Pine Grove Cemetery, 25 Gentian Path, honors the black inventor of the shoe-lasting machine. It took the young black man ten years of tireless work to perfect his invention which greatly facilitated the production of shoes. A portrait of the inventor hangs in the First Church on Lynnfield Street.

MINUTE MAN NATIONAL HISTORICAL PARK

Commemorating the battle that began the American War for Independence, this park covers lands in Concord, Lincoln and Lexington on either side of Battle Road (MA 2A). The Battle Road Visitor Center is at one end of the park and the North Bridge Visitor Center, outside of Concord, is at the other end.

On April 19, 1775, British troops on their way to Concord were attacked at the town of Lexington and at Concord Bridge by a group of patriots called Minutemen. The Minutemen fought as they had learned from the Indians, sniping from behind stone walls, hedges, trees and buildings. The red coats of the British soldiers made easy targets for their musket fire.

Black men fought side-by-side with the Minutemen, Peter Salem, Samuel Craft, Lemuel Haynes, Caesar Ferrit and his son, John, and Pomp Blackman, among others.

Battle Road Visitor Center, off MA 2A on Airport Road, serves as a starting point for visitors. A film depicts the events leading to the battle, with exhibits, and maps available for tours of the park.

Daily 8:30–5, April–Nov.; extended hours in summer.

NANTUCKET

AFRICAN BAPTIST CHURCH, at York and Pleasant streets, is the second oldest surviving African-American sanctuary in the United States. Built in 1830 by skilled craftsmen using shipbuilding techniques, it is now owned and undergoing restoration by the Museum of Afro-American History in Boston.

NANTUCKET WHALING MUSEUM, Broad Street, contains model ships, tools, logbooks, a whale skeleton, and a large collection of scrimshaw. Many black seamen worked on whaling ships, including Peter Green, second mate of the *John Adams*. When the captain and first mate were lost at sea during a violent storm, Green brought the ship safely home.

A black metalsmith, Lewis Temple, modified the design of

the whaler's harpoon in the 1840s so that lines could be securely fastened to the whale. His "toggle harpoon" doubled the catch, and the profits, of the whalers. One of the most important men on a whaler was the harpooner, who was often black.

Daily 10–5, May 28–Oct. 12; rest of the year as posted. Closed Dec. 25. Adults $3, ages 5–14 $1.

NEW BEDFORD

LEWIS TEMPLE STATUE, 613 Pleasant Street, stands in front of New Bedford Free Public Library. Lewis Temple, a black metalsmith, invented a new type of harpoon for whaling, called a "toggle harpoon," which more than doubled the profits of the whalers. Temple, however, never patented his invention and died in poverty.

WHALING MUSEUM, 18 Johnny Cake Hill, has a collection of paintings, logbooks, whaling relics, and scrimshaw, as well as a half-sized model of a fully rigged whaling bark. Whaling was one of the most important industries of early New England and New Bedford was the largest whaling port. Paul Cuffee, who lived near New Bedford, made his fortune as a black shipowner in the industry.

Included in the museum's collection is an example of Lewis Temple's toggle harpoon, and a compass used by Paul Cuffee. A whaling film is shown at 10:30 and 1:30 in summer.

Mon.–Sat. and holidays 9–5, Sun. 1–5. Adults $3.50, seniors $3, ages 6–14 $2.50.

PITTSFIELD

BERKSHIRE MUSEUM, South Street, has several rare mementos of the Peary expedition to the North Pole in 1909. Included in the exhibit is the fur suit worn by explorer

Matthew Henson on the trip as well as one of the sledges, and
other personal items. Henson was a black man, and the only
man to accompany Admiral Peary on all of his polar expeditions. Although six men started out on the expedition to the
North Pole, only Peary and Henson survived the hardships of
the trip.

Mon.–Sat. 10–5, Sun. 1–5, July–Aug. Closed Mon. rest of
year. Free.

PLYMOUTH

PARTING WAYS MUSEUM OF AFRO–AMERICAN
ETHNOHISTORY, 130 Court Street (rear). Plymouth,
birthplace of the nation, was also the site of Parting Ways, one
of the earliest free black settlements in America. In 1777 the
town of Plymouth granted 94 acres of land to Cato Howe, a
black Revolutionary War veteran, on the condition that it be
cleared and settled by himself and three other participants in
the war. The four men built their homes and lived out their
years on this land. After 1840 when the last owner passed
away, much of the land fell into disuse. Today an archaeological investigation of the settlement is underway to un-
cover a detailed picture of the lifestyle of the inhabitants of
this early black settlement.

The museum contains archaeological materials from the
Parting Ways site, along with other historical exhibits on
black history, and research materials on Afro-Americans in
Plymouth County.

Tours by appointment. Adults $1. (617-746-6028)

The PARTING WAYS ARCHAEOLOGICAL SITE is
located on Plympton Road, near the Kingston town line.
From downtown Plymouth, take MA 44 west to MA 80.
Follow MA 80 to Sacred Heart School. Parting Ways is diago-
nally across the road.

SALEM

SALEM WITCH MUSEUM, 19½ Washington Square N, is opposite the Salem Common. Slaves could be found in some unusual occupations in colonial America. There was even one slave who was accused of witchcraft.

In 1692 in Salem, then a small village, a group of young girls began acting strangely and accused Tituba, a slave, and several elderly women, of having bewitched them. Tituba and the other women were tried as witches and sentenced to death. Before the witch hysteria had ended, 19 men and women were convicted of being witches and were hanged on Gallows Hill.

Tituba initially confessed to being a witch but later admitted that she had been beaten until she agreed to testify. Although she was saved from execution, she stayed in jail for more than a year and was finally sold to pay her jail fees.

The museum depicts the witch trials of 1692. An audio-visual presentation is given every half hour.

Daily 10–7, July–Aug.; 10–5 rest of year. Closed holidays. Adults $3.50, over age 62 $3, ages 6–14 $2.

SPRINGFIELD

NAISMITH MEMORIAL BASKETBALL HALL OF FAME, 1150 West Columbus Avenue, has video stations showing highlights of professional and collegiate games, with life-size action shots of hall-of-famers, and even gives visitors a chance to test their ability at shooting baskets. One of the interesting exhibits covers the Harlem Globetrotters, the world-famous black basketball team.

Daily 9–5 Sept.–June; 9–6 July–Labor Day. Closed holidays. Adults $5, seniors $3, children under 15 $3, under 9 free.

WALTHAM

ROSE ART MUSEUM, Brandeis University, off South Street, has an excellent African art collection.
Tues.–Sun. 1–5 Sept.–June; Tues., Thurs., and Sat.–Sun. 1–5 rest of year. Closed holidays. Free.

WESTPORT

PAUL CUFFEE MONUMENT, Society of Friends Church, Central Village, honors the son of an ex-slave father and an Indian mother. Cuffee was 16 when he shipped out to sea in 1775, but by the time he was 35, he owned his own whaling ships and a farm near Central Village.

Paul Cuffee (sometimes spelled Cuffe) was one of the earliest fighters for the abolition of slavery. He and his brother refused to pay their taxes because they were denied the right to vote; they started a school for black children when their own children were not allowed to attend the village school. Using his own money, Captain Cuffee transported black American families to a colony which he started at Sierre Leone, Africa, because he felt black people could live there in freedom. The War of 1812, however, cut short his dream of colonizing a new, free land.

A lifelong Quaker, Paul Cuffee was buried in 1817 in a cemetery next to the Quaker Meeting House. The Society of Friends has dedicated a monument to his memory, which stands by his grave. There is also a plaque honoring Paul Cuffee in the town hall.

For further information about Masschusetts, contact:

Office of Travel and Tourism
100 Cambridge St., 13th floor
Boston, MA 02202
1-800-447-MASS or 617-727-3201

MICHIGAN

ADRIAN

LAURA HAVILAND STATUE, Main Street, stands outside of Adrian's city hall. The Quaker Haviland family were active abolitionists. Known as Auntie Laura, Haviland risked her life many times helping slaves to escape. Slave owners offered a $3,000 reward for her arrest. With Elizabeth Chandler, Haviland organized the first anti-slavery society in Michigan.

AUGUSTA

UNKNOWN (BLACK) SOLDIER'S GRAVE is located at Fort Custer National Cemetery, 1 mile east on MI 96. On November 11, 1986, the body of an unknown member of the 102d U.S. Colored Troops was removed from an obscure corner of the Fulton Cemetery in Grand Rapids, Michigan, and interred in the Fort Custer National Cemetery, to create the first gravesite of the black unknown soldier of the Civil War. The 102d, also known as the First Michigan Colored Infantry, was mustered into service in 1864. Some 1,387 blacks served in the unit. Flags of the 102d are among those on display in the rotunda of the state capitol at Lansing.

BATTLE CREEK

KIMBALL HOUSE MUSEUM at 196 Capital Avenue NE (North MI-66, next to Y-Center) has an exhibit case on the second floor with mementos from the life of a remarkable black woman, Sojourner Truth. No other abolitionist speaker, with the possible exception of Frederick Douglass, could sway audiences against slavery as the ex-slave Sojourner Truth. Born in 1797, she was sold four times before she received her freedom in 1827. In 1843 she renamed herself Sojourner Truth and traveled the country, speaking out against slavery whenever and wherever anyone would listen, from tiny rooms to President Lincoln's office.

During the Civil War she nursed wounded soldiers and worked with former slaves in the refugee camps. After the war, she continued to travel and lecture for the welfare of freed slaves as well as for women's rights. Finally, she retired to a cottage in Battle Creek, which served as her home and headquarters for 27 years.

Sojourner Truth died November 26, 1883, and is buried in OAKHILL CEMETERY, South Avenue and Oakhill Drive. There is a handsome historical marker on her grave inscribed with one of her most famous statements, "Is God dead?" which was the question she asked a discouraged Frederick Douglass at an anti-slavery rally. Sojourner's own faith in the ultimate victory of the abolitionists never wavered.

Museum open Tues.–Fri. 12:30–4:30; second Sunday each month except January 1–4:30. Hours subject to change. Donation.

CHAIN LAKE

CHAIN LAKE MISSIONARY BAPTIST CHURCH, Chain Lake Street, began in the homes of its members in 1838 and was formally organized in 1848. Black churches were always among the most active in the abolitionist movement and in 1853 various representatives from surrounding communities organized the Michigan Anti-Slavery Baptist Association in this building.

DEARBORN

HENRY FORD MUSEUM AND GREENFIELD VILLAGE is located at Village Road and Oakwood Boulevard (take I-94 to Oakwood Blvd. exit). This collection of historic homes and shops, moved to the village of Greenfield from all over America, is the nation's largest indoor-outdoor museum complex. Henry Ford, the pioneer automobile manufacturer, was a close friend of George Washington Carver. When Henry Ford established Greenfield Village, one of the homes he had built was a replica of the three-room log cabin in which Carver was born. Presently an exhibit is being planned which will cover Dr. Carver's contributions to agriculture.

Over 80 historic buildings may be visited at Greenfield Village, spanning more than 300 years of American history. At the reconstructed tobacco plantation, visitors learn of the life of a slave in the fields and in the big house.

At the Henry Ford Museum, the inventions of black Elijah McCoy are on display, including his hydrostatic lubricator. Many of McCoy's inventions helped Ford's new auto industry.

Daily 9–5. Closed Thanksgiving and Dec. 25; building interiors closed Jan 2.–March 16. Adults $10.50, over 62 $9.50, ages 5–12 $5.25. Extra charge for museum.

DETROIT

BETHEL A. M. E. CHURCH, 5050 St. Antoine, organized in 1839, is the oldest A. M. E. congregation in Michigan.

Bethel housed the first public school classes for black children in Detroit, and during the early twentieth century helped migrants from the South locate jobs and housing.

DETROIT HISTORICAL MUSEUM, 5401 Woodward Avenue (I-94 to Woodward Ave. exit), has a "Detroit Story" exhibit which includes material on the growth and development of the city's black community. One of the important black personages shown in the exhibit is Fannie M. Richards, the city's first black school teacher and a fighter for equal rights in the 1870s and 1880s.

The museum also has a display on local black sports heroes who have gone on to national fame, people like Thomas Tolan, Willis Ward and Joe Louis, the world's heavyweight boxing champion, 1937–1949. The JOE LOUIS ARENA, 600 Civic Center Drive, was named in honor of the Brown Bomber. Two blocks to the east, at the intersection of Jefferson and Woodward avenues, is a sculpted fist dedicated to Joe Louis in 1986. Also, at the entrance to Detroit's Cobo Hall Convention Center there is a statue of the world-famous boxer.

Museum open Wed.–Sun. 9:30–5. Closed holidays except Easter. Donation $1, seniors and under 18, 50 cents.

DETROIT INSTITUTE OF ARTS, 5200 Woodward Avenue (off I-75, 1 mile west) has one of the best African art collections in the country. The museum also has a collection of paintings by outstanding black artists such as Hughie Lee-Smith, Romare Beardon, Henry Ossawa Tanner, and Jacob Lawrence, including his series of paintings on John Brown.

Tues.–Sun. 9:30–5:30. Closed holidays. Donation.

DETROIT PUBLIC LIBRARY at 5201 Woodward Avenue, has a special collection and exhibit area honoring the achievements of Afro-Americans in music, dance, and drama. The E. Azalia Hackley Collection was named for a black Detroit music teacher who created scholarships for many talented young black musicians and revived world-wide interest in genuine black folk music.

All types of materials are included in the collection—books, manuscripts, musical scores, photographs and recordings. Many of the items are irreplaceable; autographed copies of songs by Langston Hughes and W. C. Handy, photographs of the most prominent black actors, actresses and musicians of the 1920s and 1930s, and a set of scrapbooks compiled during the Fisk Jubilee Singers' first world tour. Constantly changing displays may be found just outside the room that houses the Hackley Collection.

Mon.–Sat. 9:30–5:30, Wed. 9–9. Closed Sun. and holidays. Free.

DOUGLASS-BROWN MARKER, on East Congress Street and St. Antoine, commemorates the site of the William Webb House, where abolitionists John Brown and Frederick Douglass met with prominent black men from Detroit in March of 1859 to discuss methods of emancipating fellow blacks. It was here that Brown mapped the strategy which finally led to his raid on Harper's Ferry, West Virginia. Douglass did not become a party to Brown's plan, but opposed his course of action.

ELIJAH MUHAMMED TEMPLE NO. 1, Elijah Muhammed Boulevard (formerly Linwood Ave.). Elijah Poole, who renamed himself Elijah Muhammed when he joined the Temple of Islam, established Temple No. 1 in 1934. The religion teaches blacks to be self-sufficient and to take pride in themselves and their African heritage.

ELMWOOD CEMETERY, Elmwood Avenue at East Lafayette, is the oldest cemetery in Detroit, founded in 1846. There are many prominent black citizens buried here; abolitionists William Webb, William Lambert, George DeBaptiste; Fannie Richards, the first black teacher in Detroit's public school system; and Civil War soldiers of the 102d U.S. Colored Infantry. George DeBaptiste and William Lambert are credited with securing the safe passage of some 30,000 fugitive slaves to Canada.

GRAYSTONE INTERNATIONAL JAZZ MUSEUM, at

3000 East Grand Boulevard, is a museum specializing in jazz memorabilia from 1920 to the present. The collection includes musical instruments from the Graystone Ballroom, as well as artifacts of such great jazz artists as Count Basie, Duke Ellington, and others. The museum also organizes traveling exhibits.

Mon.–Fri. 10–5. Free.

THE MOTOWN MUSEUM (HITSVILLE U.S.A.) is at 2648 W. Grand Boulevard (take Lodge Freeway to West Grand Boulevard exit). Motown Sound was introduced to the world in the 1960s from this small home. It was a new sound, natural, rhythmic and distinctive, which became a multi-million-dollar enterprise. Berry Gordy, Jr., christened the house "Hitsville U.S.A." and his offices and recording studios remained here until the Motown headquarters moved to downtown Detroit in 1968 then to California in 1972.

The house is now a museum filled with rare photographs, vintage clothing, memorabilia and artifacts recapturing the history of this phenomenal era in American music. Exhibits feature musicians, songwriters and black singing groups such as the Original Supremes and The Temptations. The Motown Sound is playing everywhere as visitors walk through the front door.

Tues.–Sat. 10–5, Sun. 2–5; other times by appointment. Adults $3, children under 12 $2.

MUSEUM OF AFRICAN AMERICAN HISTORY is in Detroit's Cultural Center at 301 Frederick Douglass Street (take Northbound I-75 to Warren exit). Founded in 1965, the museum moved into its new $3.5 million facility in 1987. The museum's goals are to produce programs that raise black self-esteem and recover lost black heroes, as well as to correct distortions in the presentation of the rich, cultural heritage of Africa.

One of the highlights of the collection is a permanent exhibit entitled "An epic of heroism; the Underground Railroad in Michigan, 1837–1870." It displays scenes from traditional Africa, the dreaded "Middle Passage" as slaves were transported from Africa to the Americas, life in the U.S. during slavery, famous slave revolts and the escape of slaves to "free" life in the northern U.S. and Canada.

Museum programs are offered weekly on a variety of topics of interest to black Americans. Black Music Month is celebrated each June. The museum also organizes traveling exhibitions and tours of the collection.

Wed.–Sat. 9:30–5, Sun. 1–5. All tours free, but donations are welcome.

NATIONAL MUSEUM OF THE TUSKEGEE AIRMEN is located at historic Fort Wayne, 6325 W. Jefferson Avenue at the foot of Livernois Street, off I-75. This museum tells the story of the first black pilots to take to the air during World War II. The Tuskegee Airmen trained at an isolated, specially constructed air base near the town of Tuskegee, Alabama, and at Tuskegee Institute. The graduates formed the 99th Fighter Squadron, under the command of Colonel Benjamin O. Davis, Jr., who was later to become the U.S. Air Force's first black lieutenant general. Joined by three additional black fighter squadrons, the organization was redesignated the 332nd Fighter Group.

The 99th completed 1578 combat missions in North Africa, Sicily and Europe with the 12th Tactical U.S. Army Air Force. Called the "Black Birdmen" by the Germans, they were both feared and respected. The magnificent wartime record of the pilots of the 332nd Fighter Group in World War II was a major factor in causing discontinuance of the policy of segregation in the Armed Forces of the United States. Also on view at the museum are model aircraft, equipment, supplies, uniforms, and photographs.

Historic Fort Wayne is presently closed but the Tuskegee Airmen museum may be visited by appointment. (313-297-9360)

SECOND BAPTIST CHURCH, at 441 Monroe, corner of Beaubien, is one of the oldest Baptist churches in the

North. Although organized in 1836, the congregation could not afford to build a permanent building until 1857. In October 1863 black volunteers met at the Second Baptist Church to form the 1st Michigan Colored Infantry. There is a marker in front of the present building commemorating the first celebration of the Emancipation Proclamation in Detroit which was held at this church on January 6, 1863.

YOUR HERITAGE HOUSE, 110 E. Ferry Street, is a fine arts museum for youth. This collection includes African and Afro-American art works and artifacts, a library of resources on art for youth, books on Afro-American music, and a large doll and puppetry collection. There are also traveling exhibitions.

Mon.–Fri. 9:30–4:30, Sat. 10–3. Sun. by appointment. Donation.

FRANKENMUTH

MICHIGAN'S OWN, INC.—MILITARY AND SPACE MUSEUM, 1250 S. Weiss Street, honors the men and women of Michigan who fought in America's wars from World War I to Vietnam. The Korean exhibit tells of Sergeant James Thompson, a World War II veteran who was taken prisoner during the Korean War and was the last black soldier released by the North Koreans at the war's end.

Mon.–Sat. 10–6, Sun. 12–6. Adults $2.50, seniors $2, students under 18 $1.

LANSING

MALCOLM X HOMESITE, 4705 S. Logan. Lansing was the childhood home of Malcolm X. As an adult, he became a follower of Elijah Muhammed, then broke away and founded the Organization for Afro-American Unity. He was murdered in New York City in 1965. Site has a Michigan historical marker.

MICHIGAN HISTORICAL MUSEUM, at 717 W. Allegan Street in downtown Lansing, two blocks southwest of the state capitol. The museum has multimedia presentations, artifacts, photographs and changing exhibits which tell of the places and events that make up the richness of Michigan, and the various ethnic influences, including its black citizens, who contributed to the history of the state.

Mon.–Fri. 9–5, Sat. 10–5, Sun. 1–4:30. Closed Jan. 1, Thanksgiving and Dec. 25. Free.

MARSHALL

CROSSWHITE BOULDER, near Triangle Park at the junction of E. Michigan and E. Mansion streets, marks the site of an event that brought nation-wide attention to the town. In 1847, slave catchers arrived to recapture Adam Crosswhite and his family, escaped slaves from Kentucky who had lived in Marshall for several years. When the men broke down the door of the Crosswhite home and attempted to seize the family, a crowd of angry Marshall citizens gathered and successfully prevented them.

Crosswhite and his family were spirited away to safety but members of the crowd who obstructed their capture were arrested and fined for assisting escaped slaves. The action of the citizens of Marshall helped bring about the Fugitive Slave Law of 1850 which made it a federal crime to aid runaway slaves. Anger against this law rallied support for the abolitionist cause throughout the country and ultimately brought about the Civil War.

The boulder with a plaque on it lies at the approximate site of the defense of the freedom of the Crosswhite family.

MUSKEGON

JONATHAN WALKER MEMORIAL, Evergreen Cemetery, northwest entrance, honors the memory of Captain

Jonathan Walker who had "SS" (slave stealer) branded on his right hand by a federal court. Captured with seven fugitive slaves off the coast of Florida in 1844, Walker was branded and sentenced to one year in prison. Since 1955 the Greater Muskegon Urban League has given the annual Jonathan Walker Award to a citizen who has worked to improve race relations.

For further information about Michigan, contact:

Michigan Travel Bureau
Dept TPM
P.O. Box 30226
Lansing, 48909
1-800-543-2937

MINNESOTA

MINNEAPOLIS

MINNEAPOLIS INSTITUTE OF ARTS, 2400 Third Avenue, South, is a showcase of world-renowned works of art representative of diverse cultures, from prehistoric to contemporary times. African works are included in the collection.

Tues.–Wed. and Fri.–Sat. 10–5, Thurs. 10–9, Sun. noon–5. Closed holidays. Free. Guided tours available.

ORIGINAL BASEBALL HALL OF FAME MUSEUM is located across from Gate H at the HHH Metrodome, 406 Chicago Avenue, South. The museum highlights memorabilia of the Minnesota Twins, including such black players as Rod Carew, one of only two Minnesota Twins players who are included in the Baseball Hall of Fame at Cooperstown, New York. The museum also features memorabilia of well-known black baseballers who did not play for the twins, such as Jackie Robinson and Willie Mays. Jackie Robinson was the first black player in the major leagues in 1947.

Mon.–Fri. 9–5, Sat. 11–3; extended hours during Metrodome events. Free.

ST. PETER'S A. M. E. CHURCH, at 401 East 41st Street, established in 1880, was the first A. M. E. church in Minneapolis.

ST. PAUL

HISTORIC FORT SNELLING/FORT SNELLING
HISTORY CENTER, MN 5 and MN 55, via Fort Snelling
exits. Built in the 1820s, this was one of the earliest military
forts west of the Mississippi. There was a black presence at the
fort from its earliest days. Servants and slaves accompanied
the officers of the 5th Infantry and Indian agent Lawrence
Taliaferro to the area in 1819. Blacks were also involved in the
local fur trade. One black family in particular, the Bongas,
were well-known and successful among the Indians. The
Bongas had come to the territory as slaves, gained their freedom, took Chippewa brides and made a fortune in the fur
trade.

One of the most famous slaves at the fort, Dred Scott, was
owned by Dr. John Scott and lived at Fort Snelling from 1836
to 1838. He met his wife at the fort and saw his first child
born there. When he later accompanied Dr. Scott back to
Missouri, Dred Scott sued for his freedom on the grounds
that he had lived in free territories in Illinois and at Fort
Snelling and therefore should be considered a free man. The
case received national attention. Although Dred Scott finally
lost his case, the decision against him strengthened the abolitionist cause and widened the rift between the North and
South.

The black 25th Infantry Regiment was stationed at the fort
during the Indian Wars period from 1882 to 1888. Inside their
barracks, there is a uniformed mannequin representing one of
their company, along with panels picturing the service of
black soldiers on the frontier.

Today, Fort Snelling has been fully restored, including the
servant/slave quarters. Costumed tour guides portray soldiers
and civilians as they might have lived at the fort in the 1820s.
Black students occasionally play the role of the early black
pioneers in the area. There are cannon and musket drills,

blacksmithing and baking demonstrations. A history center offers exhibits and films about the fort.

An outdoor sculpture is being created which will commemorate the role of early blacks at Fort Snelling. The sculpture will be located adjacent to the main fort gate, overlooking the Minnesota River valley.

Fort open daily 10–5, May–Oct. Closed Nov.–April. History Center open daily 9:30–5 May–Oct, rest of year Mon.–Fri. 9–4:30. Admission to Fort Snelling, adults $2, seniors and ages 6–15 $1, children 5 and under free. Free admission to History Center.

MINNESOTA MUSEUM OF ART is in the Jemne Building at Kellogg Boulevard and St. Peter Street, with a branch museum in the Landmark Center, 5th and Market. Contemporary and Asian and African art are featured in two historic downtown buildings.

Tues., Wed., Fri. 10:30–4:30, Thurs. 10:30–7:30, weekends 1–4:30. Free.

PILGRIM BAPTIST CHURCH, 732 West Central Avenue, was founded in 1863 by a group of runaway slaves.

For further information about Minnesota, contact:

Minnesota Office of Tourism
375 Jackson St., 250 Skyway Level
St. Paul, MN 55101-1810
1-800-657-3700

MISSISSIPPI

BALDWYN

BRICES CROSS ROADS NATIONAL BATTLEFIELD SITE is located 6 miles west of Baldwyn on I-370. In June 1864 Union forces opposed skillfully deployed Confederate cavalry at this site. Among the Union troops were the 55th and 59th Colored Infantry regiments and a battery of the 2d Colored Light Infantry.

CLARKSDALE

DELTA BLUES MUSEUM, 114 Delta Avenue, is in the Carnegie library building in downtown Clarksdale. America's unique form of music, the blues, began in the Mississippi Delta, but the real blues began much earlier descending from the work songs and spirituals, the ring shouts and field "hollers," of the slaves. Clarksdale was home to such famed bluesmen as W. C. Handy, Charlie Patton, Muddy Waters, John Lee Hooker and many others. The Delta Blues Museum was established for the purpose of increasing understanding and appreciation of the music, which has influenced jazz, country, and rock and roll music in America.

Visitors to the museum enjoy videotape and slide-and-sound programs, photographs, recordings, books, performances, memorabilia, archives and other sources of information about the blues.

A Delta Blues Festival is held in Greenville, Mississippi, the third weekend in September.

Mon.–Fri. 9–5. Closed holidays. Free.

ROOSTER BLUES RECORDS at 232 Sunflower Avenue is a repository of obscure and vintage blues records, and provides information on blues clubs and a blues tour.

CORINTH

CORINTH NATIONAL CEMETERY, 1551 Horton Street, is the burial site of over 6,000 Civil War soldiers, including black men of the 14th, 40th, 106th, 108th and 111th Colored Infantry regiments.

GREENWOOD

COTTONLANDIA MUSEUM, 2¾ miles west on U.S. 82W bypass, has exhibits on the history of cotton production and the inhabitants of the Mississippi River Delta from pre-Columbian times to the present. Displays included are original farming implements, made and used by slaves, which represent masterpieces of craftsmanship. Without the unpaid labor of thousands of black field hands, cotton production would never have been as successful as it was in the Mississippi Delta.

Tues.–Fri. 9–5, Sat.–Sun. 2–5. Closed major holidays. Adults $2, ages 6–18, 50 cents.

FLOREWOOD RIVER PLANTATION, 2 miles west of town and south of U.S. 82 and U.S. 49E, is a recreated antebellum plantation, with costumed guides to describe the lfestyle of the 1850s. There are demonstrations of nineteenth-century trades and crafts, many of which were performed by house slaves and field hands on a large plantation. On smaller rural farms, the whites shared these tasks with the few slaves they might have owned. There is a Cotton Museum on the grounds with a restored cotton gin. The invention of the cotton gin in 1793 by Eli Whitney was the knell of doom for slaves in the South. Cotton had been a small-scale industry; after the introduction of the cotton gin, production grew to over 6,000,000 bales a year. This meant that more and more slaves were needed to work the cotton fields, as the economy of the South increasingly came to depend on the crop.

Tues.–Sat. 9–noon and 1–5, Sun. 1–5, early March–early Nov. Scheduled tours. Adults $3.50, seniors $3, ages 5–18 $2.50.

HOLLY SPRINGS

RUST COLLEGE, on MS 78, was established in 1866, as Shaw University, for the education of freed slaves. It was renamed in 1890 to honor Richard Sutton Rust, Methodist clergyman, educator and abolitionist.

JACKSON

MT. HELM BAPTIST CHURCH, southwest corner of Lamar and Church Street, formed in 1835, is the oldest black religious body in the city.

JACKSON STATE UNIVERSITY, 1400 John R. Lynch Street, was founded in Natchez in 1877 and moved to Jackson in 1882. Starting with 20 black scholars, it is now a state teachers college and has over 7,000 students. The Founder's Room in the library has historic portraits and a rare book collection.

MISSISSIPPI STATE HISTORICAL MUSEUM, N. State and Capitol streets, is housed in the Old State Capitol building. The chronological exhibits tell the story of Mississippi's history from Desoto's exploration of the territory, through

the Civil War and Reconstruction, and the civil rights movement.

Mon.–Fri. 8–5, Sat. 9:30–4:30, Sun. 12:30–4:30. Closed
major holidays. Free.

SMITH ROBERTSON MUSEUM AND CULTURAL
CENTER, 528 Bloom Street, is the first museum devoted to
black culture and history in the state. Housed in Jackson's
first public school building for blacks, the museum is named
for Smith Robertson, who was born a slave and moved to
Jackson in 1874. At a time when popular support for black
education was almost nonexistent, Mr. Robertson devoted
himself to the cause. The museum interprets the life, history
and culture of black Mississippians, including exhibits on
Farish Street Historic District, a center for black politics and
culture in Jackson; the contributions of blacks to education,
business and politics; and the work of black folk artists and
craftsmen.

Each September there is a Farish Street Festival with tours
of the historic landmarks in the district.

Mon.–Fri. 9–5, Sat. 9–12, Sun. 2–5. Adults $1, seniors
and 18 and under 50 cents.

LORMAN

ALCORN STATE UNIVERSITY, U.S. 61, south of Port
Gibson at junction with MS 552, is the first black land grant
college in the United States. The historic chapel on the campus was built in 1838. Hiram Revels, the first black man to
serve in either house of the Congress of the United States (he
filled the unexpired term of Jefferson Davis, President of the
Confederacy), returned to Mississippi to serve as president of
Alcorn College until his death in 1901.

RUINS OF WINDSOR PLANTATION, 10 miles northwest of Lorman on MS 552 in the Port Gibson area. Twenty-
three columns are all that remain of one of the most beautiful

plantation mansions in the South, built in 1860. Like many others, the house was built with slave labor; 600 slaves constructed the four-story building, which was destroyed by fire in 1890.

MOUND BAYOU

The largest black town in the United States (on U.S. 61) was settled in July 1887 by ex-slaves, hoping to find social, economic and political freedom. The home of one of the founders, Isaiah Thornton Montgomery, a member of the 1890 state convention, stands on West Main Street (not open to the public) and is now a National Historic Landmark.

NATCHEZ

DUNLEITH, 84 Homochitto Street, is the Greek Revival-style mansion where young slave John R. Lynch served as a house servant. Lynch's only formal education was four months of night school, but he secured his place in history by becoming one of the most powerful political voices in post-Civil War America. In 1872 he became Speaker of the House in Mississippi. In 1873 he was elected to the U.S. House of Representatives, and went on to become president of the Capital Savings Bank in Washington, D.C., the first black bank in the U.S. Among his many other accomplishments was the book, *The Facts of Reconstruction*.

Dunleith, today, looks much as it did when the young John R. Lynch served dinner guests in the exquisitely decorated dining room.

Mon.–Sat. 9–5, Sun. 12:30–5. Closed holidays. Adults $4, ages 6–17 $2.

EVANS-BONTURA-SMITH HOUSE, 106 Broadway, and the WILLIAM JOHNSON HOUSE, 210 State Street, were homes of free black residents of Natchez. Almost one-half of the total free black population in Mississippi resided in Natchez by the 1850s. William Johnson published a diary which is the most complete account of the life of a free black in the antebellum South. Johnson was a member of the free black aristocracy who not only entered into business deals with white landowners but, ironically, occasionally owned slaves themselves. The Smith house was the substantial residence of another free black, Robert Smith, who operated a prosperous taxi business in pre-Civil War Natchez. (Houses are not open to the public.)

HOLY FAMILY CATHOLIC CHURCH, 16 Orange Avenue, is Mississippi's oldest black Catholic church.

MOSTLY AFRICAN MARKET, at St. Catherine and Mc-Cabe streets, features African and African-American arts and crafts in an antebellum Gothic cottage.

NATCHEZ NATIONAL CEMETERY, at 61 Cemetery Road, received over two thousand black soldiers after the Civil War. Among them are landsman Wilson Brown and seaman John Lawson, both awarded Medals of Honor during the Civil War while serving in the Mobile Bay naval engagement. Hiram Revels, who served as chaplain of a Union regiment during the war and went on to become a black statesman, is also buried here. Later veterans of World War I and II, Korea and Vietnam were also buried at this cemetery.

RICHARD N. WRIGHT MARKER is located at Bluff Park on Broadway (near the bandstand). Richard Wright was born in 1908 near Natchez and is probably the world's most powerful black literary figure. The son of sharecroppers, Wright rocked the literary world with his books *Native Son* and *Black Boy*, shocking and eloquent portrayals of the black experience in America. His search for freedom finally took him to France, where he died in 1960.

ROSE HILL BAPTIST CHURCH, at 607 Madison Street, is Mississippi's oldest black Baptist church.

SLAVE MARKET SITE at St. Catherine and Liberty Road. This was one of several slave auction sites in Natchez, such as Cotton Square and the river landing on Silver Street. The tremendous expansion of the cotton empire after the War of 1812 made the slave markets at Natchez and Algiers (New Orleans) the busiest in the entire South. The population of Natchez had always included free blacks and slaves. In 1723 when the town had only 303 inhabitants, 111 of them were blacks. Cotton plantations in the Delta used large numbers of slaves; one wealthy planter, Stephen Duncan, owned 1041.

ZION CHAPEL A. M. E. CHURCH at 338 Martin Luther King, Jr. Street, was acquired in 1868 by Zion Chapel, whose minister at the time, Hiram R. Revels, became the first black U.S. Senator.

OXFORD

James Meredith became the first black student at the University of Mississippi in Oxford in October 1962. His attempt to register to study there brought about a showdown between the federal government and state's rights advocates. President Kennedy intervened on behalf of Meredith with three thousand federal troops. The setting for this dramatic confrontation was the Lyceum Building on the Ole Miss Campus.

UNIVERSITY OF MISSISSIPPI MUSEUMS are 5 blocks east of the campus on University Avenue at 5th Street. The museums house a permanent collection of more than 16,000 objects, including African and southern American folk art.

THE UNIVERSITY OF MISSISSIPPI BLUES ARCHIVE, including the B.B. King collection of memorabilia and recordings, as well as other blues collections, are housed on Ole Miss Campus, Farley Hall.

Museums open Tues.–Sat. 10–4, Sun. 1–4. Closed holidays. Free.

PHILADELPHIA

FREEDOM SUMMER MURDERS. In June 1964, the murders of three voting rights activists, the victims of a Ku Klux Klan conspiracy, provoked national outrage and led to the first successful federal prosecution of a civil rights case in Mississippi. Information about these deaths may be found on a historical marker at Mt. Zion Methodist Church on a county road about 1 mile off MS 482, 5 miles northeast of Philadelphia.

TOUGALOO

TOUGALOO COLLEGE, on I-55, was built on the grounds of a former plantation in 1869 by the American Missionary Association. Because the educational philosophy at Tougaloo was that black students should be educated not to "know" their place but to "find" it, there were those who considered the college a "hotbed of impudent blacks." During the late 1950s and early 1960s, Tougaloo became the cornerstone of the Mississippi civil rights movement, and many of the students led demonstrations and sit-ins.

Tougaloo has preserved some of its finest historic buildings and recently the Tougaloo Permanent Art Collection was started by a group of prominent New York artists and housed in Warren Hall.

Open during regular academic schedule.

TUPELO

TUPELO NATIONAL BATTLEFIELD, West Main Street, off MS 6, was the site of the last major Civil War battle fought in Mississippi. The battle at Brices Cross Road near Baldwyn, to the north of Tupelo, in which black troops were engaged, took place in June 1864. Some of those same black troops from the 59th, as well as the 61st and 68th Colored Infantry regiments, also participated in the battle of Tupelo in July 1864. The black soldiers served with such courage that the commanding general requested that the black troops be included in the forces used to capture Mobile, Alabama. The site contains monuments honoring both Union and Confederate armies.

VICKSBURG

BETHEL A. M. E. CHURCH, 805 Monument Street, was site of first African Methodist Episcopal Church (1864) and first Negro Masonic Lodge in Mississippi (1875). The present church was built in 1912.

OLD COURT HOUSE MUSEUM, at junction of Cherry, Jackson, Monroe and Grove streets, was built in 1858 by slaves. The courthouse has hosted Booker T. Washington, along with U.S. presidents and generals. A restored courtroom contains the original iron grillwork. Such beautiful ironwork was often produced by black artisans in Mississippi and Louisiana. There is a small exhibit on local blacks and their achievements in the community.

Mon.–Sat. 8:30–4:30, Sun. 1:30–4:30. Closed holidays. Adults $1.50, seniors $1, students 75 cents.

VICKSBURG NATIONAL MILITARY PARK can be entered on the east side from U.S. 80. The park adjoins Vicksburg and covers more than 1,700 acres. For 47 days in 1863 the Union army laid siege to Vicksburg. Many residents of the town retreated to live in caves to avoid the constant shelling. Several black regiments were involved in the Vicksburg campaign and their members are buried at the Vicksburg National Cemetery. The cemetery contains the bodies of over 17,000 Civil War soldiers. It lies in the north end of the park and is entered via Connecting and Union avenues.

U.S.S. *CAIRO* MUSEUM opposite the National Cemetery entrance, displays artifacts recovered from the Union ironclad *Cairo,* which was sunk north of Vicksburg in 1862. Black laborers served on the *Cairo's* crew.

The visitor center at the park entrance has a movie of the Vicksburg campaign and exhibits showing the effects of the siege on both soldiers and civilians. Within the park the original Federal siege line and the Confederate defense perimeter, along with sites of forts, trenches, artillery emplacements, scenes of combat activity and unit positions are illustrated on a well-marked self-guided tour.

Daily 8–7, June–Aug.; rest of year 8–5. $3 per car, $1 per person if entering by bus; seniors and under age 16 free. Free admission to visitor center.

For further information about Mississippi, contact:

Natchez Visitors Bureau
311 Liberty Road
Natchez, MS 39120
1-800-647-6724

Free brochure: "Historic Natchez, the African-American Experience"

Mississippi Division of Tourism
P.O. Box 22825
Jackson, MS 39205
1-800-647-2290

A statewide black heritage guide is being compiled.

MISSOURI

BRUSH CREEK

ST. PETER'S CHURCH in Brush Creek, west of Hannibal, contains a plaque dedicated to the memory of Father Augustine Tolton, who was baptized here. Although James and Patrick Healy of Boston are usually considered to be the first black Catholic priests in America, the Healy brothers were the sons of an Irish father and a mulatto mother. Father Tolton, ordained in Rome in 1886, whose parents were both Afro-Americans, is regarded as the first American black to become a Catholic priest. He is buried in St. Peter's Cemetery in Quincy, Illinois.

COLUMBIA

MUSEUM OF ART AND ARCHAEOLOGY in Pickard Hall on the University of Missouri campus (corner of University Avenue and 9th Street) has a small but excellent exhibit of African art called "Expressions of Africa." Traditional African art is not only displayed but explained in relation to its practical use. Pieces range from Ashanti fertility figures to intricately carved masks, some covering the head, some only covering the face, giving physical form to the spiritual.

Works of black artists also form part of the museum's

collection and there are often visiting African-American art
exhibits.
Tues. 9 a.m.–9 p.m., Wed.–Fri. 9–5, weekends 12–5.
Closed national holidays. Free.

DIAMOND

THE GEORGE WASHINGTON CARVER NA-
TIONAL MONUMENT is southeast of Joplin and 2½ miles
southwest of Diamond (take U.S. 71 alternate to Diamond
then west for 2 miles on County Highway V and south for a
mile on county road to the monument entrance).

The young Carver spent his childhood on the Moses Carver farm at this site. Although born a slave, George and his
brother were treated more as members of the family than
servants. The trails which young George enjoyed walking
have been preserved, along with his own private garden area.
In the midst of this garden is a bronze statue of the boy
Carver. Visitors may listen to a tape recording of Carver's last
public speech. There is also a demonstration garden containing the main crops which the noted black scientist used in
developing hundreds of products. A visitor center displays
exhibits on Carver's early life and work and the honors show-
ered upon him.

Daily 8:30–6, Memorial Day–Labor Day; rest of year
8:30–5. Closed Dec. 25. Admission $1.

INDEPENDENCE

HARRY S. TRUMAN LIBRARY AND MUSEUM,
northeast edge of Independence, on U.S. 24 at Delaware
Street. It was from Independence that many of the wagon
trains started their long, dangerous trips west. Artist Thomas
Hart Benton painted a mural called *Independence and the
Opening of the West* which may be seen at the Truman Li-

brary. In the center of the mural, a blacksmith is hard at work. The man in the painting is modeled after an actual black man, Hiram Young, who lived in Independence and made a fortune building wagons for many of the pioneers.

Another black man Major "Black" Harris, scout and Indian fighter from Independence, is not shown in the mural. He led many wagon trains west.

In the museum of the library may also be found important documents relating to the civil rights movement, executed by Harry S. Truman when he was president.

Daily 9–5. Closed Jan. 1, Thanksgiving and Dec. 25. Adults $2, under 16 free.

JEFFERSON CITY

LINCOLN UNIVERSITY, 820 Chestnut Street, was founded on the dreams of uneducated ex-slaves, the men of the 62nd Missouri Colored Volunteers who served during the Civil War. The money for the school was raised from the regiment. Enlisted men who drew only $13 a month in pay gave as much as $100. Begun as the Lincoln Institute in 1866, its first permanent building was erected in 1871. That day the men of the 62nd and 65th Missouri Colored Volunteers held a happy reunion on the campus. Today it is known as the Lincoln University and a group of buildings on campus have been declared a National Historic District.

The Inman E. Page Library has a collection of art works by noted black American artists, such as Aaron Douglas, Hale Woodruff and James Porter.

Mon.–Thurs. 8 a.m.–11 p.m., Sat. 1–5, Sun. 3–11 p.m. Free.

KANSAS CITY

BLACK ARCHIVES OF MID-AMERICA, 2033 Vine

Street, is housed in the first fire station in Missouri to be managed by blacks. The museum highlights notable black figures in sports, entertainment and politics, and serves as a regional research center and repository of records and information relating to the Afro-American experience in the midwest.

Mon.–Fri. 9–4:30; weekends by appointment. Admission 50 cents.

BRUCE R. WATKINS CULTURAL HERITAGE CENTER, at 3700 Blue Parkway (Swope Parkway and Benton Boulevard,) commemorates the history of Kansas City's black community. Bruce R. Watkins was a black community leader throughout his adult life. Among the highlights of the center are the Spirit of Freedom fountain, the Brush Creek Amphitheater and the Grand Hall of Fame. Within the hall is the Wall of Fame, which honors notable black Kansas citizens. The center offers dramatic and musical productions as well as educational and art exhibits.

Tues.–Sat. 10–6, Sun. 1–5. Exhibits free.

FOREST HILL CEMETERY, at 69th Street and Troost Avenue, is the site of a memorial tombstone at the grave of Leroy "Satchel" Paige, the black baseball great. Born in Mobile, Alabama, Paige played for Negro teams until he became the first black pitcher in the American League in 1948. He received his nickname as a young boy when he worked as a redcap and "looked like a walking satchel tree."

NEGRO LEAGUES BASEBALL MUSEUM. When this museum is completed, it will be part of the International Jazz Hall of Fame in the Vine Street Historic District. Upon arriving, the visitor will be greeted by a statue of Satchel Paige throwing his famous "hesitation pitch." Exhibits will weave black history into arrangements of artifacts and photos about the Negro League, which was organized at Kansas City, Missouri, in 1920. Call 816-924-7373 for opening date in 1992.

THE NELSON-ATKINS MUSEUM OF ART, 4525 Oak

Street, has a collection of African art as well as Afro-American pieces by Richard Hunt, Jacob Lawrence and Julian Binford.

Tues.–Sat. 10–5, Sun. 1–5. Closed holidays. Adults $3, ages 6–18 $1. Free to all on Sun.

ST. CHARLES

LEWIS AND CLARK CENTER, 701 Riverside Drive, has life-size exhibits and dioramas on the Lewis and Clark expedition which explored the West in 1804. The exhibits include information about York, the black servant of William Clark, who proved invaluable as a hunter and fisherman as well as for his ability to make friends with the Indian tribes.

Daily 10:30–4:30. Closed Dec. 25. Adults $1, children/students 50 cents.

St. Charles is also the burial site of black fur trapper Jean Baptiste Pointe Du Sable, who was the first non-Indian settler of Chicago. As the fur trapper grew older, he feared only two things; that he would not have enough money to support himself and that he would not be buried in a Catholic cemetery. His first fear came true and he died a pauper, but he was buried in the Catholic St. Charles Borromeo Cemetery in this town.

ST. LOUIS

DR. MARTIN LUTHER KING, JR. STATUE, at Fountain and Auburn streets in the Fountain Park District, was dedicated in 1978. The WASHINGTON TABERNACLE BAPTIST CHURCH, at 3200 Washington Boulevard, was the site of a major civil-rights rally in May 1963. The rally, attended by 3,000 people, took place just before the historic march on Washington.

JEFFERSON BARRACKS HISTORICAL PARK AND
NATIONAL CEMETERY is at the end of South Broadway
(Grant Road and Kingston) about 10 miles south via I-55,
South Broadway exit. In this national cemetery lie the graves
of 175 soldiers of the 56th Colored Infantry Regiment who
died of cholera while stationed at Jefferson Barracks shortly
after the close of the Civil War. More white and black soldiers
died of disease during the war than of battle wounds. An
obelisk honoring the black cholera victims is located in Section 57 of the national cemetery.

Also stationed at Jefferson Barracks, during the Spanish-
American War, was a black regiment called the 7th Regiment
of Immunes. In 1898 it was mistakenly believed that blacks
were immune to malaria and yellow fever, which were killing
many American soldiers in Cuba. Although the Immunes
never reached Cuba, the all-black 9th and 10th Cavalry and
25th Infantry regiments played a major role in the war.

Four of the original buildings at Jefferson Barracks have
been restored. There is a museum at the park which tells the
story of Jefferson Barracks from its founding in 1826.

Wed.–Sat. 10–5, Sun. noon–5. Closed Jan. 1, Thanksgiving and Dec. 25. Free.

JEFFERSON NATIONAL EXPANSION MEMORIAL,
on the waterfront at Market Street, includes not only the
world famous Gateway Arch but also the MUSEUM OF
WESTWARD EXPANSION which is housed beneath the
arch. The museum contains fascinating exhibits and interpretative programs on the pioneers and the settling of the
West, as well as the Lewis and Clark expedition. There are
exhibits on black pioneers, and the rangers who conduct
tours through the museum point out the role that black men
and women played in the westward trek.

Daily 8 a.m.–10 p.m. Memorial Day–Labor Day, 9–6 rest
of year. Closed Jan. 1, Thanksgiving and Dec. 25. Ages 17
thru 61 $1, maximum $3 per family.

THE OLD COURTHOUSE, at Broadway and Market

streets, is part of the Jefferson National Expansion Memorial. Before the Civil War, slaves were sold on the courthouse steps to settle estates. It was here that the slave Dred Scott filed suit to gain his freedom in 1846. The litigation went on for 11 years, making its way to the Supreme Court. Although Dred Scott finally lost his case, the decision handed down by Judge Taney widened the split between the North and the South over the issue of slavery. Ironically, Dred Scott himself was set free by his owner a few weeks after the decision was rendered and died a year later. He is buried in Calvary Cemetery.

The old courthouse has two restored courtrooms and five museum galleries on St. Louis history, including exhibits on the Dred Scott Case.

Daily 8–4:30. Closed Thanksgiving, Dec. 25 and New Year's Day. Guided tours available. Free.

LAMBERT ST. LOUIS INTERNATIONAL AIRPORT, Airport exit off I-70, has a mural depicting black Americans' achievements in aviation from 1917 to the present. After another mural in the airport depicting the history of manned flight was executed without black figures, an additional mural was commissioned in 1984, entitled *Black American in Flight*. The 51-foot mural was painted by Spencer Taylor and Solomon Thurman and includes 75 portraits ranging from Eugene Bullard, a black fighter pilot in World War I, to the Tuskegee Airmen of World War II, to three black astronauts, Guion Bluford, Ronald McNair, and Dr. Mae Jemison, the first black woman in space.

The mural is located on the lower level of the terminal.

QUINN CHAPEL at 225 Bowen Street, near the Mississippi River was built as a public market in 1870. The building was transferred to the Carondelet African Methodist Episcopal Church in 1880. This black congregation had formed in 1845 and called its new church Quinn Chapel, after the A. M. E.'s fourth bishop, William P. Quinn, who opened up the West to African evangelism. The church, recently designated a National Landmark, has been used by the same congregation at the same location for more than one hundred years. The original windows appear to be made of stained glass but are actually clear and lined with colored paper to produce this illusion.

ST. LOUIS ART MUSEUM stands on the top of Art Hill in Forest Park. The museum has a good collection of African art and a small collection of works by African-American artists, including Robert S. Duncanson's oil painting *View of the St. Anne's River, Canada.* Tues. 1:30–8:30, Wed.–Sun. 10–5. Closed Jan. 1 and Dec. 25. Free.

THE HISTORY MUSEUM in the Jefferson Memorial, also in Forest Park (off Lindell Boulevard), chronicles the history of St. Louis, including a display of photographs and artifacts on blacks in the city's history.

Tues.–Sun. 9:30–4:45. Closed Jan. 1, Thanksgiving and Dec. 25. Free.

ST. LOUIS SPORTS HALL OF FAME, 100 Stadium Plaza, is on the Walnut Street side of Busch Memorial Stadium, between Gates 5 and 6. This live-action museum of St. Louis sports history includes all sports, but in large part tells the story of baseball. The room honoring players of the St. Louis Cardinals team has larger-than-life-size pictures of famous black Cardinal baseball players, such as Bob Gibson and Cool Poppa Bill. World Series movies are also shown.

Daily 10–5. Open during night games to ticket holders only. Adults $2, children $1.50.

SCOTT JOPLIN RESIDENCE, 2658 Delmar Boulevard, just west of Jefferson Avenue, was the King of Ragtime's last home. One of the most creative black musicians, Joplin lived on the second floor of this house at the turn of the century, in his "St. Louis period," and composed some of his most famous works.

The house was designated a National Historic Landmark and is presently being renovated to look as it did when Joplin lived and worked there. The building will also include a museum and exhibit area for black history and culture, including a room for musical performances. The building next door, the old Rosebud Club, a favorite spot for ragtime players, has been turned into a museum of ragtime music,

Mon.–Sat. 10–4, Sun. 12–5. Adults $1.25, ages 6–12, 50 cents, ages 3–5, 25 cents.

STOWE TEACHERS COLLEGE (now HARRIS-STATE COLLEGE) 3026 Laclede, was founded a century ago as a training school for black teachers, the first black institution of higher education west of the Mississippi. Before 1866 it was illegal to educate blacks in the state of Missouri but the Rev. John Berry Meachum found a way around the law by taking his students out on a boat in the middle of the Mississippi and holding class. Stowe merged with Harris Teachers College, a training school for white teachers, in 1954. The small but excellent archives of historical black material in the library at Harris-Stowe is available to the public by appointment.

One of the Stowe's outstanding graduates was Julia Davis who went on to teach three generations of black students at the college. She contributed the Julia Davis Collection of black resource material to the St. Louis Public Library and a branch library has been named in her honor. The Julia Davis Library, 4666 Natural Bridge, has memorabilia of Julia Davis.

VAUGHN CULTURAL CENTER, 525 North Grand, has changing monthly exhibits on Afro-American history and culture. Bus tours of black St. Louis also begin at this center, led by experienced tour guides who describe black St. Louis history with fascinating stories, legend and fact.

Mon.–Fri. 8:30–5. Free. Charge and advance reservations required for bus tour. (314-535-9227)

SEDALIA

MAPLE LEAF ROOM RAGTIME COLLECTION has

a permanent home in the Learning Resources Center at State Fair Community College. Sedalia has been called the cradle of classical ragtime. It was while black composer Scott Joplin was playing his ragtime music at the Maple Leaf Club here in 1899 that John Stark, a music store owner, was intrigued by what he heard. John Stark purchased the "Maple Leaf Rag" from Scott Joplin for $50 and Joplin's royalties. The sale of the music made both John Stark and Scott Joplin financially independent . . . and ragtime music internationally famous. The "Maple Leaf Rag" became one of the first pieces of American sheet music to sell over one million copies. The original Maple Leaf Club stood at the intersection of Lamine and Main streets. A monument marks the spot.

The ragtime collection at the college contains sheet music, piano rolls, tapes of interviews, and memorabilia of Scott Joplin and other ragtime greats. The Scott Joplin Ragtime Festival is held annually in June.

Mon.–Thurs. 8–8, Fri. 8–3:30. Closed weekends. Free.

For further information on Missouri, contact:

Missouri Division of Tourism
P.O. Box 1055
Jefferson City, MO 65102
1-800-877-1234

MONTANA

FORT BENTON

In 1804 President Jefferson selected Meriwether Lewis and William Clark to lead an expedition to explore the newly purchased Louisiana Territory. Accompanying Lewis and Clark were a small group of men, including a black man, York, who was Clark's servant (actually a slave). Later an Indian woman, Sacajawea, wife of one of the interpreters, was added to the party. Sacajawea's knowledge of the Shoshone Indians and York's prowess as a hunter and fisherman, as well as his courage (he saved the lives of Clark and Sacajawea near Great Falls, Montana) determined the success of the expedition.

In 1805–1806 the Lewis and Clark expedition explored the Upper Missouri River, near what is now Fort Benton. The town was an important supply depot and jumping-off point for thousands of white and black immigrants and miners heading west in the nineteenth century. The Upper Missouri Wild and Scenic River Visitor Center, at 1718 Front Street, in Fort Benton, offers a slide presentation of Lewis and Clark's expedition as well as information about the area.

Daily 8–6 May 16–Sept. 16. Free.

GREAT FALLS

CASCADE COUNTY HISTORICAL MUSEUM, 1400
1st Avenue N. at Paris Gibson Square. Not just black men
came west as pioneers, but black women, too. One woman,
Mary Fields, made her own sort of legend in western Montana. She first worked for the Ursuline nuns at St. Peter's
Mission and went on to run a restaurant in Cascade, but is
best known for hauling freight and driving a stagecoach as
well as any man. Information and pictures of Mary Fields
may be found in the archives of the Cascade County Historical Museum.

Tues.–Fri. 10–5, weekends 10–4. Closed holidays. Donation.

HARDIN

CUSTER BATTLEFIELD NATIONAL MONUMENT
is 15 miles south of Hardin on I-90. In June 1876 General
Custer and 225 men of the 7th Cavalry Regiment were ambushed and massacred by Sioux and Cheyenne warriors at the
battle of the Little Big Horn. One of the casualties was Isaiah
Dorman, a black scout who had joined Custer only a few days
before. Dorman had lived among the Sioux. A Cheyenne
brave, describing the scene after the battle, tells of seeing
Dorman's body: "I saw by the river, on the west side, a dead
black man . . . all his clothing was gone when I saw him, but
he had not been scalped nor cut up like the white men had
been. Some Sioux told me he belonged to their people but was
with the soldiers."

Although no black soldiers died in the battle, at nearby
Custer Battlefield National Cemetery many Buffalo Soldiers
who served at forts across the West lie buried.

Battlefield includes visitor center, museum, and national

cemetery, guided battlefield tours and interpretative programs.

Monument open daily 8–sunset; visitor center open 8–7:45 in summer, 8–4:30 rest of year. Closed Jan. 1, Thanksgiving and Dec. 25. Admission $3 per vehicle, $1 per individual, over 62 free.

HELENA

MONTANA HISTORICAL SOCIETY MUSEUM is located at 225 N. Roberts. The museum recounts the history of Montana and contains one of the largest collections of the paintings of C. M. Russell, the famous Western artist. One of the paintings shows York, the black man who traveled with the Lewis and Clark expedition, being examined with amazement by the Mandan Indians. They had never seen a black man before and thought the black color of his skin would rub off. There are dioramas of the expedition, in which York may be seen, in the museum.

In addition there are exhibits and artifacts of black military regiments, black churches and black cowboys.

Mon.–Fri. 8–6, Sat.–Sun. and holidays 9–6, Memorial Day–Labor Day; rest of year Mon.–Fri. 8–5, Sat. 9–5. Closed holidays. Free.

STATE CAPITOL, 6th and Montana streets, has a painting of the Lewis and Clark expedition which shows York, the black man who accompanied them. In the Gallery of Outstanding Montana Citizens is a picture of Mattie Castner, a black woman who, with her husband, is credited with founding the mining town of Belt, Montana, in 1888.

Mon.–Fri. 8–6, weekends 9–5. Closed holidays. Free.

MISSOULA

HISTORICAL MUSEUM at Fort Missoula, Bldg. 322, South and Reserve streets, enter from South Avenue. Fort Missoula, an "open-fort," was built in 1877 and the all black 25th Infantry Regiment arrived in May 1888. One of the most interesting assignments given to them was to test the military use of the bicycle as the 25th Infantry Bicycle Corps. The corps rode their bicycles from the fort up the Bitterroot Valley, north to the St. Ignatius area and on to Yellowstone Park, to deliver dispatches. In 1897 the Bicycle Corps made a 1,900-mile trip from Missoula to St. Louis. However, the army decided that the bicycle would never replace the horse. The 25th Infantry returned to Missoula by train.

The 25th Infantry was one of the first units called to fight in the Spanish-American War. They also served in the Philippines.

The museum, with exhibits about the history of the fort, is housed in what was a quartermaster's warehouse. Other restored buildings in the complex may be visited.

Tues.–Sat. 10–5, Sun. 12–5, Memorial Day–Labor Day; Tues.–Sun. noon–5, Labor Day–Memorial Day. Free. Donations accepted. Self-guided tours.

For further information about Montana, contact:

Montana Travel Promotion Division
1424 9th St.
Helena, MT 59620
1-800-548-3390

NEBRASKA

CRAWFORD

FORT ROBINSON MUSEUM is located in Fort Robinson State Park, 3 miles west of Crawford on U.S. 20. Fort Robinson was the home of both the all-black 9th and 10th Cavalry regiments at various times. The 9th was stationed here in 1885 and some of their more famous skirmishes were against the Sioux during the Ghost Dance uprising in 1890, which culminated that December in the tragic battle of Wounded Knee. Although the 9th did not see combat in the battle, a few days later it heroically rode a hundred miles in twenty-four hours to rescue 7th Cavalry troopers pinned down at the battleground. Corporal Wilson of the 9th Cavalry received the Congressional Medal of Honor for conspicuous gallantry during this action.

In 1898 the 9th left Fort Robinson to fight with great courage in Cuba during the Spanish-American War. The 10th Cavalry replaced them, serving at the fort until 1910 when it was assigned to serve along the Mexican border.

Charles Young, who later became the first black colonel in the U.S. Army, spent part of his military career at Fort Robinson after graduating from West Point in 1889.

The Fort Robinson Museum in the old fort headquarters building has several exhibits relating to the 9th and 10th Cavalry regiments. Numerous buildings at the fort have been restored to their appearance in the nineteenth century and there are living history tours conducted by guides in period costumes, along with jeep, stagecoach and surrey rides, train excursions, and nature programs.

The Fort Robinson State Park covers 22,000 acres and is open daily, Memorial Day-Labor Day. Nebraska State Park car permit required: $2 daily. The Fort Robinson Museum is open Mon.–Sat. 8–5, Sun. and holidays 9–5, Memorial Day–Labor Day; hours vary off-season. Adults $1, under 18 with adult free. Admission fee to museum entitles you to enter other exhibit buildings.

LINCOLN

STATE MUSEUM OF HISTORY, at 15th and P streets, has three floors of exhibits on the history of Nebraska, including a "sod house," the type of frontier home in which early white and black Nebraska settlers lived. There is a special exhibit on the second floor about blacks on the frontier. Black pioneers settled in the region as early as 1867 among the Exodusters who traded the hardships of the South for the harsh, but free, life on the frontiers of Kansas and Nebraska.

Mon.–Sat. 9–5; Sun. 1:30–5. Closed holidays. Free.

NEBRASKA CITY

JOHN BROWN'S CAVE AND MUSEUM is 3 miles west on NE 2. Before the Civil War, some slaves from Missouri escaped into Nebraska Territory, then crossed the Missouri River into Iowa. This cave, named John Brown's Cave in honor of the famed abolitionist, served as a refuge for the fugitive slaves. Near the cave is the John Kagi Cabin, a small log cabin which has been documented as a station on the Underground Railroad.

Daily 10–5, May–Aug. Adults $2, children $1.

OMAHA

GREAT PLAINS BLACK MUSEUM, 2213 Lake Street, opened in 1976 as the largest black American historical/cultural institution west of the Mississippi River. The museum was the dream of Bertha Calloway whose grandfather was a cowboy who broke horses in Texas. History books, however, never said anything about black cowboys although there were many black men among the thousands who came "up the trail." They served as cooks, bronco busters, regular hands, and foremen on cattle drives. Along with their white and Mexican companions, they herded cattle to new ranges or railheads and fought Indians, blizzards, and each other. Everywhere that cattle were worked, black cowboys were found.

The museum preserves material that chronicles this largely unknown aspect of black history in the Midwest. In addition to exhibits on black cowboys, there are displays on early black settlers. The first black pioneers came to Nebraska shortly after the Civil War, locating in many counties, including Custer, Hamilton, Harlan and Cherry. Like their white neighbors, some of these pioneers dried or froze out, others, like Robert Ball Anderson, stayed to help develop Nebraska. One of the early black pioneers, Anderson was born a slave but by 1918 had become one of the largest landowners in the state.

The museum also has a music room, a section on black athletes, and on black military exploits, as well as many other fascinating exhibits. Black art, traditional African art, in addition to works of contemporary black artists, are displayed.

The museum includes an extensive manuscript research collection.

Open Mon.–Fri. 8–4:30. Donation of $1 requested; special rates for students.

For further information about Nebraska, contact:

Division of Travel and Tourism
P.O. Box 94666
Lincoln, NE 68509
1-800-228-4307

NEW HAMPSHIRE

HANOVER

HOOD MUSEUM OF ART is connected to Hopkins Center and Wilson Hall, on the south side of the Green on the campus of Dartmouth College. The museum has displays of native American and African art, as well as twentieth-century works.

Tues.–Fri. and Sun. 11–5, Sat. 11–8. Closed holidays. Free.

Dartmouth College was founded in a log cabin in 1769 by the Rev. Eleazar Wheelock to spread Christian education "to the Indians and other youth." The town of Hanover was strongly opposed to slavery, so much so that when a president of Dartmouth College wrote of slavery as a divine right, he was forced to resign. The first black graduate was Edward Mitchell in 1828. When the trustees were reluctant to admit him, the student body pled his case and persuaded the trustees to change their mind.

JAFFREY

AMOS FORTUNE may not have been the most famous black American but he certainly was one of the most determined. He bought his freedom from slavery and his family's in 1770 when he was sixty years old. At the age of seventy, when most men would have retired, he started a tannery business in Jaffrey. A highly respected citizen of the town, he left his small fortune to the local Quaker church and school district when he died.

The white clapboard Quaker meeting house, built in 1773, is the site of the Amos Fortune Lectures, an annual public speaking contest. Prizes for the lectures come from the fund left to the school district in 1801 by Fortune.

There were many like Amos Fortune in America's history, men and women who by sheer grit, courage and determination rose from slavery to respected citizenship. Most of their names are unknown, but on the headstone of the grave of Amos Fortune can still be read: "Sacred to the memory of Amos Fortune, who was born free in Africa, a slave in America, he purchased liberty, professed Christianity, lived reputably, and died hopefully. Nov. 17, 1801."

Amos Fortune's grave is in the Old Burying Ground in Jaffrey Center next to the Quaker meeting house.

JAFFREY PUBLIC LIBRARY, 111 Main Street. In 1795 Amos Fortune founded the Jaffrey Social Library. Today, the Jaffrey Public Library has Fortune's freedom papers as well as newspaper clippings and other reference material about this leading citizen of the community.

Mon., Wed., Fri. 11–5:30, Tues. and Thurs. 1–8 p.m., Sat. 2–5:30. Free.

For further information about New Hampshire, contact:

New Hampshire Office of Vacation Travel
105 Loudon Rd., Prescott Park,
P.O. Box 856
Concord, NH 03301
603-271-2666

NEW JERSEY

BURLINGTON

BETHLEHEM A. M. E. CHURCH, founded in 1830, is one of the oldest black churches in the state. The cemetery contains the graves of black Civil War veterans. A pastor of the church was an early civil rights activist, suing the state in 1883 so that his children could attend an all-white school.

Burlington, itself, was on the Underground Railroad route that passed through Philadelphia and Camden. Oliver Cromwell, black Revolutionary War veteran, lived in the town. George Washington signed his discharge in 1783. Cyrus Bustill, an ancestor of the noted black singer Paul Robeson, lived in Burlington during colonial times. He helped found the Free African Society in 1787. Later he moved to Philadelphia, from where he supplied bread to the Continental Army at Valley Forge.

CAMDEN

FETTERSVILLE in Camden was established as a black settlement in 1833, and the MACEDONIAN A. M. E. CHURCH in Fettersville, founded in 1832, is the oldest black congregation in Camden. (Another small, early black settlement in New Jersey was Timbuctoo in Westampton, established in the 1820s, the only black settlement in the country named after an actual West African city.)

Also in Camden is the Ulysses S. Wiggins Riverfront Park, named in honor of an active leader in the local chapter of the NAACP. The riverfront park is located where slave ships docked in colonial days.

FREEHOLD

MONMOUTH BATTLEFIELD STATE PARK is 3 miles west on NJ 33. On a blistering hot day in June 1778, British forces were withdrawing from Philadelphia to the safety of New York through Monmouth County when they were attacked by American troops. The British finally retreated under cover of darkness.

For number of troops engaged, Monmouth was one of the largest battles in the Revolutionary War. There were at least 700 black soldiers among the 13,500 Americans in the Monmouth campaign. By 1778 Washington's Continental Army averaged about 50 black soldiers per battalion. One of them was a young black woman, Deborah Gannet, who enlisted in the 4th Massachusetts Regiment as "Robert Shurtliff." Although she did not fight at Monmouth, she served for seventeen months in the Continental Army before her gender was discovered. After the war she was cited "for an extraordinary instance of female heroism."

THE MONMOUTH BATTLE MONUMENT stands on the site where some of the fiercest fighting took place. At the park visitor center, presently being renovated, information about the battle may be obtained.

The Park is open daily 8–8 Memorial Day-Labor Day, 8–4:30 rest of year. Visitor center open daily 10–6, Memorial Day–Labor Day, 10–4 rest of year. Free.

LAWNSIDE

Lawnside was an early, almost all-black community. Established in the late 18th century, incorporated in 1926, today it is one of the few historically all-black towns in America. In the 1930s the town was an entertainment center, with many well-known all-black nightclubs, such as Lawnside Park. Lawnside was such an important station on the Underground Railroad that for a while in 1840 the town changed its name to Free Haven.

William Grant Still, a free black and successful businessman, lived in Lawnside and was one of the founders of the Pennsylvania Society for the Abolition of Slavery. His home, like many other homes of free blacks, was a station on the Underground Railroad. He kept stocks of clothing and food for the fugitive slaves who came to his door. Although it was dangerous for Underground conductors to keep written records, Still documented the escaping slaves who passed through his house so that families could be reunited later. In 1871, William Still wrote *The Underground Railroad*, a definitive history of the movement.

The MOUNT PISGAH A. M. E. CHURCH, Warwick and Mouldy roads in Lawnside, was built about 1800 as a Methodist church for black and white worshippers, and continued to grow after the white members withdrew in 1815. Like many black churches in the North, Mount Pisgah was also a station on the Underground Railroad. Black veterans of America's wars are buried in the Mount Pisgah Cemetery, including a navy veteran of the War of 1812 who served on the U.S.S. *Constitution*.

JERSEY CITY

THE AFRO-AMERICAN HISTORICAL AND CULTURAL SOCIETY OF JERSEY CITY, at 1841 Kennedy

Boulevard, has a collection of African and Afro-American art, civil rights posters, quilted coverlets, lifestyle exhibits and photographs of prominent black New Jersey citizens from 1890 to the present. Guided tours, lectures, films.

Mon.–Sat. 10–5. Closed holidays. Free but donations encouraged.

MOUNT LAUREL

JACOB'S CHAPEL A. M. E. CHURCH congregation dates from 1813, although the church was built in 1859. Today this original building is used as a social hall. Several prominent black families are buried in the churchyard, including Dr. James Still, who in the 1840s was one of the first black doctors in New Jersey. Dr. Still was so successful with his herbal medicine that he attracted both white and black patients.

NEWARK

NEWARK MUSEUM, at 49 Washington Street, was one of the first museums to hold an Afro-American art exhibition in 1944. The museum has an excellent collection of paintings and sculpture by black Americans with works by Henry Ossawa Tanner, Charles W. White, and Hale Woodruff; a rare Joshua Johnston portrait, and *Monument to Malcolm X, II* by Barbara Chase-Riboud. There is also a fine collection of African art and artifacts, ranging from Yoruba carvings to beadwork from Cameroon and masks of Zaire.

Tues.–Sun. noon–5. Closed holidays. Free.

PRINCETON

THE HISTORICAL SOCIETY OF PRINCETON is located in the Bainbridge House, 158 Nassau Street. The library has papers and documents from the black community, including autobiographical material on prominent black citizens of Princeton.

Library open Tues. and Fri. noon–4. Free.

WITHERSPOON PRESBYTERIAN CHURCH, 124 Witherspoon Street in Princeton's black historic district, was the pulpit of Paul Robeson's father. Paul Robeson, the famous singer, was born in Princeton and was valedictorian of his class at Rutgers College in New Brunswick, New Jersey. Although Robeson's later career was clouded by his political philosophy, he is still regarded as one of America's outstanding singers.

TENAFLY

AFRICAN ARTS MUSEUM, 23 Bliss Avenue, is run by the S. M. A. Father, Society of African Missions, Inc. The collection includes items from over 40 West African cultures: scrulptures, masks, textiles, household utensils, musical instruments, wood and metal artifacts, religious headdresses, and bronze Ashanti goldweights. There are guided tours and programs for children and adults. Library open by appointment only.

Mon.–Sat. 10–5, Sun. 10–12. Closed holidays. Donation.

TRENTON

WASHINGTON CROSSING STATE PARK is 8 miles northwest on NJ 29, then northeast on County Road 546 to the entrance. Although recruitment of blacks into the Continental Army was discouraged at the time of the battle of Trenton, two black men, Prince Whipple and Oliver Cromwell, crossed the frozen Delaware River with General Washington on Christmas Day, 1776. The Hessian mercenaries were defeated at Trenton by Washington's small army, who marched 9 miles over icy roads in a freezing rain to take them by surprise.

Blacks had already fought at Bunker Hill, Lexington, Concord, and helped cover Washington's retreat at the battle of Long Island in August 1776. Blacks, slave and free, had also gone over to the British army. In 1776 the British army on Staten Island had 800 former American slaves among its ranks.

In 1777 the Continental Congress approved enlistment of blacks in the army, and in the same year a Hessian officer wrote home that there was no regiment among the Americans "in which there are not Negroes in abundance, and among them are able-bodied, strong and brave fellows."

The Continental Lane, over which the half-frozen Colonial troops marched to capture Trenton, extends almost the full length of the park and is marked with historical memorials. There is also a reenactment of Washington crossing the Delaware, which begins on the Pennsylvania side at 2 p.m. on December 25.

The visitor center has a museum with hundreds of artifacts from the Revolutionary War period. The cooperplate engraving of Thomas Sully's painting *Washington Crossing the Delaware* which shows black Prince Whipple in Washington's boat, may be seen at the museum. There are also several historic homes, a nature arboretum, and an open air theater in the park.

Park open daily 8–8 Memorial Day weekend–Labor Day; rest of year 8–4:30. The visitor center is open daily 9–5 Memorial Day–Labor Day; rest of year Wed.–Sun. 9–4:30. Admission with $2 parking fee Memorial Day weekend–Labor Day, free after Labor Day.

MT. ZION A. M. E. CHURCH, 135 Perry Street, was founded in 1811 as the Free African Society of Trenton. It joined the A. M. E. Church in 1817 and the famous black minister Richard Allen conducted the first service. Mt. Zion was also involved in nineteenth-century black political and abolitionist activity.

WILLINGBORO

MERABASH MUSEUM (Museum for Education and Research in American Black Art, Science and History) is located in the William Allen School, built in 1868 and presently under renovation. The collection includes Afro-American and African artifacts, a library of rare books and resource materials on blacks, and a "Please Touch" display for children.

Open by appointment only. (P.O. Box 752, Willingboro, New Jersey 08046, or phone 609-877-3177.)

TOUR OF BLACK HISTORIC SITES IN NEW JERSEY. Group tours may be arranged through Giles R. Wright, 16 Madestone Lane, Willingboro, NJ 08046; normally arranged at least three months in advance. Prices vary.

For further information about New Jersey, contact:

New Jersey Division of Travel and Tourism
20 W. State Street
CN 826
Trenton, NJ 08625
609-292-2470

NEW MEXICO

ANGEL FIRE

DAV VIETNAM VETERANS NATIONAL MEMO-
RIAL on U.S. 64. Although the Vietnam Veterans Memorial
in Washington, D.C., is better known, this beautiful cur-
vilinear structure built on a hilltop overlooking the Sangre de
Cristo Mountains is a striking memorial to those who lost
their lives or who were disabled in the conflict. Of the 47,253
who died in Vietnam, 5,681 were black members of the military.

The chapel is always open; visitor center is open daily 6:30–
5:30. Free. Angel Fire, itself, is a year-round resort offering a
series of classical and jazz concerts from mid-August to Sept.

COLUMBUS

In March 1916, Pancho Villa and his Mexican guerrillas
crossed the border and attacked Columbus and its military
outpost, killing ten civilians and eight soldiers. Within a
week, General John "Black Jack" Pershing had retaliated by
marching 6,000 troops into Mexico. Among them were members of the 10th U.S. Cavalry. Their supplies running low, the
white and black troopers were forced to live off the land while
they pursued the Mexican band, finally attacking Villa and his
men at Carrizal, Mexico. Although they never captured Villa,

the military experience gained in Mexico, with such novelties as field radios, motorized vehicles and airplanes, proved useful to America in World War I.

THE COLUMBUS HISTORICAL MUSEUM in the restored Southern Pacific Depot and historical markers at the PANCHO VILLA STATE PARK on NM 11 present information about the Villa raid, the last hostile action by foreign troops within the continental United States.

Museum open daily 9–5. Closed Christmas, New Year's, Thanksgiving and Easter. Free.

LAS CRUCES

FORT SELDON STATE MONUMENT is located 15 miles north on I-25 to exit 19, then ¼ mile west. Fort Seldon, established in 1865, was one of ten New Mexican forts at which black soldiers of the United States regular army were stationed after the Civil War. Black soldiers, along with white soldiers, helped build the fort. About a thousand Buffalo Soldiers passed through or were stationed there during the twenty-six years of its existence. They were involved in countless engagements against the Apaches, who resisted the growing presence of white settlers in West Texas, New Mexico and Arizona.

In 1875 almost the entire 9th Calvary regiment passed through Fort Seldon on its way from Texas to other forts in New Mexico. The army's effort to subdue the Apaches culminated in the Victorio War (1879 and 1880) when the 9th Cavalry in New Mexico and the 10th Cavalry in Texas participated in the defeat of the Warm Springs Apaches and Chief Victorio.

Fort Seldon was put out of commission in 1891 and all that remains today are the adobe walls and a few buildings. A museum displays military artifacts and gives descriptions of life at the military post in its earlier days, including a photo exhibit on the Buffalo Soldiers of the 9th Cavalry Regiment. Self-guided walking tour. On summer weekends, rangers in period uniforms demonstrate late nineteenth-century military life.

Open daily, 9–6 May 1–Sept. 15, rest of year 8–5. Closed major holidays. Adults $2 ages 6–16 $1.

LINCOLN

OLD LINCOLN COUNTY COURTHOUSE on U.S. 380 was the center of the Lincoln County Cattle War of 1877–1878. The climax of the war was a three-day gun battle in Lincoln between rival cattle men, that involved William Bonney, alias Billy the Kid, as well as Buffalo Soldiers from nearby Fort Stanton. After the battle, small detachments of the 9th continued to aid civil officials in running down the desperados and outlaws still roaming Lincoln County. Billy the Kid was finally captured but killed his guards and escaped from the Lincoln County courthouse in 1881. Several months later he was killed by Sheriff Pat Garrett.

The old Lincoln County courthouse has been turned into the Museum of Frontier History and there are conducted tours. There is also an HISTORICAL CENTER in Lincoln with exhibits about the black soldiers of the 9th Cavalry and the role they played in the Lincoln County Cattle War.

Daily 9–5. Courthouse open all year round. Historical Center closes December. Admission varies for both museums throughout the year. Call 505-653-4372.

VADO

VADO, located on U.S. 80, 15 miles southeast of Las Cruces, is one of the black communities settled in the West after World War I. The town's origins, however, are much older. Henry Boyer, a black wagoner who fought at the battle of Brazito in the Mexican War with Colonel Doniphan's regiment, returned to his home in Georgia and told of the uncrowded land he had seen in the new territory. His son, Francis, in 1896 walked west to the New Mexico Territory "to find a place for colored people to live and to be their own free agents. Nobody to help you and nobody to hinder you."

The first black settlement, at Blackdom, failed and in 1920 the Boyer family moved on to what is now the town of Vado. Other black families followed them, working from sunrise to sunset to build their farms and community. When their children were refused admission to white schools in the area, they built their own high school/college in Vado. Today, Vado survives, a small, quiet town brought into existence by a dream.

WATROUS

FORT UNION NATIONAL MONUMENT is located 8 miles northwest of Watrous on NM 161. The original fort was built in 1851 to protect travelers on the Santa Fe Trail. In the mid-1860s during the Indian Wars, it became the largest supply depot in the West. Several companies of the U.S. 9th Cavalry were stationed at Fort Union, guarding telegraph and supply lines and fighting Apaches. During the Indian Wars, 14 Congressional medals of honor were awarded to black regular soldiers, 11 of them to members of the 9th Cavalry. Nine of the medals of honor were awarded for combat action in New Mexico between 1877 and 1881.

A self-guiding tour explores the 100 acres of adobe ruins at Fort Union. There is a visitor center with a historical museum. During the summer there are living history demonstrations of life at the fort.

Open daily 8–6 Memorial Day to Labor Day, rest of year 8–5. Closed Jan. 1 and Dec. 25. Admission $3 per car, $1 per person.

ZUNI

ZUNI PUEBLO is intersected by NM 53 and is near Gallup, New Mexico. In 1536, four men looking like savages, more dead than alive, reached the headquarters of the Spanish government in Mexico. Three of the men were white; the fourth was a black man named Estevan, sometimes called Estevanico. They were the sole survivors of the 500-man Narvaez expedition sent from Spain to explore the northern coast of the Gulf of Mexico.

Estevan's stories of his adventures, particularly the tales he had heard from the Indians about Cibola, or the "Seven Cities of Gold," made the Spanish governor decide to send an expedition to search for this treasure trove. Father Marcos de Niza led the exploratory party. Estevan was chosen to be the guide.

Estevan scouted ahead of the expedition, sending back information to Father Marcos, but he was never to reach the Seven Cities of Gold. He was killed as he entered an Indian village. Estevan had stumbled on the Pueblo city of the Zuni Indians. Although Estevan's discovery brought no gold to the Spaniards, his early mapping and exploration of Arizona and New Mexico paved the way for later explorations of the southwest by Coronado and de Soto.

Visitors are welcome to the Zuni Pueblo during daylight hours. Permission must be obtained to view masked ceremonial dances held throughout the year.

To the east of Zuni, several miles north of Albuquerque off NM 85 is the town of Bernalillo. One mile northwest of Bernalillo on NM 44 off I-25 is the CORONADO STATE MONUMENT. The visitor center museum traces the route of Spanish exploration (following the maps of Estevan) and has exhibits on the cultural changes in the Indian's world brought about by the arrival of the Spaniards.

Daily 9–6 May 1–Sept. 15, 8–5, Sept. 16–April 30. Closed state holidays. Adults $2, under 16 free.

For further information about New Mexico, contact:

New Mexico Tourism Division
The Joseph Montoya Bldg.
P.O. Box 20003
1100 St. Francis Dr.
Santa Fe, NM 87503
1-800-545-2040

NEW YORK

ALBANY

ISRAEL A. M. E. CHURCH, 381 Hamilton Street, has a congregation that dates back to the 1820s, although the present church dates from the 1880s. The original church was used as a stop on the Underground Railroad, spiriting runaway slaves north to the safety of Canada.

AUBURN

HARRIET TUBMAN HOME, 180–182 South Street, where she lived the last years of her life, has been restored and is maintained as a museum by the Auburn A. M. E. Zion Church. Some of Mrs. Tubman's possessions are still in the house. One of the truly heroic figures in American history, Harriet Tubman, an escaped slave herself, courageously risked her own life to return to the South time and time again, to guide other fugitive slaves, including her family, to safety. Rewards of up to $40,000 were offered for her capture but she was never caught nor did she ever lose any of her passengers in transit.

Harriet Tubman, called "the Moses of her people," died in 1913 and was given a military funeral at Fort Hill Cemetery in Auburn. The next year the city unveiled a plaque in her honor at the Auburn Courthouse.

Harriet Tubman's home is open to the public by appointment. (315-253-2621)

BROOKLYN and the BRONX, *see New York City.*

BUFFALO

ALBRIGHT-KNOX ART GALLERY, just south of junction of NY 198 and Elmwood Avenue, has a collection of paintings and sculpture dating from 3000 B.C. to the present. Its contemporary collection includes paintings by black artists Horace Pippin and Jacob Lawrence, and sculpture by Richard Hunt.

Tues.–Sat. 11–5, Sun. noon–5. Closed Jan. 1, Thanksgiving and Dec. 25. Donation $2.

THE KUSH MUSEUM OF AFRICAN AND AFRICAN-AMERICAN ART AND ANTIQUITIES, Langston Hughes Institute, Inc., 25 High Street, is a new museum, presently in the process of developing its collection of African artifacts, gathering and disseminating information on the largely unknown history and culture of the African peoples, and showcasing works of art by contemporary African and African-American artists.

The museum recently sponsored an exhibit by local African-American artists and an African film festival.

Mon.–Fri. 10–5. Free.

CANASTOTA

INTERNATIONAL BOXING HALL OF FAME, 1 Hall of Fame Drive, a quarter-mile off exit 34 of the New York State Thruway, traces roots of boxing to the early 1800s. One of the earliest prizefighters in America was Tom Molineaux, a young slave in Virginia who won his freedom by defeating the champion fighter on a neighboring plantation. In time, Tom Molineaux became the self-styled first heavyweight boxing champion of America. However, early white American boxing champions like John L. Sullivan refused to face black boxing challengers. It wasn't until 1892 that interracial prizefighting once again took place in America. Black George Dixon won the world featherweight boxing championship that year, Joe Walcott the welterweight in 1901, Joe Gans the lightweight in 1901, and Jack Johnson the heavyweight in 1908.

The International Boxing Hall of Fame has a variety of artifacts from the boxing world, fist impressions of champions from 1920s to present, hand wraps from Joe Louis, trunks and robes from Joe Frazier and Floyd Patterson, even two of Mike Tyson's mouthpieces. There are also videos of famous fights shown continuously.

Daily 9–5. Adults $3, seniors $2.50, 9–15 $2, under 8 Free.

COOPERSTOWN

NATIONAL BASEBALL HALL OF FAME AND MUSEUM, Main Street, chronicles the history and development of baseball with more than 1,000 photographs, artifacts, films and tape recordings. Included is memorabilia of famous black baseball players, Jackie Robinson, Monte Irvin, Josh Gibson, Satchel Paige, and others. Jackie Robinson won a new type of civil right in 1947 when he joined the Brooklyn Dodgers and became the first black player in major-league baseball.

Visitors to the museum can watch a 15-minute action-packed video in the Grandstand Theater, and computer screens that call up information on any inductee. There is a Great Moments Room, Ballparks Room, World Series Room and the "Baseball Today" display. There is also a section in the museum devoted to the black teams that played in the old Negro League.

Daily 9–9, May–Oct., rest of year 9–5. Closed Jan. 1, Thanksgiving and Dec. 25. Adults $5, ages 7–15 $2.

CORONA

LOUIS ARMSTRONG HOUSE AND ARCHIVES, 34–56 107th Street, was the last home of Louis Armstrong, one of the most famous and talented black musicians in America. He lived in this house from 1943 until his death in 1971 and the house remains almost exactly as the Armstrongs kept it, with their personal photographs and furnishings. The small archives contains some of Armstrong's original music and letters.

Mon.–Fri. 9–5. Tours of house by appointment only. (718-478-8274)

HEMPSTEAD, LONG ISLAND

AFRICAN AMERICAN MUSEUM OF NASSAU COUNTY, 110 North Franklin Street, traces the history, cultural heritage and contributions of African American Long Islanders through art, books and documents. The museum also receives changing exhibits from the Smithsonian Institution, the Brooklyn Museum and others.

Tues.–Sat. 9–4:45, Sun. 1–4:45. Donation.

LAKE PLACID

JOHN BROWN FARM STATE HISTORIC SITE is 2 miles south on NY 73 then ¾ mile on John Brown Road. John Brown, the militant abolitionist, was hanged on Dec. 2, 1859, for his raid on the arsenal at Harper's Ferry in West Virginia. His final wish was to be buried on his farm in New York State. The farm was part of thousands of acres set aside by wealthy abolitionist Gerritt Smith as a free community for ex-slaves. The settlement did not succeed because the climate was too harsh and there were no markets for the farm products.

Today the home has been restored to its appearance when the Brown family lived there. John Brown and several of his sons and companions who died at Harper's Ferry are buried in a grave site near the home. (Three of the black men who fought with Brown are buried in Westwood Cemetery, Oberlin, Ohio.)

Wed.–Sat. 10–5, Sun. 1–5, early May to late Oct. Free.

NEW YORK CITY

BRONX

BRONX MUSEUM OF THE ARTS, 1040 Grand Concourse, has a strong collection of works by noted black artist Romare Bearden.

Sat.–Thurs. 10–4:30, Sun. 11–4:30. Adults $2, children/seniors $1.

BROOKLYN

BROOKLYN MUSEUM, Eastern Parkway and Washington Avenue, has a large collection of African art as well as works by black American artists, such as Jacob Lawrence, Richard Mayhew and Ernest Crichlow.

Wed.–Mon. 10–5. Closed Tues., also Jan. 1, Thanksgiving and Dec. 25. Suggested donation, adults $4, students $2, seniors $1.50, under 12 free with adult.

WEEKSVILLE, 1698 Bergen Street, was a black community in Brooklyn that reached its height from 1838 to 1883. The Society for the Preservation of Weeksville and Bedford-

Stuyvesant History maintains four Hunterfly Road properties from the nineteenth century, including house furnishings, costumes, archival materials, and numerous photographs from 1900 to present.

Mon.–Fri. 9–5. All tours by appointment. (718-756-5250)

LOWER MANHATTAN

FRAUNCES TAVERN, 54 Pearl Street at Broad. During slave days there were many free black men and women who successfully engaged in all sorts of occupations. Samuel Fraunces, of black and French parents, operated a tavern in New York City that is still in use today. Before the Revolutionary War the Sons of Liberty met at Fraunces Tavern and plotted revolution.

Legend has it that Black Sam's daughter, Phoebe, saved the life of George Washington. She stopped him from eating a dinner poisoned by one of his bodyguards. It was at the Fraunces Tavern that General George Washington bade farewell to the officers of the Continental Army in 1783. When Washington was elected president, Sam Fraunces was steward of the first presidential mansion in New York.

Today, there is still a restaurant on the first floor of Fraunces Tavern. A museum about the tavern's history and the Revolutionary War occupies the upper floors.

Mon.–Fri. 10–4, phone for weekend hours 212-425-1778. Closed Jan. 1 and Dec. 25. Donation to museum $2.50, under 12 and seniors $1.

MIDTOWN MANHATTAN

AMERICAN MUSEUM OF NATURAL HISTORY is at Central Park West at 79th Street. One of the most interesting collections on African culture is housed in this museum. The many exhibits in the Hall of Man in Africa show all phases of the life of African men, women and children, and explain the wide diversity of peoples and social systems on the continent. There are at least 1,000 culturally distinct groups in Africa, each of which may have a language and way of life very different from its nearest neighbor.

Music is an important part of African life and there are several exhibit areas given over to African musical instruments, including clapping sticks, wooden drums, harps, lutes and zithers as well as flutes and horns. The hall also has exhibits interpreting the various African tribal religions.

Daily and holidays 10–5:45, also Wed., Fri. and Sat. to 9 p.m. Closed Thanksgiving and Dec. 25. Adults $4, children $2, Fri.–Sat. 5–9 free. Free highlight tours.

CENTER FOR AFRICAN ART, 54 East 68th Street, is housed in two restored turn-of-the-century townhouses. The museum is dedicated to increasing the understanding and appreciation of the richness and variety of African culture. Some of its recent exhibitions have been "African Masterpieces from Munich," "Africa and the Renaissance," "Lessons in the Art of Seeing Africa" and "20th-Century African Art." The museum also develops educational programs for children and adults.

Tues.–Fri. 10–5, Sat. 11–5, Sun. 12–5. Adults $2.50, students/seniors/children $1.50.

COOPER-HEWITT MUSEUM, 2 East 91st Street at 5th Avenue, is the Smithsonian Institution's National Museum of Design. In its collection of over 165,000 decorative art objects from around the world can be found African examples such as Kente cloth, raffia cloth from Zaire, a Zulu basket and tie-dyed woman's skirt from the Ivory Coast. The museum has also offered lectures and seminars on African-American design.

Tues. 10 a.m.–9 p.m., Wed.–Sat. 10–5, Sun. 12–5. Closed

major holidays. Adults $3, seniors and students over 12 $1.50. Free admission Tues. 5–9 p.m.

METROPOLITAN MUSEUM OF ART, Fifth Avenue and 82nd Street, has paintings by contemporary as well as nineteenth-century black artists in its enormous holdings of world art. A few of the better-known works by black artists in the collection are *Victorian Interior* by Horace Pippin, *Blind Beggar* by Jacob Lawrence, *The Woodshed* by Romare Bearden, sculpture by Richmond Barthe, and photographs by Gordon Parks.

In the Mertens Galleries of this great museum can be found the Crosby Brown Collection of Musical Instruments of all Nations, with one of the most complete collections of African musical instruments in the world. Some of the instruments are not only centuries old but exceedingly rare, such as the *kissars* or lutes made from the skulls of enemies, horns carved from ivory elephant tusks from Zanzibar, gourd rattles, thumb pianos, and "talking" drums. A listening device enables the viewer to hear the instruments while looking at them.

Sun. and Tues.–Thurs. 9:30–5:15, Fri.–Sat. 9:30 a.m.– 8:45 p.m. Closed Jan. 1, Thanksgiving and Dec. 25. Suggested donation includes admission to the Cloisters in Upper Manhattan; adults $5, seniors and students $2.50, under 12 free.

MUSEUM OF MODERN ART, 11 West 53rd Street. Perhaps the best-known works by black artists in this collection are thirty of the sixty panels entitled *The Migration of the Negro* by the great social-protest artist Jacob Lawrence. The rest of these panels are in the Phillips Collection, Washington, D.C. The museum's extensive holdings also includes other drawings, prints, paintings, sculptures and photographs by Afro-American artists.

Fri.–Tues. 11–6, Thurs. 11 a.m.–9 p.m. Closed Wed. Adults $7, students, seniors $4, under 16 free with adult. Thurs. 5–9 pay what you wish.

WHITNEY MUSEUM OF AMERICAN ART, 945

Madison Avenue at 75th Street. Black artists Jacob Lawrence and Charles White are included in this museum's collection of great American art, along with Richmond Barthe's graceful statue entitled *The Blackberry Woman.*

Weds.–Sat. 11–5, Tues. 1–8, Sun. 12–5. Adults $5, seniors $3, under 12 with adults free. Tues. 6–8 free.

UPPER MANHATTAN/HARLEM

Harlem's geographical boundaries extend south to north from 96th Street to 170th Street, and east to west from the Harlem to the Hudson rivers. The most widely known section is Central Harlem, from 110th to 155th streets and from Fifth to Amsterdam avenues.

The best way to see Harlem is with a walking or bus sightseeing tour. There are at least a half-dozen tours available, day and night, such as a Harlem spirituals tour, which includes a soul food dinner and live show, or a Sunday morning tour to a church service complete with traditional black music. There is a Harlem Renaissance tour which takes in cultural, historical and entertainment sites. There is also a Harlem Economy tour and a Harlem on Foot tour.

To find out about these various tours, contact the HARLEM VISITORS AND CONVENTION ASSOCIATION, 1 West 125th Street, Room 206, New York, NY 10027, or the NEW YORK VISITORS BUREAU, at 2 Columbus Circle, New York, NY 10019. The offices are open Mon.–Fri. 9–5, weekends 10–6. There is another office of the New York visitors bureau at 158 W. 42nd Street, near Times Square, open Wed.–Fri. 9–6, weekends 10–6. Usually there is a charge for tours.

AFRO ARTS CULTURAL CENTER, 2192 Adam Clayton Powell, Jr., Boulevard at 130th Street is a combination cultural/educational facility. The center presents recitals, jazz concerts, operas and other performances, along with an African museum.

Daily 9–5. Donation.

APOLLO THEATRE, 253 West 125th Street, at 125th Street between 7th and 8th avenues. The first theater in America organized by a group of free blackmen, where black actors and actresses could perform serious dramas was the African Grove Theatre on Bleecker Street in Greenwich Village. The Grove Theatre closed in 1830 shortly after it opened but blacks continued as entertainers in vaudeville. It wasn't until the black cultural explosion at the turn of the century that more black theaters opened, this time in Harlem. The Lafayette Theatre on Seventh Street became a proving ground for many fine young black actors and actresses.

Then in the 1930s the Apollo Theatre began presenting variety shows featuring leading black entertainers, such as Louis Armstrong, Ella Fitzgerald, Duke Ellington, Count Basie, Cab Calloway, and soon became the center of black entertainment in Harlem and in the country. It still presents musical performances. Contact the theater for schedule (212-749-5838).

AUNT LEN'S DOLL AND TOY MUSEUM, 6 Hamilton Terrace between 141st and 142nd streets, is a unique museum which houses over 10,000 black and multi-ethnic dolls from throughout the world. Tours by appointment only. (212-281-4143)

BLACK FASHION MUSEUM, 157 West 126th Street. between Lenox Avenue and Adam Clayton Powell, Jr., Boulevard. Another one-of-a-kind museum which contains the most outstanding collection of memorabilia about black fashion to be found anywhere in the country, including books, photographs, textiles, clothing, jewelry, oral history tapes and furniture.

Mon.–Fri. 12–8 p.m. Adults $1, 50 cents for children over 12.

There are many historic and famous churches in Harlem. The following are only a select few.

ABYSSINIAN BAPTIST CHURCH, 132 W. 132th Street between Lenox Avenue and Adam Clayton Powell, Jr. Boulevard. Thomas Paul began the movement for establishing independent black Baptist churches in the United States. In 1808 he formed a separate black Baptist congregation in New York, which has come to be known as the Abyssinian Baptist Church. In 1921 it moved to its present location and built a magnificent Gothic structure of New York bluestone. Today, it has the largest black Protestant congregation in the United States.

One of the well-known leaders of this church was Adam Clayton Powell, Jr. who, in addition to becoming pastor of the church after his father's retirement, served as a member of the United States Congress. There is a small exhibit devoted to Powell's career in the church. Call for museum hours. (212-862-2626)

CATHEDRAL CHURCH OF ST. JOHN THE DIVINE, Amsterdam Avenue and 112th Street, begun in 1892, is surrounded by 13 acres of beautiful greenery. When completed it will be the world's largest Gothic structure. A Biblical Garden contains more than 100 plants mentioned in the scriptures.

Tours Tues.–Sat. at 11 and Sun. at 12:45. Open daily 7–5. Free.

MALCOLM SHABAZZ MASJID (Mosque of Islam) at 116th Street and Lenox Avenue. This four-storied mosque is the East Coast headquarters for the Moslem faith and was named in honor of Malcolm X, the late black leader.

MOTHER A. M. E. ZION CHURCH, 140-146 West 137th Street, between Lenox Avenue and Adam Clayton Powell, Jr. Boulevard, was the first church organized in New York City by and for black Americans, in 1796. The original church was built in 1800 at 156 Church Street with money donated by Peter Williams, an ex-slave. The church moved several times before reaching its present location.

The church helped runaway slaves during slavery and among its celebrated members were Frederick Douglass, Harriet Tubman and Paul Robeson. Another famous member was a woman known simply as Isabella. One day she stood up in the middle of a service and said that henceforth she would be known as Sojourner Truth. "Sojourner because I am a wanderer, Truth because God is Truth."

ST. PHILIP'S EPISCOPAL CHURCH, 240 West 134th Street, between Adam Clayton Powell, Jr. Boulevard and Frederick Douglass Boulevard. After the Revolutionary War, the original members of St. Philip's worshipped at primarily white Trinity parish. Then, refusing to be segregated, they secured their own separate place of worship in 1818. The congregation moved into its present building in 1918.

COUNTEE CULLEN REGIONAL BRANCH, NEW YORK PUBLIC LIBRARY, 104 West 136th Street, is named for the prominent black poet who was one of the leaders of the Harlem Renaissance of the 1920s and 1930s when writers and artists began realistically portraying life in black America.

The library has the James Weldon Johnson Reference Collection for Children, books that give an accurate, well-rounded picture of black life in all parts of the world. In addition, there is an African-American/Black Culture reference collection.

For library hours, call 212-491-2070.

HARLEM RENAISSANCE AUTHORS' HOMES. Some of the authors of the Harlem Renaissance in the 1920s and 1930s, whose writings brought about a new understanding of black life in America, lived in Harlem. James Weldon Johnson lived at 187 W. 135th Street, Langston Hughes at 20 East 120th Street, and Claude McKay at 180 West 135th Street.

The homes are National Historic Landmarks but are privately owned and are not open to the public.

JACKIE ROBINSON PARK, at West 145th to 155th streets, is named for the legendary baseball player. A recreational park, it has a pool, basketball and volleyball courts and softball field and playground.

MARCUS GARVEY MEMORIAL PARK, 120th to 124th streets between Mount Morris Park West and Madison Avenue. Marcus Garvey, who settled in Harlem in 1916, was the flamboyant leader of the United Negro Improvement Association, which has been called the first mass movement among Negroes. Garvey was a segregationist, opposing all integration with the white race, and his spellbinding oration convinced his black audiences that they should take pride in being black. Although the UNIA lasted only a few short years, by the mid-twenties, it had more than a million members.

There is a watchtower in the park, built in 1856, which is the last remaining fire watchtower in Manhattan. The park contains an Olympic size swimming pool and a recreation center.

MUSEUM OF THE CITY OF NEW YORK, 1220 Fifth Avenue between 103rd and 104th streets, is a popular museum of memorabilia and exhibits covering over 300 years of New York City history, including black history. A gallery is reserved for the Theater and Music Collection, with an enormous number of programs, pictures, playbills, costumes and scene designs of Broadway shows, including material on black performers and musicians.

Tues.–Sat. 10–5, Sun. 1–5. Closed Jan. 1, Thanksgiving and Dec. 25. Free, although donations accepted: adults $4, seniors/children/students $2, families $6.

SCHOMBURG CENTER FOR RESEARCH IN BLACK CULTURE is located at 515 Lenox Avenue at 135th Street. Begun in 1926 with a collection compiled by Arthur Schomburg, a Puerto Rican of African ancestry, the center has become one of the most important in the world for the study of black people. The Schomburg Center has materials ranging from rare items from the earliest African kingdoms to contemporary civil rights materials, books, magazines, photographs, manuscripts, playbills, that document the black experience in every possible way.

The center also has an excellent collection of African folk music, indexed by tribe, song and instrument, in addition to several thousand phonograph records and tape recordings of musical works by black people. The jazz, rhythm and blues collections are exceptional.

On permanent display are a wide variety of African art and cultural objects as well as works by such noted black American artists as Jacob Lawrence and Romare Bearden, and four murals painted by Aaron Douglas depicting black America's history from its African origins to the great migration of blacks from the South to the North.

Mon.–Wed. 12–8 p.m. and Thurs.–Sat. 10–6. Tours by appointment (491-2214). Free.

STRIVERS ROW, at West 137th to 139th streets between Adam Clayton Powell, Jr. Boulevard and Frederick Douglass Boulevard. The elegant townhouses along this street were originally built in 1891 for New York's wealthy white families. In the early twentith century, as whites moved out of the area and blacks moved in, Strivers Row became home for such prominent Harlemites as Eubie Blake, W. C. Handy, prizefighter Harry Wills, comedian Stepin Fetchit, and Father Divine. The district takes its name from the fashionable blacks who lived there and were striving for status.

STUDIO MUSEUM IN HARLEM, 144 West 125th Street between Lenox Avenue and Adam Clayton Powell, Jr. Boulevard, is dedicated to collecting and exhibiting the paintings, sculpture, photography and folk art of African American artists, the well-known as well as gifted but unknown artists. It also conducts workshops, concerts, film programs and organizes traveling exhibits.

Tours by appointment, Wed.–Fri. 10–5, Sat. and Sun. 1–6.
Adults $2, seniors/students/children $1. (212-864-4500)

*A select few of the many other art galleries in Harlem
specializing in African and African-American art are:*
ADAM CLAYTON POWELL, JR. GALLERY, 163
West 125th Street (2nd floor); BENIN GALLERY, 240
West 139th Street, MEHU GALLERY, 21 West 100th
Street, GENESIS II MUSEUM OF INTERNA-
TIONAL BLACK CULTURE, 509 Cathedral Park-
way; and GRINNELL GALLERY, 800 Riverside
Drive. Check for hours of operation. Usually free.

NORTH TARRYTON

PHILIPSBURG MANOR, on U.S. 9 and VAN CORT-
LANDT MANOR, off U.S. 9. From the New York State
Thruway (I-87) take exit 9 for Tarrytown and proceed north 2
miles to Philipsburg Manor and north another 9 miles to Van
Cortlandt Manor.

While touring both these historic sites, run by the Historic
Hudson Valley, visitors are made aware of the role that slaves
played as skilled labor during the colonial period in New
York State. Philipsburg Manor relied on tenant farmers and
slaves to operate the grist mill on its huge estate. At Van
Cortlandt Manor, visitors touring the grounds are shown the
work done by slaves in the main house and work areas.
School tours to these sites sponsored by the Historic Hudson
Valley explore the importance of African-Americans in the
history of the area, and the elements of their culture that they
were able to retain.

Daily 10–5 April–Nov.; Wed.–Mon. 10–5 Dec.; Sat.–Sun.
10–5 March. Closed Jan. and Feb. and holidays. Adults $5,
seniors $4.50, ages 6–17 $3. For information about tours,
phone 914-631-8200.

ROCHESTER

FREDERICK DOUGLASS MONUMENT, Highland Park Bowl, is one of the most impressive monuments to the black leader of the many around the country, and was dedicated in 1899 by the then New York governor, Theodore Roosevelt. The youngest Douglass son, Charles, posed for this handsome bronze statue of his father. Bronze tablets around the base have excerpts from speeches by Douglass.

FREDERICK DOUGLASS GRAVE is in Mount Hope Cemetery, 79 Mount Hope Avenue. Although Douglass died of a heart attack at his home, Cedar Hill, in Washington, D.C., he is buried in Rochester, which is where he began publishing his abolitionist newspaper, *The North Star*, in 1847.

SCHUYLERVILLE

SARATOGA NATIONAL HISTORICAL PARK is 8 miles south of Schuylerville on U.S. 4 and covers more than 2,000 acres. The battles of Saratoga were fought here in September and October 1777. These American victories are considered the turning point of the American Revolution. Ironically, Benedict Arnold, who later turned traitor and joined the British, helped to secure success here.

Blacks fought on both sides on these battles. Free blacks served in the Continental Army, and the Hessian forces supporting the British side used blacks as servants and teamsters.

A visitor center on Fraser Hill offers a view of the battlefield, as well as theater programs and self-guiding tours.

Daily 9–5. Closed Jan. 1, Thanksgiving and Dec. 25. $1 per person or $3 per car, under 17 free.

SARATOGA SPRINGS

NATIONAL MUSEUM OF RACING AND HALL OF FAME, Union Avenue and Ludlow Street, contains chronological exhibits on the past, present and future of thoroughbred racing in America, honoring horses, jockeys and trainers. Isaac Murphy, a black jockey, was the first jockey to be voted into the Jockey Hall of Fame. He was also the first jockey to win three Kentucky Derbies, in 1884, 1890 and 1894. At the museum, in a simulated racetrack area, videos of famous trainers and jockeys explain their race riding techniques.

Mon.–Sat. 10–4:30, Sun. noon–4:30, Memorial Day-Thanksgiving weekend, extended hours in August; rest of year Tues.–Sat. 10–4:30. Adults $2, seniors and students $1, under 5 free.

STONY POINT

STONY POINT BATTLEFIELD STATE HISTORIC SITE is 2½ miles northeast off U.S. 9W on Park Road. The British garrison of 600 men at Stony Point was captured by American troops in a violent hand-to-hand struggle. Among the captured British soldiers were several black men.

Although by 1779 all the colonies had black troops in uniform (with the exceptions of Georgia and South Carolina), slaves still continued to escape to the British lines. In 1778 Thomas Jefferson estimated that 30,000 slaves had escaped from Virginia since 1776. Tragically, many of the slaves who joined the British and left America with them hoping for freedom were instead sold by British officers as captured booty in the West Indies.

At Stony Point, however, a slave named Pompey Lamb worked for the American cause by serving as a spy before the battle. He sold his vegetables to the British garrison and then returned to the American forces with information which helped them surprise their enemy.

A museum and walking tours interpret the battle.

Wed.–Sun. 8:30–5, late April–late Oct. Free.

SYRACUSE

EVERSON MUSEUM OF ART, 401 Harrison Street, has historical displays as well as art dating from the eighteenth century, including African art.

Tues.–Fri. and Sat. 10–5, Sun. noon–5. Donation.

TICONDEROGA

FORT TICONDEROGA is reached via an entrance one mile northeast of Ticonderoga on NY 74. In 1775 Ethan Allen and his Green Mountain Boys took the British fort of Ticonderoga in a surprise attack. There were several blacks with the Green Mountain Boys, including Lemuel Haynes, Primus Black and Epheram Blackman. Some of the cannons were taken from the fort, and in the dead of winter transported 300 miles to provide much-needed armament for the Continental Army.

The fort has been restored with a museum containing one of the finest collections of weapons, uniforms and historic battle mementos in America. There is a well-marked battleground, guided tours, cannon-firing demonstrations, and fife and drum music offered in the summer.

Daily 9–6 July–Aug., 9–5 May 10–June 30 and Sept. 1–Oct. 21. Adults $5, ages 10–13 $3, which includes admission to adjoining battle sites.

For further information about New York, contact:

Division of Tourism
One Commerce Plaza
Albany, NY 12245
1-800-225-5697

New York Visitors and Convention Bureau
2 Columbus Circle
New York, NY 10019-1823
212-397-8222

Harlem Visitors and Convention Association
1 West 125th St., Rm. 206
New York, NY 10027
212-427-7200

NORTH CAROLINA

ASHEVILLE

YMI CULTURE CENTER, 39 South Market. After building the showplace of Asheville, the Biltmore estate, with its 250 room French Renaissance-style chateau and 35 acres of gardens, George Vanderbilt in 1892 commissioned a three-story recreation center in the town to show his appreciation toward the black craftsmen who helped build his magnificent mansion. Today, the center has been turned into a vocational education institute for young blacks and is in the process of organizing an African-American museum and library on the premises. There are monthly exhibits of works by Afro-American artists.

Mon.–Fri. 9–5. Free.

THE BILTMORE ESTATE, U.S. 25, 3 blocks north of exit 50, mansion and grounds, is open daily for guided tours, 9–5. Closed holidays. Adults $17.50, ages 12–17 $13.

CHARLOTTE

AFRO-AMERICAN CULTURAL CENTER, 401 North Myers Street (near intersection of 7th and McDowell), promotes and preserves African-American culture through visual arts exhibits, music and theatrical productions and provides space for community events.

Tues.–Sat. 10–6, Sun. 1–5. Free, although some ticketed events.

CRESWELL

SOMERSET PLACE STATE HISTORIC SITE is on Lake Phelps, 9 miles south of Creswell via U.S. 64 and county roads. This splendid nineteenth-century coastal plantation was begun by Josiah Collins in 1785. Hundreds of slaves were bought, and with their labor the thousands of acres of useless swamp land were cleared of trees, and a canal 6 miles long and 12 feet wide was dug by hand. Within two years the swamp land had been drained and could be used to grow rice, making a fortune for Josiah in a matter of decades.

Although many slaves died of disease and exhaustion in the labor of building the canal, the black men and women on the Collins plantation were treated better than many slaves of the time. They were provided with chapel, minister and medical care and reasonably comfortable living quarters.

The Civil War ruined Somerset Place and it was not until the 1950s that restoration work was begun on the mansion and outbuildings. Archaeological studies have exposed the remains of slave buildings, including the hospital and chapel and the overseer's house.

Guided tours of the mansion, garden and restored outbuildings give visitors a feeling of how both master and slave lived on a nineteenth-century Southern plantation.

Mon.–Sat. 9–5, Sun. 1–5, April–Oct., rest of year Tues.–Sat. 10–4, Sun. 1–4. Closed Thanksgiving and Dec. 24–25. Free.

DURHAM

NCCU ART MUSEUM, North Carolina Central University, has a collection which focuses on African-American works of art, paintings, sculptures and minor arts. Five temporary shows are offered each year.

Tues.–Fri. 9–5, Sun. 2–5. Free.

STAGVILLE CENTER, NC 1004 (the Old Oxford Highway), 7 miles northeast of the intersection of NC 1004 and NC 501 Business (Roxboro Road). Slaves who were brought to America, and to the Stagville plantation in North Carolina, were generally of West African origin and came from family-based, agrarian societies. The large African city states with standing armies were not usually invaded by slave raiders. Stagville itself, originally a plantation of several thousand acres, lay at the center of an enormous estate owned by the Bennehan-Cameron family, which totalled almost 30,000 acres and 900 slaves by 1860.

There were several slave communities on the estate. The Horton Grove slave quarters housed perhaps one hundred men, women and children in its two-story, four-room cabins. More commonly, one- and two-room cabins sheltered slaves. Slaves not only worked in the field and the big houses but were artisans and craftsmen, such as those who built the large barn at Stagville and other buildings on the plantation. Slaves also managed to maintain vestiges of their culture. Some scholars believe that a walking cane found wedged between the two sections of the Benneham House may reflect the secret religious practices of slaves at Stagville. Perhaps hidden in the house by a conjurer, the cane could either have placed a curse on its occupants or provided a blessing.

Although slaves did toil from sunrise to sunset, away from the master, the slave community had the responsibility of educating its children. In addition they cultivated their own small vegetable plots, cleaned their cabins, cared for family members, hunted and fished, and planned community affairs. Slaveholders liked to think that they alone cared for their slaves but the evidence shows that slaves worked and cared for themselves. This attitude of self-reliance was passed on to each generation.

After the Civil War, many of the former slaves and their children continued to farm Cameron-held lands, working as sharecroppers and living much as they had in the nineteenth century.

Stagville today is an historic property of 70 acres owned by the state of North Carolina. Stagville Center offers a wide array of seminars, workshops and conferences on topics such as historic preservation and African-American studies. A few of the nineteenth-century buildings are still standing, some in the Horton Groves Slave Area. There are also relics of folk magic that the slaves brought with them from West Africa.

Mon.—Fri. 9–4. Free.

The town of Durham today has more successful black businesses than almost any other Southern city. One of the most successful is the NORTH CAROLINA MUTUAL LIFE INSURANCE COMPANY, 501 Willard St. The building is a National Historical Landmark. Started by blacks in 1898 during the repressive days of Jim Crow, it managed to become one of the largest black-owned and operated businesses in the country.

FAYETTEVILLE

EVANS METROPOLITAN METHODIST CHURCH, 301 Cool Spring Street, was built in 1803 and was the first Methodist church in the city.

FAYETTEVILLE STATE UNIVERSITY, 1200 Murchison Road, was originally a teachers' college, founded by local blacks, and is the oldest normal school for white or black students in the South.

GREENSBORO

THE MATTYE REED AFRICAN HERITAGE CEN-TER is located on the main campus of the North Carolina A & T State University. The center has a growing collection of over 6,000 items from some 35 African countries, New Guinea and Haiti. Many of the pieces on display, pots, baskets, dishes, jewelry, weapons and fabrics, are of a functional nature. They reflect traditional and contemporary lifestyles of various African cultures. Also part of the main museum collection are masks, icons, bronze, ivory and wood sculptures.

The center is used as a resource center for students and researchers, and offers tours, lectures, seminars, music workshops, slides and films.

The university itself was founded in 1890 and was originally called the Agricultural and Mechanical College for the Colored Race. Before 1970 North Carolina had more predominantly black colleges than any other state in the country.

Mon.–Fri. 9–12, 2:30–3:30, and by appointment. Free.

Greensboro was the site of a wave of sit-ins, then a new form of civil rights protest, which began in February 1960 when four black college students refused to move from a Woolworth lunch counter when they were denied service. By September 1961 more than 70,000 students across the country, white and black, had participated in sit-ins.

RALEIGH

JOHN CHAVIS MEMORIAL PARK, East Lenoir and Worth streets, was named in honor of a free black teacher and Presbyterian minister who was educated at Princeton University. He taught and preached to both blacks and whites in Raleigh in the early 1800s. After the Nat Turner Rebellion, John Chavis was forced to give up the ministry and stop teaching black students. So brilliant was John Chavis as a teacher, that one of his white students went on to become a senator and another a governor. There is a plaque in the park honoring John Chavis.

NORTH CAROLINA MUSEUM OF ART is at 2110 Blue Ridge Boulevard off I-40 (Wade Avenue exit) via signs. The museum is arranged in historical sequence through eight major collections, including one of African art and sculptures, along with art from early Egypt.

Tues.–Sat. 9–5, Fri. 9 a.m.–9 p.m., Sun. noon–5. Closed state holidays. Free.

NORTH CAROLINA MUSEUM OF HISTORY, 109 E. Jones Street, includes a collection of furniture crafted by black cabinet maker Thomas Day. A free black, Day had his own factory in the town of Milton, North Carolina, where he trained black and white carpenters. The furniture he produced was so highly sought after that when Day threatened to leave Milton because black laws wouldn't allow him to bring his wife (a free black woman) into the state, the citizens of Milton were granted a special exemption for Mrs. Day from the legislature.

Tues.–Sat. 9–5, Sun. 1–6. Closed major holidays. Free.

ST. AUGUSTINE'S COLLEGE, 1315 Oakwood Avenue, was founded in 1867 for black students by the Protestant Episcopal church. Some of the buildings on the tree-shaded 110-acre campus have been named historical landmarks, including the college chapel and Taylor Hall.

SHAW UNIVERSITY, 118 East South Street, was founded in 1864 by a Civil War veteran who had saved his army pay, a woolen goods manufacturer, and the Freedmen's Bureau. Shaw was one of the first schools to train black lawyers and doctors. The buildings on the campus are both historic and modern.

ROANOKE ISLAND

NORTH CAROLINA AQUARIUM is on Airport Road

at Mateo, which is on historic Roanoke Island. Manteo may be reached by causeway from the east or west. Along with the displays of live fish, turtles and other sea animals that live in North Carolina, there is a small display honoring Captain Richard Etheridge. Captain Etheridge began life as a slave and rose to become the first black commander of the Pea Island Lifesaving Station. One of the rescues performed by Etheridge and his black crew was to save the crew and passengers of the *E. S. Newman,* blown onto the rocks by a storm in 1895. The exhibit tells the story of Etheridge and the commanders who followed him at the station until it closed in 1952. (The exhibit on the all-black Pea Island Lifesaving Station occasionally travels.)

Mon.–Sat. 9–5, Sun. 1–5. Closed Thanksgiving and Dec. 25. Free.

SALISBURY

LIVINGSTONE COLLEGE, West Monroe Street, was begun in 1879 by black orator and leader Dr. Joseph Price. The first black inter-collegiate football game was played on the campus lawn in 1892. The W. J. Walls Heritage Hall has an African Culture room and a Black History Room. Some of the African artifacts were collected by Bishop W. J. Walls during his travels in Africa. There is also a Christian Heritage Room with documents and manuscripts relating to the history of the A. M. E. Zion church.

Daily 9–4:30. Tours available on Thurs.

SEDALIA

CHARLOTTE HAWKINS BROWN MEMORIAL, 6135 Burlington Road. Sedalia is east of Greensboro via I-85; take exit 135 north or U.S. 70 east from Greensboro. The granddaughter of slaves, Lottie Hawkins established a day and boarding school for black students in 1902. Under her 50-year leadership, the Palmer Institute in Sedalia became nationally recognized, first for its vocational training and then for its emphasis on cultural education and the worth of each individual student.

The Palmer Institute closed its doors in 1961. Today it is a state historic site with exhibits, tours of historic structures, and audio-visual presentations emphasizing the contributions black citizens have made to education in North Carolina.

Tues.–Sat. 10–4, Sun. 1–4. Free.

WINSTON-SALEM

WINSTON-SALEM DELTA FINE ARTS, INC., offers visitors of all ethnic backgrounds exhibits, lectures, and workshops developed from the black perspective. Most of the programs are held at the DELTA ART CENTER, 1511 East Third Street. A recent program was an exhibition of paintings by renowned 20th-century artist Lois Mailou Jones, along with a poetry reading by Pulitzer Prize-winning author Gwendolyn Brooks.

Delta Fine Arts, Inc., funded the purchase of the Thomas Day Collection of furniture for the North Carolina Museum of History, and established at the library at Winston-Salem State University a permanent collection of paintings and sculptures by nationally known North Carolina-born black artists.

Center open Mon.–Fri. 10–5:30. Generally admission is not charged to activities.

MUSEUM OF EARLY SOUTHERN DECORATIVE ARTS, located at 924 South Main Street within the Old Salem restoration. The museum is dedicated to the study and collection of decorative art objects made in the South before 1821.

Although black artisans, slave and free, were cabinetmakers, silversmiths, potters, weavers, and wood carvers, the identities of these men and women remain largely unknown. However, a recent computer search of the database at this museum has produced a list of 2,836 slave and free black artisans who worked in southern states through 1820.

Tours Mon–Sat. 10:30–4:30, Sun. 1:30–4:30. Closed Thanksgiving and Dec. 24–25. Adults $6, ages 6–14 $3.

For further information about North Carolina, contact:

Travel and Tourism Division
430 North Salisbury St.
Raleigh, NC 27611
1-800-847-4862

NORTH DAKOTA

WASHBURN

FORT MANDAN is 3 miles via county road 17 in Fort Mandan Park. The famous Lewis and Clark expedition, which included the black slave York, arrived at a Mandan Indian village in the Dakotas in October 1804. They immediately began felling cottonwood trees for cabins. They were forced to endure five months of bitter cold, short rations and raging blizzards, but there were moments of gaiety. On New Year's Day, York and fourteen others went to the Mandan village and danced to amuse the Indians. The Indians had never seen a black man before and were much impressed with York's strength and agility.

It was at Fort Mandan that the Lewis and Clark party was joined by the pregnant Indian girl, Sacajawea, and her husband. Her baby was born at the fort and accompanied his mother on the entire journey to the Pacific Ocean and back. The Indian girl, like York, proved of great service to the expedition, particularly in fostering good relations with the Indians they met along the way.

The original Fort Mandan was washed away by the Missouri River but a full-size replica of the 1804–05 campsite, with a visitor center, has been built.

At 610 Main Avenue in downtown Washburn, the McLEAN COUNTY HISTORICAL MUSEUM displays

Indian artifacts, and maps and information on the Lewis and Clark expedition.

Fort Mandan open year round. Museum open only in summer. Free.

WILLISTON

FORT BUFORD STATE HISTORIC SITE is 2 miles west of junction of U.S. 2 and U.S. 85, then 17 miles southwest on ND 1804. The fort was built in 1866 and during its first four years was almost continuously under siege by the Sioux. In the 1870s and 1880s it served as a supply base for other western forts and guarded railway construction crews from hostile Indians. Fort Buford was also the site of the surrender of Chief Sitting Bull in 1881.

The units stationed at the post included two companies of the all-black 10th Cavalry and 25th Infantry. After the fort was discontinued in 1895, the black soldiers were transferred to Fort Assiniboine, Montana.

A life size cutout of black infantryman Carter Huse greets visitors as they enter the museum, which is in the original field officers' quarters. The museum tells the fort's story with pictures and exhibits. There is also a military cemetery nearby and a stone powder magazine.

Daily 9–6 May 16–Sept. 1. By appointment rest of year. Closed major holidays. Adults $1.50, children 6–15, $.75, free to children under 6.

FORT UNION TRADING POST NATIONAL HIS-TORIC SITE, a few miles from Fort Buford, is located 24 miles southwest of Williston via U.S. 2 and ND 1804. This was the principal fur-trading depot in the Upper Missouri River region from 1829 to 1867. Traders employed by the fort, which was owned by John Jacob Astor's American Fur Company, were sent to the Indian camps during the winter and returned in the spring, hopefully with a load of furs and no leftover trade goods. In its heyday, Fort Union Trading Post was a busy place with a cosmopolitan mix of Americans, including blacks, Englishmen, Germans, French, Spanish, Italians and Russians.

One of the blacks who worked out of the fort was the mulatto James Beckwourth, born in Virginia of a slave mother and a Revolutionary War officer father. Although there is no special exhibit on Beckwourth at the fort, records show that in the 1830s he was handchosen by Kenneth McKenzie, the man in charge of Fort Union, to trade with the Crow Indians. In 1825, while traveling with General Ashley on the first overland trapping expedition across the plains, Beckwourth had been captured and had lived with the Crows, thus forming a good relationship with the Crow people.

The restless Beckwourth led a colorful, exciting life as a mountain man, trapper and explorer, and in 1850 discovered a pass through the Sierra Nevada in California. The pass, used by many immigrants heading west, was named after him.

Fort Union has been reconstructed and furnished as it might have appeared in the early 1850s. A visitor center has exhibits on the history of the fort, as well as displaying artifacts uncovered during the excavations.

Daily 8 a.m.–8 p.m. Memorial Day–Labor Day, rest of year 9–5:30. Free.

For further information about North Dakota, contact:

Tourism Promotion Division
Liberty Memorial Bldg.
600 E. Boulevard Avenue
Bismarck, ND 58505
1-800-437-2077

OHIO

AKRON

JOHN BROWN HOUSE, at 514 Diagonal Road, was home to abolitionist John Brown for two years during the 1840s. The two public rooms in the two-story-white frame house display items relating to Brown's abolitionist activities. At Perkins Park is the JOHN BROWN MEMORIAL, a monument to this man who many Afro-Americans consider their true emancipator. Cut into the monument are these words: "He died to set his brothers free and His Soul goes marching on."
Tues.–Sun. 1–5. Free.

SOJOURNER TRUTH MONUMENT, Danner Press Building at 37 N. High Street, is one of the few monuments to the noted black woman orator. It stands at the site where Sojourner Truth gave her famous "Ain't I a woman?" speech in 1851.

ALLIANCE

MOUNT UNION COLLEGE, 1972 Clark Avenue, was established in 1846 to provide young people, including young blacks, with a liberal arts and Christian education. The college is located in the Mount Union Historic District, which was an abolitionist center and station on the Underground Railroad shortly after 1845.

ATHENS

MT. ZION BAPTIST CHURCH at the corner of Congress and Carpenter, was built in 1872 by former slaves and the children of slaves. Near Athens, on Township Road 232, is the KILVERT COMMUNITY CENTER which is located in a tiny settlement of 50 people, all descended from escaped slaves and Cherokee Indians who established the community in 1830.

CANTON

PRO FOOTBALL HALL OF FAME, 2121 George Halas Drive N.W., next to Fawcett Stadium (Fulton Rd. exit off I-77 and U.S. 62) is a four-building complex dedicated to the recipients of football's highest honor. The Hall of Fame offers something of interest for every football fan, of every team and every age.

A section is dedicated to black National Football League players, starting with some who played before the formation of the NFL. Of the 155 members in the Pro Football Hall of Fame, 32 are black. They include such athletes as Kenny Washington and Woody Strade, the first blacks to sign with the LA Rams in 1946, and Marion Motley and Bill Willis who signed with the Cleveland Browns in 1946. The visitor can also listen to sound recordings and watch motion pictures of outstanding pro football events.

Daily 9–8, Memorial Day–Labor Day, 9–5 rest of year. Closed Dec. 25. Adults $4, over 65 $2, ages 5–13 $1.50.

CINCINNATI

CINCINNATI ART MUSEUM is 1¼ miles northeast of U.S. 22/OH 3 (Gilbert Avenue) in Eden Park; from I-71, use exit 2. This was the first major art museum in America to display African art. The museum also has several paintings by early Afro-American artist Robert Duncanson. Duncanson's best works are the romantic landscapes which were so popular in nineteenth-century America. He studied and traveled abroad, but the early years of his career were spent in Cincinnati.

Tues.–Sat. 10–5, Wed. 5–9, Sun. 1–5. Closed holidays. Adults $3, students $2, seniors $1.50, under 18 free. Free to all on Sat.

CINCINNATI MUSEUM OF NATURAL HISTORY, 17209 Gilbert Avenue, near the entrance to Eden Park, has special exhibits and programs on African art and culture.

Tues.–Sat. 9–5, Sun. noon–5, June–Sept.; rest of year, Tues.–Fri. 9–5, Sat.–Sun. noon–5. Closed holidays. Adults $3, under 12 $1.

DR. MARTIN LUTHER KING, JR. MEMORIAL at the corner of Reading Road and Martin Luther King, Jr. Drive, pays tribute to the slain civil rights leader.

STOWE HOUSE STATE MEMORIAL is located at 2950 Gilbert Avenue. It was while living in Cincinnati from 1833 to 1850 that Harriet Beecher Stowe gained the background material on slavery that she used in her famous book *Uncle Tom's Cabin.* The Stowe home has now been restored as a cultural and educational center promoting black history and displaying authentic documents and fascinating exhibits on slavery and the plantation system, the Underground Railroad, and the antislavery movement.

Tues.–Thurs. 10–4. Free. Tours are offered.

TAFT MUSEUM, 316 Pike Street, has in its entrance hall the only known murals of Robert Duncanson, the most prominent black American painter of the nineteenth century.

Built in 1820, the property was originally the home of philanthropist Nicholas Longworth. A generous friend of Robert Duncanson, Longworth commissioned him to paint the murals when Duncanson was still a relatively unknown artist.

Mon.–Sat. 10–5, Sun. and holidays, 2–5. Closed Jan. 1, Thanksgiving and Dec. 25. Adults $2, seniors and students $1.

CLEVELAND

AFRICAN AMERICAN MUSEUM, at 1765 Crawford Road. For visitors seeking out Ohio's black history, this museum is a must. Established in 1956, it features photographs, tape recordings, records, books, speeches and paintings that celebrate the black church, black music and the achievements of individual African-Americans. The museum also has a collection dealing with blacks in aviation. Films and guided tours.

Mon.–Thurs. 12–3, Fri. 12–8, Sat. noon to 3. Adults $2, children $1

CLEVELAND MUSEUM OF ART, 11150 East Boulevard, has holdings that represent many cultures, including a good African art collection.

Tues.–Fri. 10–5:45, also Wed. 5:45–9:45, Sat. 9–4:45, Sun. 1–5:45. Closed holidays. Free.

HARRIET TUBMAN MUSEUM, 9250 Miles Park, is named after one of the most distinguished and valiant heroines in American history. After Harriet escaped slavery, she returned South to help her parents escape. Although her mother didn't want to leave behind a feather bedtick and her father clung to his tools, Harriet bundled up bedtick, tools, mother, father and all, and landed them in Canada. She was so successful in leading hundreds of slaves to safety, that rewards for her capture began at $1,000 and reached as high as

$40,000. The museum has information on Harriet Tubman and over 5,000 artifacts covering black history from slavery through the 1960s, along with information on outstanding black men and women from Cleveland. There is also a small archive of slave documents and deeds, books and newspapers.

Cleveland has a long list of illustrious firsts in black American history. Among many others: Carl B. Stokes was elected the first black mayor of a major American city in 1967; Garrett Morgan, a black native of Cleveland, invented the gas mask and electric traffic light; Lawrence Doby was the first black baseball player in the American League; and James "Jessie" Owens set five world records in track and field.

Tues.–Thurs. by appointment. Sat. and Sun. 1–4. Guided tours for groups by appointment. Adults $3, children $2. (216-341-1202)

KARAMU HOUSE THEATRE, at 2355 E. 89th Street, was the first professional black theater established outside New York. This community theater now offers productions by internationally known directors. The adjoining art gallery, open one hour before performances and Sun. 2–3, displays work by local and national artists.

COLUMBUS

COLUMBUS MUSEUM OF ART, 480 East Broad Street, has on permanent display a collection of works of the black, internationally-renowned woodcarver Elijah Pierce. Pierce's works have appeared in the Museum of Modern Art and the Whitney Museum in New York City, and at an international showing in Zareb, Yugoslavia.

Tues.–Fri. and Sun. 11–5, Sat. 10–5. Closed Mon. and holidays. Adults $3.50, seniors and students and ages 6–17 $1. Free on Fri.

MARTIN LUTHER KING, JR. CENTER FOR PERFORMING AND CULTURAL ARTS, 807 Mt. Vernon

Avenue, was designed by black architect Samuel Plato in 1926 and opened for its present use in 1987. Big name black entertainers performed in the first floor theater during the 1930s and 1940s, including Duke Ellington and Cab Calloway.

For schedule of exhibits and performances, call 614-252-5464.

DAYTON

CARILLON PARK, at 2001 S. Patterson Boulevard, is a 65-acre historical park which traces the history of transportation, including a replica of the 1905 Wright brothers airplane. African-American history is displayed in the Rubicon Building.

Tues.–Sat. 10–6, Sun. 1–6 from May to Oct. Free.

DAYTON ART INSTITUTE, Forest and Riverview avenues, has African art, along with Asian, European and American pieces exhibited in a building designed like an Italian villa.

Tues.–Sun. noon–5. Adults $2, seniors and students $1, under 18 free.

OLD COURTHOUSE MUSEUM, at 3rd and Main streets, contains exhibits on the Wright brothers, who were natives of Dayton, along with county history, including information on Dayton's black history.

Tues.–Fri. 10–4:30, Sat. noon–4. Closed holidays. Free.

PAUL LAURENCE DUNBAR HOME, 219 N. Summit Street, is the restored home of the internationally acclaimed black poet who was called the "Poet Laureate of his race." Today his poetry may seem old-fashioned but he caught the warmth and love of black family life as few ever have.

In his home may be seen the study, with desk and books where Dunbar did much of his writing, along with his personal belongings and many original manuscripts of his poems.

Wed.–Sat. 9:30–5, Sun. and holidays, noon–5, Memorial

to Labor Day; weekends only thru Oct. 31, Sat.9:30–5, Sun. noon–5. Adults $2.50, children 6–12 $1.

UNITED STATES AIR FORCE MUSEUM at Wright-Patterson Air Force Base, 6 miles northeast of Dayton. May be reached via I-70, exiting at OH 4 south towards Dayton, 8 miles to the Harshman Road exit; entrance to the museum is on Springfield Pike. The oldest and largest . . . and certainly one of the most fascinating . . . military aviation museums in the world has more than 200 aircraft and thousands of artifacts under 10 acres of roof.

Tuskegee Airmen of World War II (be sure to see also the five-foot-high monument to the Tuskegee Airmen in the Memorial Park) and other black flyers are recognized throughout the museum. These include World War I's Eugene Bullard, the world's first black pilot. Among other exhibits about blacks in USAF history is one on integration in the USAF. The air force was the most progressive of the three military services in integrating African-American into its ranks.

Daily from 9–5. Closed Thanksgiving, Christmas and New Year's Day. Free.

FINDLAY

BLACK HERITAGE PUBLIC LIBRARY, at 839 Liberty Street, features African-American art and artifacts, and the Smithsonian Institution's "Black Wings" exhibition.

Tues. 6–8 and by appointment. Free. (419-423-4303)

GALLIPOLIS

JUNIOR FAIRGROUNDS, at 384 Jackson Pike, is the site of an annual two-day celebration of the emancipation of black people from slavery. The celebration has been held every year except one since the Civil War, on the weekend nearest September 22.

MAUMEE

OHIO BASEBALL HALL OF FAME, one mile north of U.S. 24 on Key Street in the Lucas County Recreation Center, has exhibits of memorabilia from Ohio teams and players such as famous black players Satchel Paige, Frank Robinson, and Vada Pinson.

Mon.–Fri. 10–8, weekends 12–5 April–Sept.; rest of year Mon.-Fri. 10–5. Hours subject to change. Closed major holidays. Adults $2, seniors $1.50, children under 12 $1.

OBERLIN

MONUMENT TO THREE OF THE BLACK MEN WHO DIED AT HARPER'S FERRY WITH JOHN BROWN is located in City Park. The residents of Oberlin who had long been active in the abolition movement and the Underground Railroad were proud of the fact that several of their sons had fought at Harper's Ferry with John Brown— Lewis Leary, a native of Oberlin, John Copland, Jr., a student at Oberlin College, and Shields Green, a fugitive slave from South Carolina. In 1859 a cenotaph to these three black men was erected in Westwood Cemetery alongside their graves. The monument was later moved to the City Park, where it was rededicated in October 1972.

OBERLIN COLLEGE was involved in the Underground Railway movement before the Civil War. A statue commemorating the Underground Railroad is located on campus. The Oberlin College library has an outstanding collection of antislavery pamphlets and documents.

Oberlin College was also one of the first fully accredited co-educational institutions of higher learning to accept black students and to award degrees to women. Lucy Sessions was the first black woman in the U.S. to earn a college degree in 1850 from Oberlin. ALLEN MEMORIAL ART MUSEUM on the Oberlin College campus includes an African art collection as well as works by contemporary African-American sculptors like Richmond Barthe.

Tues.–Fri. 10–5, Sun. 1–5 during academic year. Closed holidays. Free.

The college maintains a visitors information center in the Student Union, Wilder Hall, on West Lorain Street. During the summer, guided tours of the campus are conducted.

PIQUA

ROSSVILLE MUSEUM, at 8250 McFarland Street, has a wealth of information on black history. The town of Piqua dates from the mid-1700s and the French and Indian War.

Sun.–Fri. Hours vary. Free.

PUT-IN-BAY

PERRY'S VICTORY AND INTERNATIONAL PEACE MEMORIAL at Put-in-Bay may be reached during the summer by automobile ferry from Catawba, and by passenger ferry or plane from Port Clinton. In the naval battle fought here in September 1813, Oliver Hazard Perry and his fleet of nine vessels won a decisive victory over a British naval squadron. His success gave America control of Lake Erie, which was vital to winning the War of 1812.

One-fourth of the men aboard Perry's small fleet of ships were black. Initially Perry had not been enthusiastic about using black sailors, but after the battle he said of his black crew members, "They seemed absolutely insensible to danger."

The monument commemorating the battle of Lake Erie is a granite column 352 feet high. Carved on the walls inside the rotunda at the base of the monument are the names of the sailors killed or wounded in the conflict. The column is floodlit at night and is one of the world's most impressive battle monuments.

Daily 9–6 mid-June to Labor Day, 10–5 late April to mid-June and day after Labor Day–late Oct. Adults $1, over 61 and under 17 free.

RIPLEY

RANKIN HOUSE STATE MEMORIAL, on 1824 Liberty Hill, north off OH 52, was built in 1828 by Presbyterian minister John Rankin. The house overlooks the town of Ripley and the Ohio River. A wooden staircase climbed up the hillside from the river to the house. Each night a light beamed from an upstairs window, serving as a beacon to guide fugitives across the river from the slave state of Kentucky to a safe haven in Ohio. After the Fugitive Slave Law was passed and escaped slaves were no longer safe even in a free state like Ohio, a cellar was dug beneath the barn behind the house. There fugitive slaves were hidden when pursuers approached too near.

From 1824 to 1865 several thousand slaves were sheltered in the Rankin house, fed, clothed and sent north to freedom in Canada. Eliza, a character in *Uncle Tom's Cabin*, was supposedly patterned after a slave who found refuge here after crossing the frozen Ohio River.

The home has been restored to look as it did when the Rankin family lived there. Visitors may even follow the route of the escaping slaves by climbing the newly built "staircase to liberty."

Wed.–Sun. 12–5, Memorial Day–Labor Day. After Labor Day–Oct. weekends 12–5. Adults $1, seniors 60 cents, ages 5–12, 25 cents.

TOLEDO

ELLA P. STEWART SCHOOL AND MUSEUM, at 707 Avondale, was named for the first black woman pharmacist to graduate from the University of Pittsburgh. In addition to running a pharmacy in Toledo with her husband, Mrs. Stewart was a leader in the human and civil rights movement from the mid-1930s and traveled widely serving on United Nations committees and as a goodwill ambassador for the U.S. State Department. She was among the first group inducted into the Ohio Women's Hall of Fame. There is a small museum in the school with artifacts and photographs from Mrs. Stewart's life and travels.

Museum open by appointment. (419-246-7881)

UPPER SANDUSKY

WYANDOT MISSION CHURCH, at 200 E. Church, was established in 1816 by John Stewart, a black minister who served as a missionary among the Wyandot Indians. Although poor and uneducated, Stewart was so inspiring that a church was built among the Wyandot Indians as a result of his labor. The church, restored in 1889, is today a Methodist historical shrine. John Stewart's grave is on the mission grounds.

WESTERVILLE

BENJAMIN HANBY HOUSE, 160 W. Main Street, was a station on the Underground Railroad and home to composer Benjamin Hanby. After learning about fugitive slave Joe Selby, who had to leave behind the woman he loved when he escaped on the Underground Railroad, Hanby wrote the song "My Darling Nellie Gray" to immortalize the story. The home has been restored to represent the 1850s era.

Sat. 10–4, Sun. 1–5, May–Oct. Adults $1.50, ages 6–12, 50 cents.

WILBERFORCE

NATIONAL AFRO-AMERICAN MUSEUM AND CULTURAL CENTER is at 1350 Brush Row Road, ½ mile west of U.S. 42 in Wilberforce. Completed in 1988, it is one of the largest African-American museums in the country. For thousands of visitors its exhibits preserve, detail and interpret African-American history and culture. A permanent exhibit, "From Victory to Freedom: Afro-American Life in the Fifties" chronicles the crucial period of American history from 1945 to 1965, from victory in World War II to the passage of civil rights legislation. Part of the exhibit is an award-winning film on black music of the period.

The museum exhibits focus on black inventions, military involvements, dolls and toys, arts and crafts, sports, businesses, institutions, and African ceremonial objects. Eventually the museum will include a children's mini-museum, library, art gallery, and more. Guided tours available.

Tues.–Sat. 9–5, Sun. 1–5. Closed holidays, except Martin Luther King, Jr. Day. Adults $1, under 17, 50 cents.

WILBERFORCE UNIVERSITY, 1055 North Bickett, is adjacent to U.S. 42 South, 20 miles east of Dayton, 3 miles northeast of Xenia. Wilberforce was the first institution of higher education in the United States to be owned and operated by Afro-Americans. The school was begun in 1856 with funds donated by the African Methodist Episcopal church. Its first students were freedmen or escaped slaves, and sometimes the mulatto children of Southern planters.

The school was named for William Wilberforce, an early British abolitionist who helped bring the English slave trade to a close in 1807. Memorabilia of William Wilberforce, as well as historical items that relate to black history and culture, and source material on early black church leaders, such as Daniel Alexander Payne, may be seen in the Carnegie Library on the campus. Daniel Payne was elected a bishop in the A. M. E. church in 1852 and was the first president of Wilberforce University. The library also has a gallery of works by black American artists.

Mon.–Thurs. 8 a.m.–9 p.m., Fri. 8–4:30, Sat. 1–5, Sun. 2–6. Closed holidays and summers. Free.

XENIA

BLUE JACKET OUTDOOR DRAMA is performed at Caesar Ford Park Amphitheatre, 5 miles southeast of U.S. 35 on Jaspar Road, then ¼ mile north on Stringtown Rd. This 2½-hour performance tells the true story of white Shawnee war chief Blue Jacket, and the courageous black warrior Caesar who, having been adopted by the Shawnee, joined in the Indians' fight to protect their lands and customs.

Performances mid-June to Labor Day, Tues.-Sun. at 8:30 p.m. Adults $10, $11 on Sat., ages 3–10 $6. Reservations recommended.

For further information about Ohio, contact:

Division of Travel and Tourism
PO Box 1001
Columbus, OH 43266-0101
1-800-BUCKEYE

Ask for brochure: "Ohio Cross-Cultural Guide"

OKLAHOMA

BOLEY

The black migration into Oklahoma began in the 1880s as soon as the Oklahoma Territory was opened for settlement. Oppression in the black belt of the South drove thousands to seek a new "promised land" in the southwest where they could own their own land and manage their own separate black communities. Boley and Langston, Oklahoma, were two such communities. Primitive frontier towns like many white settlements of the time, they only differed by being run by black mayors, with black sheriffs and black teachers and pupils.

Booker T. Washington, visiting Boley in 1905, commented that on summer nights from the hills beyond the town there could still be heard the shrill cries of Indian dancers. He also reported that the first town marshal of Boley had been killed in a gun duel with a horse thief.

Not all the black communities survived. They often faced new oppressions from Jim Crow laws, and were refused the right to vote. However, the towns of Boley and Langston, along with other all-black towns such as Clearview, Tatums, Red Bird and Tullahasse, are still in existence today.

Boley is south of Tulsa on U.S. 62 off of I-40 between Shawnee and Henryetta. The Boley Historic District was designated a National Historic Landmark in 1975. The town hosts an annual Black Rodeo during Memorial Day weekend. Write for current information to the Boley Chamber of Commerce, 125 South Pecan Street.

FORT GIBSON

FORT GIBSON MILITARY PARK, 110 East Ash Street, is one mile north of U.S. 62 on OK 80. The oldest military post in Oklahoma, the fort was built in 1824 in wild and sparsely settled country where Kiowa and Comanche Indians raided, and whiskey peddlers plied their illegal trade. Life here was so harsh that in its first 11 years 570 men died, earning the fort the name "Graveyard of the Army." In 1867 Buffalo Soldiers from the 10th Cavalry were stationed here, and the 1st Kansas Colored Regiment was attacked by Indians, on their way to the fort.

There is a reconstructed log stockade on the original site of the fort. Within the stockade are living quarters, blockhouses and a guardhouse.

Stockade is open Tues.–Fri. 9–5, Sat.–Sun. 1–5. Closed holidays. Free.

LANGSTON

Langston is north of Oklahoma City off OK 33, just east of Guthrie. Edwin P. "King" McCabe came west hoping to carve an all-black state out of Oklahoma in what had been Indian Territory. Although his dream of a state for black people failed, McCabe was the first black man to be appointed to the Oklahoma Territorial Cabinet. He founded the all-black town of Langston City and then LANGSTON UNIVERSITY in 1897, the first African-American A & M College.

LAWTON

FORT SILL MILITARY RESERVATION AND NA-
TIONAL HISTORIC LANDMARK is 5 miles north on
U.S. 62/277/281 to Key Gate entrance. The historic Old Post
area is located just east of the Main Post. Work on Fort Sill
(then called Camp Wichita) was begun in 1869 by the black
troopers of the 10th Cavalry. (There were 13 forts built in
Oklahoma Territory before 1869, most of which were built by
the 10th Cavalry.) The construction was constantly inter-
rupted because the Buffalo Soldiers had to take off on Indian
expeditions, escort duty, surveys and the pursuit of lawless
bands of renegades who infested the border area.

After the fort was finished, the soldiers stationed there were
involved in the Red River campaign against the Comanches,
Kiowas and Southern Cheyenne Indians, a war that finally
ended in 1875.

Today Fort Sill is the U.S. Army Field Artillery Center, but
the Old Post area has been preserved as a historic site. The
Old Stone Corral contains relics of frontier days. The
Geronimo Guardhouse and Cannon Walk display weapons
from battlefields around the world.

FORT SILL MUSEUM in the Old Post buildings reflects
the history of this frontier cavalry post. Some of the more
prominent displays concern the Buffalo Soldiers who played
an important part in early garrison life at Fort Sill. A theater
shows a slide program about the fort daily, at 10 and 2.

Not far from the Old Post area are the grave sites of
Geronimo and Sitting Bear, along with other valiant Indian
chiefs who were buried with military honors at Fort Sill. The
Chiefs' Knoll, as the burial site is known, has been called the
"Indian Arlington."

The Fort Sill Museum is open daily 9–4:30. Closed Jan. 1
and Dec. 25. Free.

NORMAN

UNIVERSITY OF OKLAHOMA MUSEUM OF ART, 410 W. Boyd Street, includes paintings and other works of art from Africa, Europe, the Americas, and the Orient.

Tues.–Wed. and. Fri. 10–4:30, Thurs. 10–9, Sat.–Sun. 1–4:30. Closed holidays and between semesters. Free.

OKLAHOMA CITY

CALVARY BAPTIST CHURCH was the starting point of the first peaceful civil rights march in Oklahoma in August 1958. The church is on the National Historic Register.

NATIONAL COWBOY HALL OF FAME AND WESTERN HERITAGE CENTER occupies 31 acres at 1700 N.E. 63rd Street, ½ mile west of I-35 on I-44. The center is a memorial to the men and women who pioneered the West. The complex contains the Rodeo Hall of Fame, paying tribute to the greatest rodeo stars of all time.

Black cowhands and rodeo riders were always part of the western scene. One of the best known was Bill Pickett (1870–1932), who originated the sport of bulldogging. Pickett had a unique style. He would leap from his horse, grab the steer around the neck or by the horns, and then sink his teeth into the animal's upper lip.

Pickett was employed at the famous 101 Ranch (now a National Historic Landmark) five miles south of Ponca City, and was the last of the original 101 hands to die. He is buried on the ranch.

Pickett was elected to the National Cowboy Hall of Fame, along with Jesse Stahl (1883–1938), a black Tennessee-born bronc rider.

Daily 8:30–6 May 30–Sept. 7, 9–5 rest of year. Closed Jan. 1, Thanksgiving and Dec. 25. Adults $4, senior citizens $3, ages 6–12 $1.50.

OKLAHOMA STATE MUSEUM OF HISTORY, southeast of the capitol at N.E. 19th Street and Lincoln Boulevard. There are extensive exhibits on the state's history including the contributions of Indians, the early pioneers, and black men and women.

Mon.–Sat. 9–5. Closed holidays. Free.

SANAMU AFRICAN GALLERY is located on the second floor in the Kirkpatrick Center Museum Complex (in Lincoln Park Country), 2100 Northeast 52nd Street. The Sanamu Gallery features an excellent collection of traditional arts and crafts from sub-Saharan Africa, with the purpose of promoting a better understanding and appreciation of African life and culture. The museum provides tour guides, sponsors seminars and institutes, and presents special exhibits and programs.

Daily 10–5, Sun. 12–5. Closed Thanksgiving and Christmas.

Also in the Kirkpatrick Center is an Air Space Museum, American Indian exhibits, a Planetarium, and a garden and greenhouses, among many other attractions.

The center is open in the summer Mon.–Sat. 9–6, Sun. noon to 6 in the summer; shorter hours in the winter. Admission to all the museums and attractions, adults $5, ages 5–12 and over 64, $3, children under 5 free.

TULSA

GREENWOOD CULTURAL CENTER at 322 N. Greenwood. Greenwood Avenue was the scene of one of America's worst race riots in June 1921. Over 35 city blocks were looted and burned to the ground, and more than 1,000 homes destroyed. Today Greenwood Avenue has been renovated and has become the hub of black culture in Tulsa.

The center includes the Mabel B. Little Heritage museum, with art, photographs and artifacts of North Tulsa's history and a second-story gallery containing works of local black artists. The OKLAHOMA JAZZ HALL OF FAME is housed in the Chappelle-Goodwin Gallery, attached to the center. Some of the greatest jazz names in the country have come out of Oklahoma, including the Oklahoma City Blue Devils, organized in the 1920s, and recently inducted into the Jazz Hall of Fame. The Blue Devils brought many innovations to jazz and greatly influenced Count Basie. A jazz festival is offered in June of each year at Greenwood. (918-582-1741)

Tues.–Sat. 1–5 and upon request. Free. For information about the restored area of Greenwood Avenue contact *The Oklahoma Eagle*, 624 East Archer, the oldest black-owned newspaper in Oklahoma.

PHILBROOK MUSEUM OF ART, 2727 S. Rockford Road (1 block east of Peoria Street), is an elaborate estate set among 23 acres of formal gardens. Its extensive collection of art includes an excellent African exhibit.

Tues.–Sat. 10–5, Sun. 1–5. Closed holidays. Adults $3, Seniors $1.50, students thru grade 12 free.

For further information about Oklahoma, contact:

Oklahoma Tourism and Recreation
500, Will Rogers Bldg.
Oklahoma City, OK 73105
1-800-652-OKLA

For information on black tours:
Territorial Tours Limited
1636 S.W. 79th Terr.
Oklahoma City, OK 73159

OREGON

ASTORIA

FORT CLATSOP NATIONAL MEMORIAL, 5 miles southwest of Astoria off U.S. 101, is where the Lewis and Clark expedition spent the winter after finally sighting the Pacific Ocean in November 1805. The exhausted party took a vote on where they should build their camp. Clark's black servant, York, and the Indian woman Sacajawea, having proven themselves on the long, perilous trip, voted with the rest. In the spring, Lewis took a part of the group northwest to explore a route across the Continental Divide, while York and the rest of the expedition followed Clark home, exploring the Yellowstone along the way. They returned to St. Louis in September 1806.

Despite his courageous service to the expedition, York remained Clark's slave. Two years later Clark gave York his freedom and the black explorer's final fate is uncertain. One account has him dying of cholera, another has York returning west and becoming a black chief with the Crows.

The Fort Clatsop National Memorial features an exact full-scale replica of the log fort built by Lewis and Clark in the winter of 1805. At the visitor center a narrated slide program takes the viewer along the explorers' route from St. Louis to Fort Clatsop. An exhibit room contains artifacts from the expedition. York's role can be seen in both the exhibits and

the slide show. During a living history program, June 16–
Labor Day, buckskin-clad park rangers show the clothing,
equipment and lifestyle of the expedition.

Visitor center and grounds open daily, 8–6 mid-June to
Labor Day, rest of year 8–5. Closed Dec. 25. Adults $1,
maximum of $3 per family, children and seniors enter free.

OREGON CITY

OREGON TRAIL INTERPRETIVE CENTER, Fifth
and Washington streets, contains artifacts and exhibits recall-
ing the difficult journey made by 300,000 pioneers over the
Oregon Trail. Among their number were black slaves of the
pioneers, and free blacks.

Tues.–Sat. 10–4, Sun. noon–4. Closed Jan. Adults $2,
seniors, $1.50, students $1.

PORTLAND

CHILDREN'S MUSEUM, 3037 Southwest 2nd Avenue,
has hands-on learning opportunities for children of all ages,
including a visit to an authentic African village.

Tues.–Sat. 9–5, Sun. 11–5. Donation.

OREGON HISTORICAL SOCIETY, 1230 Southwest
Park Avenue, has an exterior mural which includes a picture
of the black servant and explorer York, who came to Oregon
with the Lewis and Clark expedition. Exhibits within the
museum cover the history of Oregon from prehistoric times
to the present. In the library are documents and books on the
history of blacks who homesteaded in the Pacific Northwest
in the late-nineteenth century.

Mon.–Sat. 10–4:45. Donation.

PORTLAND MUSEUM OF ART, 1219 Southwest Park
at Jefferson, includes many outstanding paintings and sculp-

tures, including artwork by Indians of the Pacific Northwest as well as a very good West African art collection with a strong emphasis on the Cameroon culture.

Tues.–Sat, 11–5; Sun 1–5, also 5–9 P.M., the first Thurs. of each month. Adults $3, students and over 62 $1.50, ages 6–12 free. Free on Thurs after 5.

Painted on a building at the northeast corner of Shaver Street and Martin Luther King Boulevard are murals entitled *Now's the time—The time is now*, painted by a group of amateur and professional artists led by artist Shamsud-Din. The powerful murals celebrate black leadership and history.

For further information about Oregon, contact:

Tourism Division
775 Summer St., N.E.
Salem, OR 97310
1-800-547-7842

PENNSYLVANIA

CHADDS FORD

BRANDYWINE BATTLEFIELD PARK runs along the north side of U.S. 1, ¼ mile east of junction PA 100. In the fall of 1777 Washington lost 1,200 men in this battle and was forced to retreat, losing Philadelphia to the British. Edward Hector, a black soldier attached to the 3d Pennsylvania Artillery, (with only a few exceptions, black soldiers in the Revolutionary War served in integrated units), took a notable part in the battle of Brandywine.

When Hector's regiment was ordered to pull back, he disobeyed and, making use of weapons discarded by fleeing soldiers, he saved his ammunition wagon for the Americans. Many years later the Pennsylvania legislators voted him a forty-dollar reward.

There are restored buildings on the battlefield and the visitor center has an audio-visual program and exhibits about the battle.

Grounds open daily 9–8 in summer; rest of year Tues.–Sat. 9–5, Sun. 12–5. Free. Visitor center and historic buildings open Tues.–Sat. 9–5, Sun. 12–5. Closed all legal holidays. Adults $1, seniors 75 cents, ages 6–17, 50 cents.

CHEYNEY

CHEYNEY UNIVERSITY, Cheyney and Creed roads, was established in 1837 exclusively for the training of black teachers, and is considered the nation's oldest black university. The school prospered under the leadership of Fanny Jackson Coppin, one of the first black woman college graduates in America. In 1920 the operation was transferred to the Commonwealth of Pennsylvania with the assurance that Cheyney graduates would be allowed to teach in either white or black schools in Pennsylvania, a promise that was not fulfilled until the 1950s.

There are few historic buildings still standing on this campus but there are many interesting new buildings, including the George Washington Carver Science Center with a planetarium attached, and a World Culture Center which contains a museum of African and other cultures.

Open during regular academic hours. Closed summers.

ERIE

ERIE HISTORICAL MUSEUM, 356 W. 6th Street (6th and Chestnut), highlights local history, including a multimedia presentation of the battle of Lake Erie. Commander Perry defeated the British fleet in this naval battle during the War of 1812. Twenty-five percent of the sailors in Perry's fleet were black.

Tues.–Fri. 10–5, Sat. and Sun. 1–5, June–Aug.; rest of year Tues.–Sun. 1–5. Adults $1, 6–12, 50 cents.

PERRY MEMORIAL HOUSE (THE DICKSON TAVERN) 201 French Street. Built in 1809, the Dickson Tavern was one of Erie's finest inns. The port cities along Lake Erie were used by escaping slaves as exit points to Canada and there were several Underground Railway stations in the town of Erie. Legend has it that one of those stations, where fugitives hid until they could secure ship's passage was the Dickson Tavern. There were even rumors that the walls of the tavern-inn were honeycombed with secret passages, although this has never been proven.

Today the building has been restored, featuring a tavern setting and rooms furnished with nineteenth-century objects.

Tues.–Fri. 10–5, summer only; Sat. and Sun. 1–5, year round. Free.

PERRY MONUMENT, Presque Isle State Park at Misery Base (park may be reached by PA 832 or by boat). This stone shaft monument is dedicated to the white and black men who fought and died in the battle of Lake Erie in 1813. Across the road near a little bridge is Graveyard Pond where Perry's men, who did not live through the terrible winter of 1813–14, were buried under the ice of the backwater. The dead include British captives from the battle of Lake Erie at Put-in-Bay. (See also Perry's Victory Memorial at Put-in-Bay, Ohio.)

Daily 8 A.M. to sunset.

U.S. BRIG *NIAGARA*, foot of State Street and Public Dock, was Commodore Perry's flagship in the naval battle fought against the British in September 1813 for control of Lake Erie, during the War of 1812. When Perry's original flagship, which bore the brunt of the fight, was put out of action, he transferred to the *Niagara* and hoisting his battle flag, "Don't give up the ship," continued the fight.

One-quarter of the sailors aboard Perry's small fleet of nine vessels were blacks. Before the battle Perry complained of the reinforcements sent him, "a motley crew of blacks, soldiers and boys." His commanding officer, Commodore Chauncey, answered tartly, "I have yet to learn that the color of the skin or the cut and trimmings of the coat can affect a man's quality or usefulness." After winning the battle against the much larger British navy, Perry praised the courage of his black crew members. The square-rigged, wooden U.S. Brig *Niagara* has recently been completely restored to fully operable, sailing condition and may be toured by visitors. Mention is made on these tours of the role of blacks in the naval victory.

Mon.–Sat. 9–5, Memorial Day to Labor Day. Adults $1.50.

GETTYSBURG

GETTYSBURG NATIONAL MILITARY PARK surrounds the city of Gettysburg and has its main entrance at the National Park Visitor Center on PA 134. Although black troops did not fight in this, the bloodiest battle of the Civil War, they were involved behind the scenes as supportive troops, building barricades and roads and serving as carpenters, hospital attendants and blacksmiths. It was only shortly after the Gettysburg campaign in July 1863 that black troops were enlisted in the Union army. Some 8,600 black Pennsylvanians had served in its ranks before the end of the war. Most of them were trained at Camp William Penn on the outskirts of Philadelphia. By the end of the war, 180,000 black men had joined the Union army.

The visitor center/museum serves as the starting point for tours of the battlefield. The museum contains the nation's largest collection of Civil War artifacts as well as an exhibit on U.S. Colored Troops who served in the war. The Soldiers' National Monument in the Gettysburg National Cemetery stands near the spot where Lincoln delivered his famous dedication address in November 1863.

Park roads open daily 6 a.m.–10 p.m. Visitor center daily 8–5. Closed Jan. 1, Thanksgiving and Dec. 25. Adults $2, over 61 $1.50, under 16 free.

MERION

BARNES FOUNDATION, on Latches Lane, has one of

the finest private art collections in the world, including items from Africa, and paintings by African-Americans such as Horace Pippin. Visitors must call ahead for times and reservations. (215-667-0290)

MERION CEMETERY, Bala Cynwyd, contains the grave site of James Bland, the black minstrel singer and composer of over 600 songs, including "Carry Me back to Old Virginny," the official state song of Virginia, and "Oh, Dem Golden Slippers." Upon his death, there was no money for even a modest funeral or a grave marker. It wasn't until 1941 that an overdue tribute was paid to Bland; he was given an honorary burial in the Merion Cemetery by the governor of Virginia.

NEW HOPE

WASHINGTON CROSSING STATE PARK on PA 32 and PA 532 is about 7 miles southeast of New Hope on the Delaware River. On Christmas night 1776, General Washington crossed the Delaware River from Pennsylvania to New Jersey with 3,400 soldiers. He went on to victory at Trenton, New Jersey, but Pennsylvania has preserved Washington's embarkation point.

Although blacks had fought at Bunker Hill, Lexington and Concord, black soldiers were not officially recruited into the Continental army at that time. Nevertheless, two black men, Prince Whipple and Oliver Cromwell, crossed the Delaware with Washington. The following year Washington asked the Continental Congress to approve enlistment of Negroes in the army and his request was granted.

The Memorial Building at the embarkation point houses a copy of Emanuel Leutze's famous painting *Washington Crossing the Delaware,* and shows Prince Whipple in Washington's boat. A reenactment of the crossing of the Delaware is held at the park at 1 P.M. on Dec. 25. The Memorial Building also has a film depicting the crossing. The park with several restored historic buildings is open daily 9–5. Closed legal holidays. Park and Memorial Building are free.

OXFORD

LINCOLN UNIVERSITY, on U.S. 131, is 45 miles southwest of Philadelphia, between Oxford and West Grove. Lincoln, begun in 1854, is considered the oldest college in America established for the purpose of providing a liberal education for black students, and has been interracial since 1866. The many famous graduates of Lincoln University include Supreme Court justice Thurgood Marshall, musician Gil Scott-Heron, and the poet Langston Hughes.

The oldest building on campus, Lincoln Hall, was built in 1866. One of the newest buildings is the Langston Hughes Memorial Library, which contains the poet's personal papers and his library. The library also has a large collection of black-related literature and a collection of African art and artifacts.

Library is open school hours during the academic year. Free.

PHILADELPHIA

A brochure, *African-American Historical and Cultural Attractions in Philadelphia* is available at the visitor center at 16th Street and John F. Kennedy Boulevard. Open daily 9–6.

AFRO-AMERICAN HISTORICAL AND CULTURAL MUSEUM, northwest corner of 7th and Arch streets, is the first museum specifically built to house and interpret collections on African-American culture. The achievements of black men and women are documented through historical artifacts, photographs, multimedia presentations and the work of black artists. There are exhibits relating to the slave trade and blacks in the American Revolution. There are also

African sculpture and artifacts and an archive of African-American history and literature. Since the museum's opening in 1976, it has attracted over one million visitors. An African-American Heritage Tour of Philadelphia starts at the museum.

Tues.–Sat. 10–5, Sun. 1–6. Closed Mon. and major holidays. Adults and ages 13–18 $3.50, over 61 and ages 5–12 $1.75.

AFROAMERICANS FOR CULTURAL DEVELOPMENT, INC., 2247 North Broad Street, produces "The Africamericas Festival," which includes a cultural parade, art exhibits, a film festival and concerts attracting participants from across the nation and the world. (215-232-2900)

ALL-WARS MEMORIAL TO BLACK SOLDIERS, West Lansdowne Drive, Fairmount Park, was erected by the state of Pennsylvania in 1934 to honor the black soldiers from Pennsylvania who had fought in America's wars.

AMERICAN WOMEN'S HERITAGE SOCIETY/MUSEUM is at 2000 Belmont Mansion Drive, West Fairmount Park. The Belmont Mansion was built in 1742 and entertained such notables as Washington, Franklin and Madison during the Revolutionary War. It is located in Fairmount Park, now the largest landscaped city park in the world. In 1986 the American Women's Heritage Society began using the mansion as a showcase for the contributions of African-American women to the growth of Philadelphia and to the country. There are also general exhibits on black history and culture.

Tues.–Sat. 10–4:30. Donation.

FRANKLIN INSTITUTE SCIENCE MUSEUM, 20th Street and Benjamin Franklin Parkway, honors Philadelphia's greatest citizen and one of the first opponents of slavery. In 1785, Franklin became the president of the Pennsylvania Society for Promoting the Abolition of Slavery and the Relief of Free Negroes Unlawfully Held in Bondage. The museum has four floors of hands-on exhibits dedicated to making science and technology fun for all ages, such as walking through a giant heart, or sitting behind the controls of a jet fighter. The museum also has many of Franklin's personal effects.

Mon.–Fri. 1:30–4:30, weekends 10–5. Closed major holidays. Adults $5.50, ages 4–11 $4.50.

COALITION OF AFRICAN-AMERICAN ORGANIZATIONS, 2253 N. Broad Street, provides a cultural calendar of black institutions in Philadelphia, featuring performing arts, exhibitions, lectures, tours and workshops.

Historical Black Churches in Philadelphia:

CHURCH OF THE ADVOCATE, 18th and Diamond streets, is known as the Freedom Church because it was the site of many important civil and human rights meetings in the 1960s. The church hosted the second Black Power Convention and the last National Convention of the Black Panther Party. Bishop Barbara Harris, the first female bishop in the entire Episcopal church, was ordained here.

FIRST AFRICAN PRESBYTERIAN CHURCH, 42nd and Girard Avenue, was established in 1811 as the first of its kind in Philadelphia. Originally located at 7th and Bainbridge streets, the church moved twice before settling at its present location.

MOTHER BETHEL AFRICAN METHODIST EPISCOPAL CHURCH, 419 S. 6th Street, is one of the oldest black churches in America. The church was founded by Richard Allen in 1794 because he refused to worship in segregated congregations. The land on which the church stands is the oldest parcel of real estate continuously owned by black people in the United States. Richard Allen became the first bishop of the African Methodist Episcopal Church in 1816.

From the pulpit of the Mother Bethel A. M. E. Church, many prominent abolitionists have spoken out against slavery, among them Lucretia Mott, Frederick Douglass, William Still and James Forten. Forten served in the Revolutionary War and, with Allen, raised a force of 2,500 free blacks to help defend Philadelphia during the War of 1812. Forten spoke out from Mother Bethel A. M. E. in opposition to the idea of resettling slaves in Africa. He also helped put up the funds which William Lloyd Garrison needed to found his abolitionist paper, *The Liberator.*

The lower level of the church, where escaped slaves were sheltered, contains the tomb of Bishop Richard Allen and a small museum displaying historical articles.

SAINT THOMAS EPISCOPAL CHURCH, 401 N. 52nd Street, was formed in 1791 when Absalom Jones withdrew from St. George's Methodist Church rather than sit in segregated pews. St. Thomas formally opened its doors in 1794, and received a charter from the state of Pennsylvania in 1796, thus becoming the first incorporated body of African-Americans in the United States.

With Richard Allen, Absalom Jones formed the Free African Society and also helped found a black militia to defend Philadelphia during the War of 1812. In its 200-year history, the church has moved several times from its original site at 5th and St. James streets.

ZOAR UNITED METHODIST CHURCH, 12th and Melon streets, was founded in 1796 (originally called the African Zoar Methodist Episcopal Church) and is the oldest established church of black Methodists in the area.

JOHNSON HOUSE, 6306 Germantown Avenue was built in 1768 as the home of Quaker Samuel Johnson. The house served as a station on the Underground Railroad and runaway slaves were hidden in the basement and the attic. The house was also used as a meeting place for such important underground operators as William Still and Harriet Tubman.

Tues.–Sat. 10–4, or by appointment. Adults $1.50, children 75 cents.

LIBERTY BELL PAVILION, Market Street between 5th and 6th streets, Philadelphia's most famous landmark, is now enclosed in glass. The bell was first referred to as the Liberty

Bell in 1839 by an anti-slavery society called The Friends of Freedom. Tapes in English and 15 other languages narrate the bell's history.

Daily 9–5, extended hours in summer. The bell can be viewed from outside 24 hours a day. Free.

MOST WORSHIPFUL PRINCE HALL GRAND LODGE OF PENNSYLVANIA (MASONIC HALL) 4301 N. Broad Street, was established in 1787 by Absalom Jones and Richard Allen. The lodge is named for Prince Hall, a black veteran of the Revolutionary War. Prince Hall was inducted into the Masonic Lodge by a group of British soldiers stationed in Boston, although no American lodge would accept him. In 1787 he received permission from the Mother Grand Lodge in England to start the first African lodge No. 459 in Boston. Thus Prince Hall became the founder of the oldest social organization among blacks in the United States. Today the lodge in Philadelphia is headquarters for the 8,000 Prince Hall members of Pennsylvania. The present structure was dedicated in 1975.

PENNSYLVANIA ACADEMY OF FINE ARTS, Broad and Cherry streets, has a fine collection of paintings by black artists, including religious pieces by Henry Ossawa Tanner, and one of Horace Pippin's most important works, *John Brown Going to His Hanging*. Painted into the foreground is the figure of Pippin's grandmother, turning sadly away from the scene of abolitionist John Brown riding a wagon to his death.

Tues.–Sat. 10–5, Sun. 11–5. Closed holidays. Guided tours Tues.–Fri. 11 and 2, weekends at 2. Adults $5, senior citizens $3, students $2, under 5 free. Free to all Sat. 10–1.

PHILADELPHIA DOLL MUSEUM, 7257 North 18th Street, is a collection of black doll memorabilia, as well as a clearinghouse for black doll makers, with workshops and seminars.

Open by appointment. (215-934-3121)

PHILADELPHIA MUSEUM OF ART is located at the

end of Benjamin Franklin Parkway at 26th Street. One of the world's major art museums, the collection includes African art as well as works by nineteenth- and twentieth-century black American artists such as *The Lynching* by Samuel Brown, *The End of the War* by Horace Pippin and *The Annunciation* by Henry Ossawa Tanner.

Tues.–Sun. 10–5. Closed Mon. and holidays. Adults $5, over age 61, age 5–18 and students $2.50. Free on Sun. 10–1.

THE PHILADELPHIA TRIBUNE, 522 S. 16th Street, was founded in 1884 by Christopher Perry and is the nation's oldest black-owned newspaper.

CHARLES L. BLOCKSON AFRO-AMERICAN COLLECTION, Temple University Library, Broad Street and Montgomery Avenue. The Blockson collection comprises over 43,000 items concerning notable African-Americans, such as slave narratives, letters, posters, photographs, original recordings and archive collections of the private papers of prominent figures. Collection open for research only.

WASHINGTON SQUARE, 6th to 7th streets and Walnut to Locust streets, was once known as Congo Square because it was a meeting place for free blacks. The square is the burial place for hundreds of Revolutionary War dead, including black soldiers. The Tomb of the Unknown Soldier of the Revolutionary War lies in the square beside an eternal flame.

PITTSBURGH

CARNEGIE MUSEUM OF ART, 4400 Forbes Avenue, contains works by contemporary black artists like Norman Lewis and John Wilson, as well as nineteenth-century artists such as Horace Pippin and Henry Ossawa Tanner. The institute also has an excellent collection of African art.

Tues.–Sat. 10–5, Fri. 5–9, Sun. 1–5. Closed Mon. and holidays. Adults $4, ages 3–18 and students $2.

SHARON HILL

BESSIE SMITH'S GRAVE SITE is at Mt. Lawn Cemetery, Sharon Hill, Delaware County. Queen of the blues and one of the most famous blues singers in America's musical history, Bessie Smith died from injuries suffered in an auto accident in Tennessee, after being refused admission to a hospital close to the scene. Her body was shipped north for burial. For many years the site was neglected until the late singer Janis Joplin provided a tombstone for the grave.

VALLEY FORGE

VALLEY FORGE NATIONAL HISTORICAL PARK extends east from the village of Valley Forge along PA 23. In December 1777, after a series of defeats, Washington and his army went into winter quarters at Valley Forge. Here, exhausted, often starving and ill-clothed, one-quarter of the 10,000 soldiers died.

Black soldiers suffered and died along with white soldiers at Valley Forge, including Salem Poor, who had fought at Bunker Hill and other engagements. Miraculously, Washington was able to hold his ragged, unpaid army together during that terrible winter. It was from Valley Forge that General James Varnum left in the spring of 1778 to raise a black regiment from Rhode Island.

Today the remains of the lines of entrenchments, fortifications and huts may be seen at Valley Forge, as well as national and state monuments honoring the men who endured the terrible winter of 1777. The museum has exhibits and mementos of the native-born and foreign-born white, black and American Indian soldiers who supported the cause of independence. Buses take visitors on a narrated ride covering points of interest in the park.

Daily 8:30–5. Closed Dec. 25. Free.

For further information about Pennsylvania, contact:

Bureau of Travel
453 Forum Bldg.
Harrisburg, PA 17120
1-800-847-4872

For a brochure on Philadelphia's African-American attractions:

Visitor Center
1525 John F. Kennedy Blvd.
Philadelphia, PA 19102
1-800-321-WKND

RHODE ISLAND

BRISTOL

HAFFENREFFER MUSEUM OF ANTHROPOLOGY, Brown University, near junction of Metacom Avenue (RI 136) and Tower Road, contains cultural and archaeological items from Africa, as well as the Pacific and North and South America.

Tues.–Sun. 1–5, June–Aug.; weekends 1–5, Sept.–Dec. and March–May. Adults $1, seniors and ages 4–12, 50 cents.

NEWPORT

OLD COLONY HOUSE, built in 1739 on Washington Square, was where the first law in the United States prohibiting the importation of slaves was passed in 1774 by Newport's General Assembly. Rhode Island was one of the most independent of the early colonies. Although the federal Constitution was ratified at the Old Colony House in 1790, Rhode Island had initially opposed it, until succumbing to pressure from the other colonies.

During the Revolutionary War, the British made their headquarters at Newport. In July 1777 in a daring raid on the headquarters, a small group of colonial soldiers captured British general Richard Prescott, who was still asleep in his bed.

Jack Sisson, a black soldier, was the first to arrive at the bedroom and broke down the door.

Mon.–Sat. 10–4, Sun. and holidays 12–4, June 15–Labor Day. Free.

PORTSMOUTH

BUTTS HILL FORT, off Sprague Street, is the site of Rhode Island's only major land battle in the Revolutionary War. In August of 1778, General Washington sent a large force of militia and a portion of the French fleet to attack the British at Newport, Rhode Island. The French fleet were unable to support the Americans because of a severe storm at sea, and although the militia attacked as planned, they were forced to withdraw under cover of night, pursued by British and Hessian soldiers.

Among the New England militia which attacked the British garrison was the 1st Rhode Island, a newly raised regiment of more than 200 black soldiers.

A few old redoubts can be seen at the battle site today, and a marker telling of this Revolutionary War battle.

MEMORIAL TO BLACK SOLDIERS, RI 114, is just to the left of the junction of northbound RI 114 and RI 24. During the battle of Rhode Island, the Hessians attacked a line held by the all-black 1st Rhode Island Regiment, thinking it would be the easiest to break. Instead the regiment was commended for showing "desperate valor" in repelling three "furious assaults" for four bitter hours. When the commander of the Rhode Island Regiment was cut down by enemy fire, the Hessians had to kill a faithful guard of black soldiers before they could reach his body. The 1st Rhode Island Regiment was the first black regiment to fight for the American flag and they made their gallant stand at the spot marked here by a flagpole.

PROVIDENCE

MUSEUM OF ART, RHODE ISLAND SCHOOL OF DESIGN, 224 Benefit Street, is one of the nation's finest small museums. Included in the collection are contemporary and historic black American art works, sculpture and paintings. Seven landscapes by the nineteenth-century black artist Edward Bannister may be seen. Bannister lived in Providence and was one of the seven founders of the famed Providence Art Club.

Tues.–Wed. and Fri.–Sat. 10:30–5, Thurs. noon–8 and Sun. and holidays 2–5, Sept. 1–June 15; rest of year Wed.–Sat. noon–5. Closed holidays. Adults $1, seniors 50 cents, ages 5–18, 25 cents.

OLD STATE HOUSE, 150 Benefit Street, was where the General Assembly in 1784 passed the first legislation in the United States providing for the gradual emancipation of slaves. Even earlier, in 1674, Rhode Island had been the first of the American colonies to pass a law regulating slavery.

Mon.–Fri. 8:30–4:30. Free.

RHODE ISLAND BLACK HERITAGE SOCIETY, One Hilton Street, founded in 1974, is an archive/library, gallery and historical society for black history in Rhode Island. A recent exhibit called "Creative Survival" focused on the Underground Railroad in Providence and the black experience there in the nineteenth century. Also arranges traveling exhibitions and hosts black history tours of the area.

Mon.–Fri. 9–4:30, Sat.–Sun. by appointment. Free.

For further information about Rhode Island, contact:

Rhode Island Tourism Division
7 Jackson Walkway
Providence, RI 02903
1-800-556-2484 or 401-277-2601

SOUTH CAROLINA

BEAUFORT

ROBERT SMALLS MONUMENT is at Baptist Tabernacle Church, 907 Craven Street, in this historic port town.
One of the naval heroes of the Civil War was an ex-slave,
Robert Smalls, who was a crewman aboard the Confederate
gunboat *Planter*. On a night in May 1862, while it was
moored in Charleston harbor, loaded with guns and ammunition for the Confederates, and all the white officers had gone
ashore, Smalls and the other black crewmen left aboard, took
command and piloted the ship under the guns of Fort Sumter
and out of the harbor. "I thought the *Planter* might be of
some use to Uncle Abe," he said, as he delivered it into Union
hands.

Smalls was invited to Washington to meet the president and
was given command of the vessel. During the war it carried
the black men of Higginson's 1st South Carolina Volunteers
on raids along the South Carolina and Georgia coasts. After
the war, Smalls served in the state legislature and as a representative from South Carolina to the U.S. Congress.

His home at 511 Prince Street is a National Historic Landmark but is not open to the public.

PENN SCHOOL HISTORIC DISTRICT AND MU-

SEUM is on Land's End Road, St. Helena Island, which is a short distance from Beaufort on U.S. 21. When federal troops took control of St. Helena Island in 1861, they confiscated the property of plantation owners including some 10,000 slaves listed as "contraband of war." Funded primarily by Northern abolitionists, missionaries and teachers began arriving to provide schools for the ex-slaves, adults and children. The first school for freed slaves in the South was the Penn School, created in 1862. By the late 1800s, Penn was teaching agriculture, homemaking and industrial arts.

Today the school is the Penn Community Services Center. In addition to tutoring black residents on the island, the Center is used as a bi-racial conference center. Dr. Martin Luther King, Jr., was a frequent visitor. The Penn Center is listed on the National Register of Historic Places and some of the historic wooden and tabby structures dating from the 1860s are being renovated.

YORK BAILEY MUSEUM is at Frogmore in the Penn Center Historic District on St. Helena. The museum has exhibits on the culture and history of the black residents of the sea islands. The exhibits chronicle island life from the 1800s, including oral histories, folk art, photographs and a collection of tools used in everyday life on the island.

Daily 9–5. Closed holidays. Adults $2, ages 6–17 $1.

CHARLESTON

AVERY RESEARCH CENTER FOR AFRICAN-AMERICAN HISTORY AND CULTURE, is located at the College of Charleston, 125 Bull Street. The center is developing materials on African-American history from the coastal region between Savannah, Georgia, and Myrtle Beach, South Carolina. In this region, the African-American or "Gullah" culture is distinguished by heavy retention of African and

Caribbean traditions, expressed in the Gullah dialect. The dialect, a mixture of seventeenth- and eighteenth-century English and Irish with languages from the west coast of Africa and the Caribbean, is still used today. The center also presents lectures, workshops and exhibits.

Tours of the center are provided at 2, 2:30, 3 and 3:30. Group tours by appointment. Reading room hours, Mon., Tues., Thurs., 9–1; Mon.–Fri. 2–4. Donation. (803-727-2009)

BOONE HALL PLANTATION is 9 miles north of Charleston on U.S. 17. Begun in 1676, this was one of the largest cotton plantations in the South before the Civil War, spreading over 17,000 acres and requiring more than a thousand slaves for its operation.

Handmade bricks and tiles produced by slaves were used to construct the white-columned manor house, gin house, smokehouse, garden walls—and the street of small cottages near the mansion for the house slaves. Nine of the original tile-roofed slave cabins still stand, constituting the only intact "slave street" in the southeast. The field hands lived in less comfortable quarters elsewhere.

Boone Hall remains a working farm today but sections of the plantation, the gardens and mansion house, and some of the outbuildings including the slave quarters, are open to the public.

Mon.–Sat. 8:30–6:30, Sun. 1–5, April 1–Labor Day; rest of year Mon.–Sat. 9–5, Sun. 1–4. Closed Thanksgiving and Dec. 25. Adults $6, seniors $5, ages 6–12 $2.

CABBAGE ROW, 89–91 Church Street, was the model for Catfish Row in Dubose Heyward's novel *Porgy* which later became the basis for Gershwin's opera *Porgy and Bess*. The row of tenements got their name Cabbage Row from the vegetables which black residents displayed for sale on their windowsills.

Continue down Church Street to St. Michael's Alley, turn

left through the alley then right on Meeting Street, and most days locally woven sweetgrass baskets can be found for sale. Of all the arts that black men and women brought with them from Africa, that of basket weaving was preserved in its purest form. The sweetgrass baskets sold in Charleston are practically the same coil basketry that you would find in West Africa. The only difference is that the South Carolina basketweavers have added the brown needles of the long-leaf pine for decoration.

CHARLESTON MUSEUM, at 360 Meeting Street, at the corner of John Street, was established in 1773 and is considered to be the nation's oldest museum. It features displays mainly relating to Charleston and the South Carolina "low country," along with exhibits of natural history, archaeology, and a children's "Discover Me" room. There is also a permanent collection of artifacts from slavery, with changing exhibits on the lifestyles and crafts of African-Americans.

Mon.–Sat. 9–5, Sun. 1–5. Closed holidays. Adults $3, seniors $2.70, ages 3–12 $1.50.

DENMARK VESEY HOUSE, 56 Bull Street, was the home of a free black Charleston carpenter who, in 1822, plotted a slave revolt which involved a large group of black city workers. An informer revealed the plan and 36 participants were executed. The Vesey home is a National Historic Landmark, privately owned.

There were dozens of small slave uprisings and at least nine large-scale slave revolts in America between 1691 and 1865. In Charleston County, near Rantowles, the Stono River Slave Rebellion erupted during the Colonial period. Some 100 escaped slaves burned plantations and murdered whites before they could be stopped by the militia.

DRAYTON HALL, 9 miles northwest on SC 61. Built for the Drayton family, 1738–1742, by European and African-American artisans, the hall was designed in the Georgian Palladian style. Never modernized with electricity, central heating or even plumbing, the house is virtually in its original condition and was the only Ashley River house to survive the Civil War intact.

A guided tour is offered of the plantation house and grounds, which emphasizes the contributions of African-Americans at Drayton Hall and in the low country of South Carolina. Documentary and archaeological surveys of the plantation are being conducted, including sites relating to slavery. Special events at Drayton Hall focus on African-American culture.

Daily 10–5 March–Oct., rest of year 10–3. Closed holidays. Adults $6. children 6–18 $3.

MIDDLETON PLACE is northwest of Charleston on SC 61, 14 miles from its junction with U.S. 17. It took 100 slaves 10 years to complete the landscaped gardens at Middleton, the oldest landscaped gardens in America. The main portion of the home was destroyed in the Civil War. There are restored outbuildings which have demonstrations of spinning, weaving, blacksmithing, candlemaking, carpentry, and pottery making. All these tasks would have been performed by the plantation slaves. Visitors can see how a plantation was run in the eighteenth and nineteenth century.

Gardens and outbuildings daily 9–5; house tours Mon. 1:30–4:30, Tues.–Sun. 10–4:30. Gardens and outbuildings $8, ages 6–12 $4; house $4 extra. Admissions slightly higher mid-March to mid-June.

MORRIS ISLAND, with its massive fortress of Fort Wagner, controlled every sea approach to Charleston during the Civil War. In July 1863, the all-black 54th Massachusetts, under Colonel Robert Gould Shaw, led the assault on Fort Wagner. Despite being caught in a deadly crossfire, the men of the 54th stormed the walls of the fort, fighting with bayonets and clubbed rifles against artillery, rifle fire and grenades. Of the 650 black troops who fought that day, 272 lost their lives.

Colonel Shaw was one of those killed and was buried with

his men at Fort Wagner. Sergeant William Carney, although wounded several times, saved the regimental flag and was awarded the Medal of Honor for his bravery that day. The actual battlesite of Fort Wagner no longer exists.

It was under the guns of nearby FORT SUMTER that black pilot Robert Smalls captured the Confederate ship *Planter* and piloted her out of Charleston harbor. Fort Sumter, where the first shot of the Civil War was fired, is now a National Monument. Tours of Fort Sumter are conducted by the National Park Service and there is a museum with artifacts from the fort. Hours vary according to season. Fort Sumter may be reached by tour boats from Charleston City Marina on Lockwood Boulevard in Charleston, and from Patriots Point Naval Museum in Mount Pleasant. Schedules vary. Adults $7.50, ages 6–11 $3.75.

SLAVE AUCTION BUILDING, 6 Chalmers Street, was where slaves, real estate and other property were sold before the Civil War. The city of Charleston did not allow slaves to be sold out in the street. Instead, they had to be sold inside licensed markets, such as the building on Chalmers Street, once called Ryan's Mart. There is another building at State and Assembly streets where slaves were once sold.

SULLIVAN ISLAND is across the channel from Fort Sumter and may be reached from Charleston via U.S. 17 and SC 703. Forty percent of blacks who arrived in America during the early 1800s came through Sullivan's Island. The island was used as a clearing house, similar to Ellis Island in New York City, for slaves bound for plantations throughout the mainland.

The OLD SLAVE MART LIBRARY, which was previously located in Charleston at the Old Slave Mart Museum, is now on Sullivan's Island. The collection consists of over 24,000 items, books, pamphlets, documents, maps, engravings, prints, letters, audio-visual material, by and about Afro-Americans and Africans. Some of the items date back to the late seventeenth century.

Open by appointment only. P.O. Box 459. (803-883-3797)

COLUMBIA

MANN-SIMONS COTTAGE, MUSEUM OF AF-RICAN-AMERICAN CULTURE is located at 1403 Richland Street in an historic house which was first owned by a black freewoman, Celia Mann. Built in 1850, the house remained in the Mann family until 1970. The collection includes period furnishings, family portraits, art works by local artists, artifacts found during restoration of the cottage, African art and sculpture and African-American artifacts and documents from mid-nineteenth to twentieth centuries. Guided tours, a library of South Carolina black history, and an annual Jubilee Festival held the last Saturday in September.

Tues.–Fri. 10–4, Sat. 11–2. Adults $1, seniors, students and children 50 cents.

McKISSICK MUSEUM on the University of South Carolina campus, two blocks south of the State House near the intersection of Bull and Pendleton streets. The collection focuses on southern folk art and culture, including black history and culture. Permanent and changing exhibits.

Mon.–Fri. 9–4, Sat. 10–5, Sun. 1–5. Closed holidays. Free.

SOUTH CAROLINA STATE MUSEUM, 301 Gervais Street, beside the Gervais Street Bridge, has four floors of exhibits and artifacts chronicling the natural history and history of the state. There is a permanent exhibit entitled "Antebellum Society," which includes a study of slavery, and exhibits on black funerals and mourning customs. There are changing exhibits throughout the year on Afro-American culture.

Mon.–Sat. 10–5, Sun. 1–5. Closed holidays. Adults $3, seniors, students $2, ages 6–17 $1.25. Under six free.

FLORENCE

FLORENCE MUSEUM OF ART, Graham and Spruce streets, contains Oriental and Western art as well as a small collection of African art. The Hall of South Carolina History traces the development of the state.
Tues.–Sat. 10–5, Sun. 2–5. Closed in Aug. Free.

GREENVILLE

GREENVILLE COUNTY MUSEUM OF ART, 420 College Street. In its modern American collection, the museum has works by black artist Romare Bearden.
Tues.–Sat. 10–5, Sun. 1–5. Closed holidays. Free.
GREENVILLE CULTURAL EXCHANGE CENTER, 700 Arlington Avenue at Sumner Street, is dedicated to the preservation of black history with its major emphasis on the Greenville area. Included in the museum is the Jesse Jackson Hall of Fame. Jackson is a native of Greenville.
Tues.–Fri. 10–5, Sat. 11–4. Free.

ORANGEBURG

I. P. STANBACK MUSEUM AND PLANETARIUM, at South Carolina State College, 300 College Street. This new museum focuses on history, science, and the fine arts, and the main gallery can be adapted to a variety of exhibits. The permanent collection includes Afro-American art of William Johnson, Elton Fox, Romare Bearden, Jacob Lawrence, as well as bronzes from Benin and art pieces from Cameroon. There is also a photo collection on black life and history from the 1800s and 1900s. One of its latest photographic exhibits was "Harlem on my mind."

The domed planetarium can seat 80 people and is located directly across the lobby from the museum.

Mon.–Fri. 9–4:30. Closed in summer. Donation.

ROCK HILL

MUSEUM OF YORK COUNTY, west on SC 161 from I-77 exit 82A, then north on Mount Gallant Road. The unusual displays in the Stans African Hall feature large mounted African animals, star-gazing safaris, and art and handicrafts from Africa. There is also a planetarium and nature trails.

Tues.–Sat. 10–5, Sun. 1–5. Closed on Mon. and major holidays. Adults $2, seniors $1, children under 5 free.

SHELDON

OYOTUNJI AFRICAN VILLAGE, U.S. 17–21, 50 miles south of Charleston, 45 miles north of Savannah. The village is patterned after the ancient Yoruba tradition. Volunteers live in the African-style village full-time. Visitors to the Oyotunji Village can meet the king and his wives in the palace, visit the village museum with art objects and crafts from Yoruba and Benin, and take a stroll down Temple Row where they will be introduced to ancient gods and goddesses of southwestern Nigeria. There is a Trader's Bazaar of quaint shops. Colorful drum festivals with Yoruba temple dancers are celebrated monthly. African luncheon and lodging available by reservation.

Daily winter–fall 9–5, spring–summer 9–8. Adults $3.50, children 6–16 $2.50. Guided tours for groups of 10 or more. (803-846-8900/9939)

For further information about South Carolina, contact:

Division of Parks and Tourism
1205 Pendleton Street
Columbia, SC 29201
803-734-0122

SOUTH DAKOTA

DEADWOOD

DEADWOOD GULCH is 26 miles past Rapid City. Take Alt. 14 off I-90 at Sturgis then 11 miles west. Deadwood is America's most famous living gold camp, filled with the history and legends of the Old West. ADAMS MEMORIAL MUSEUM, Deadwood and Sherman streets, had exhibits on the pioneer life in the Black Hills. Not only black men came west in the gold mining days, but black women, too. Sally Campbell was the first woman in the Black Hills, arriving in 1874. She staked out a gold claim and lived in Galena, South Dakota, until her death in 1888. Her grave marker occupies a place of honor in the museum.

Another black woman whose picture can be seen in the museum is Lucretia Marchbank, better known as Aunt Lou. Although she was only a housekeeper for the Father de Smet miners, it was said that she could run the mine as well as any man.

Several cowboys claimed the title "Deadwood Dick," including the flamboyant Nat Love, a black cowboy who won prizes for his riding and markmanship at a Fourth of July celebration at Deadwood in 1876. Born a slave in Tennessee in 1854, Nat Love ran away from home at age 15 and headed west. He wrote an autobiography about his colorful life which included riding with the long cattle drives north from

Texas and fighting off Indians, wild animals and desperate men. Although, like other Western sagas of the time, the book is filled with exaggeration, it catches the freewheeling, hard-driven life of the cowboy in the West, whether he was black or white.

There is an annual rodeo and historical parade in Deadwood in which Nat Love is portrayed.

Museum: Mon.–Sat. 9–6, Sun. 9–5, June–August. Mon.–Sat. 9–5, May and Sept. Donation.

GHOSTS OF DEADWOOD GULCH, WESTERN HERITAGE MUSEUM, Old Towne Hall on Lee Street, has costumed wax figures portraying life during the gold rush in Deadwood.

Daily 8–6 May 15–Oct. 1. Adults $2.75, students $2.25, under 12 free.

BOOT HILL (MOUNT MORIAH CEMETERY) is about 1 mile from town via a marked route from the business section. Boot Hill contains graves of such western legendaries as Wild Bill Hickok and Calamity Jane.

Daily 9–7 June–Oct. Adults $1, children 50 cents, free rest of year.

LAKE CITY

FORT SISSETON STATE HISTORIC PARK is 10 miles southwest off SD 25, and contains well-preserved stone fort buildings and breastworks built during the Sioux uprisings in the 1860s. Buffalo Soldiers of the 24th and 25th Colored infantries were stationed here from 1884 to 1888. The guard house contains bricks carved with the names of members of the 25th.

Visitor center open daily 11–7, Memorial Day–Labor Day. Free.

LAURENCE COUNTY

NIGGER HILL/NIGGER GULCH is on the Wyoming border, 15 miles northwest of Spearfish, S.D. Black miners were sent into this area in 1879 by white miners because they believed there was no gold there. Ironically, the area in fact contained a rich vein of gold and the black miners became quite wealthy.

STURGIS

OLD FORT MEADE MUSEUM is 1 mile east on SD 34. This fort was built in 1878 to control the Sioux and to protect the Black Hills miners. It was a key command post during the Sioux struggle. The famous 7th Cavalry was stationed here, and it was at Fort Meade that Major Reno, whose command was detached from Custer's at the Little Bighorn, was court martialed.

Several companies of the all-black 25th Infantry were stationed at Fort Meade from 1880 to 1888. Thirteen Buffalo Soldiers are buried at the Fort Meade Cemetery.

Some of the original buildings remain intact. There is a museum at the visitor center with a video presentation giving an overview of fort life, and an exhibit on the black troops that were stationed here.

Museum open daily 9 a.m.–8 p.m., Memorial Day weekend–Labor Day. Out of season tours can be arranged. Adults $1, under 16 free.

VERMILLION

SHRINE TO MUSIC MUSEUM, at Clark and Yale streets, run by the University of South Dakota, is a center for the study of historic musical instruments. The museum includes more than 2,500 antique pieces, including ancient instruments from Africa. Other exhibits cover slave music in America and later forms of Afro-American music, such as jazz.

Mon.–Fri. 9–4:30, Sat. 10–4:30, Sun. 2–4:30. Closed holidays. Free.

YANKTON

ALLEN CHAPEL A. M. E. CHURCH, at 508 Cedar Street, was built in 1885 and was the first church to be established in Dakota Territory by blacks.

Tours by appointment only.

For further information about South Dakota, contact:

Department of Tourism
Capitol Lake Plaza
Pierre, SD 57501
1-800-843-1930

TENNESSEE

CHATTANOOGA

CHATTANOOGA AFRO-AMERICAN MUSEUM AND RESEARCH CENTER, 730 Martin Luther King Boulevard, is devoted to the study of black culture. The museum has exhibits from the black history of Chattanooga, Afro-American and African exhibits, historical documents, photographs and a library. There is also a special Bessie Smith collection. A native of Tennessee, Bessie Smith was called the "Queen of the Blues" and since her death in 1937 her recordings have become collectors' items. Memorabilia of Bessie Smith, including her upright piano, may be seen at the museum. Eventually expansion of the museum will add the Bessie Smith Hall as a performance showcase.
Mon.–Fri. 9–5. Free.

HENNING

ALEX HALEY HOUSE AND MUSEUM is located at 200 S. Church Street and Haley Avenue. Henning is 45 miles north of Memphis on TN 209. The family history handed down by Haley's grandmother and aunts in Henning inspired him to research his ancestors who had been brought to America as slaves; figures such as Kunta Kinte, sold into slavery at sixteen in West Africa, and Chicken George, who led the family from North Carolina to Tennessee. The novel that resulted, *Roots,* won Haley the 1976 Pulitzer Prize and international acclaim. *Roots* has been translated into over 30 languages and not only has made readers aware of the suffering that blacks endured under slavery but has inspired millions of people around the world to search for their own roots.

The boyhood home of Alex Haley is the first state-owned historic site devoted to the Afro-American in Tennessee. Visitors may tour the home which features the life and work of Haley along with family portraits, mementos and furnishings.

Tues.–Sat. 10–5, Sun. 1–5. Adults $2.50, students $1.

BETHLEHEM CEMETERY, Durhamville Road, one mile east of Henning. The second entrance to the cemetery will lead visitors directly to the Haley family plot where Chicken George is buried.

FORT PILLOW STATE HISTORIC AREA is approximately 18 miles east of Henning on TN 87, then a short distance north on TN 207. On April 12, 1864, 1,500 Confederate cavalrymen overwhelmed Fort Pillow. Half of the 500 men at the garrison were black troops. After their surrender, scores of the black soldiers and some of the white soldiers were murdered. For black soldiers, "Remember Fort Pillow!" became a rallying cry, spurring them to fight to the death and to offer no quarter.

Today, the still-visible earthworks of the fort form part of the scenic Fort Pillow State Historic and Recreational Area. An interpretative center with an audio-visual program gives information about the battle.

Park hours 8 a.m.–10 p.m. Interpretative center 8–4:30. Free.

JACKSON

CASEY JONES HOME AND RAILROAD MUSEUM, at junction of I-40 and U.S. 45, bypass exit 80A, honors the legendary locomotive engineer. The song, "Casey Jones," which immortalized the brave engineer and is a part of America's musical folklore, was written by Wallace Saunders, a black fireman aboard Jones' locomotive. Blacks have played a large, unsung role in building and running America's trains, from laying tracks to acting as firemen, waiters in the dining cars, and the pullman porters, who helped to make railroad travel so memorable.

The museum has memorabilia of railroading, along with a sister engine and tender to Casey's Old 382.

Daily 8–8 June–Sept.; rest of year Mon.–Sat. 9–5, Sun. 1–5. Closed holidays. Adults $3, ages 6–12 $2.

KNOXVILLE

BECK CULTURAL EXCHANGE CENTER, 1927 Dandridge Avenue, consists of a museum, small library, gallery and cultural center in a historical home. The collection covers the first 100 years of the black history of Knoxville, through photographs, documents and black newspapers from 1840s–present, black American art works, and books on the African-American experience, some written by local black authors.

Tues.–Sat. 10–6. Free.

KNOXVILLE COLLEGE, 901 College Street, is one of the first black colleges founded in Tennessee, in 1875.

MEMPHIS

BEALE STREET TOURS. There are brochures for self-guiding tours and various commercial tours of Beale Street's day and night life, which introduce visitors to the musical history of Memphis as well as the city's black history and heritage. Check with the Memphis Visitors Center at 207

Beale Street, open Mon.–Sat. 9–5, Sun. 11–4. Also the Holiday Inn Crowne Plaza Hotel Lobby, 250 North Main Street, offers information on black heritage tours daily 9–8. Charge for conducted tours.

BEALE STREET HISTORIC DISTRICT, located downtown off Riverside Drive, is an entertainment district stretching several blocks east from the Mississippi River. Beale Street was the heart of the music scene in the early 1900s, when W. C. Handy played at PeeWee's Saloon, and Bessie Smith performed at various night spots. The blues, a unique African-American contribution to American music, got its start here in 1909 when W. C. Handy wrote a political song called "Mr. Crump" for a mayorality candidate. The song was such a hit that Handy turned the piece into the "Memphis Blues," the first blues ever published. This was soon followed by his "Beale Street Blues" and "St. Louis Blues."

Today, Beale Street has restaurants, shops, parks and nightclubs, including B. B.'s Place, owned by the legendary blues great, B. B. King, and the Memphis Music and Blues Museum.

W. C. HANDY'S HOME, 352 Beale Street, is where Handy was living when he wrote his most famous compositions. Although born in Florence, Alabama, William Christopher Handy spent a great deal of his life on Beale Street. There is a collection of Handy memorabilia on display at the house.

Hours vary. Call 901-527-2583, or check with Memphis visitors center, 207 Beale Street.

W. C. HANDY PARK on Beale Street has a bronze statue of the Father of the Blues with his horn raised, overlooking the Beale Street that he made famous. Special musical events are offered during the summer at Handy Park.

GRACELAND, 3765 Elvis Presley Boulevard, 1½ miles south of junction I-55, exit 5B, was the home of Elvis Presley, who made himself and Memphis famous by singing with a black rhythm and blues sound. Elvis' family moved to Memphis when he was 12 years old. Tours of the mansion, his gravesite, his private jets and car collection, and the Elvis Up Close museum.

Daily 8–7 June 15–Aug. 10; 8–6 June 1–14 and Aug. 11–31; 8–5 May 1–31; 9–5 rest of year. Closed holidays and on Tuesdays, Nov.–Feb. Reservations are suggested. Mansion tour, adults $7.50, ages 4–11 $4.75. Elvis Up Close museum $1.75.

A statue of Elvis Presley may be seen at the corner of Maine and Beale, in Elvis Presley Plaza.

IDA B. WELLS PLAQUE may be seen at the First Baptist Beale Street Church, 379 Beale Street, the site where she published her newspaper, *Free Speech*. The paper took a courageous stand against the injustices endured by black people in the early 1900s. Mrs. Wells was one of the first black women to publish a newspaper.

LORRAINE HOTEL is at 406 Mulberry Street. It was on a balcony of this motel that Dr. Martin Luther King, Jr., was murdered on April 4, 1968. Today the building is being turned into THE NATIONAL CIVIL RIGHTS MUSEUM, which provides the most comprehensive overview of the American civil rights movement in the United States. The museum fills a long-neglected gap in the study of America's recent history by covering the civil rights movements from the 1950s and 1960s, along with earlier and later periods of African-American history. Audio-visual programs will supply the background for the dramatic events covered in the interpretative exhibits.

Presently a massive steel sculpture entitled *The Mountain Top* at the north end of Civic Center Plaza honors Martin Luther King, Jr.

Mon.–Sat. 10–5, Sun. 1–5, closed Tues. Adults $5, Students $4, ages 6–12 $3.

SUN STUDIO, 706 Union Avenue (near Beale Street) is the recording studio founded by Sam Phillips, at which the bluesmen of Beale Street originally recorded their music. Blues legends Howlin' Wolf, Muddy Waters, B. B. King and

Little Milton all began their careers here. The studio is also where the first rock 'n' roll recording was cut in 1952. Other stars who recorded at Sun were Elvis Presley, Jerry Lee Lewis, Johny Cash, Carl Perkins and Roy Orbinson.

Open daily 10–6. Adults $4, children 4–12 $3, children under 4 free. Recordings conducted during the evenings from 6 P.M. until midnight.

TOM LEE MEMORIAL, on the riverbank near Beale Street, is a monument to the memory of a black man who, in 1925, saved 32 people from disaster when an excursion boat capsized on the Mississippi River.

NASHVILLE

BATTLE OF NASHVILLE. In December 1864, Union and Confederate forces fought outside of Nashville. Eight black regiments, recruited mainly from Tennessee and Missouri, formed a part of the Union army.

The 13th U.S. Colored Infantry led the line of Union troops which attacked strongly fortified Overton Hill. They had to fight up the hill against musket fire while threading through tangled fences of knife-sharp branches placed in their way. Within thirty minutes, 25 percent of the black brigade had been lost, but the remainder succeeded in reaching the summit of the hill.

Some of the old forts and trenches, as well as monuments and historic markers, may be seen on a portion of the Nashville battlefield. A map showing the location of battle sites and markers may be secured from the Metropolitan Historical Commission, Stahlman Building, Nashville.

COUNTRY MUSIC HALL OF FAME AND MUSEUM is at 4 Music Square East, 1½ blocks south of exit 209B off I-40. Nashville is the "country music headquarters" of the world, and this museum honors white and black singers and writers who have contributed to the sound. RCA's Studio B offers a behind-the-scenes look at the recording process. Among the exhibits in the museum is the harmonica played by Deford Bailey, a black musician who accompanied country bands between 1925 and 1941. A monument to Bailey may be found at Greenwood Cemetery.

Daily 8–8 June–Aug., rest of year 9–5. Closed holidays. Adults $6.50, ages 6–11 $1.75.

FISK UNIVERSITY, 17th Avenue North, about 2 miles northwest of downtown Nashville, was founded in 1866 as a school "equal to the best in the country," primarily for the newly freed slaves. Its Meharry Medical School was the first black medical school in the nation. There are many interesting historical buildings on campus, including the Little Theater, the oldest building, which was used as a hospital during the Civil War.

CARL VAN VECHTEN GALLERY OF FINE ARTS on Fisk Campus is on the third floor of the library. One of the outstanding African-American art galleries in the country, it holds the MacDonald Collection of African sculpture, contemporary black American art from the Alfred Stieglitz collection, and murals by Aaron Douglas.

Gallery open Tues.–Fri. 10–5, Sat.–Sun. 1–5. Adults $2.50, students free.

On the second floor of the Fisk University library is an extensive collection of materials on the black man in Africa, America and the Caribbean. The original manuscripts and literary effects of such black authors and leaders as Charles Waddell Chesnutt, W. E. B. Du Bois, Jean Toomer and Langston Hughes are preserved here.

Also in this library are mementos from the first group of JUBILEE SINGERS. When Fisk University almost ran out of funds shortly after it opened, a professor of music took a group of students with outstanding voices on a concert tour to raise money. At first the students sang traditional concert songs, but in 1871 their performance of the spiritual "Steal away to Jesus" received a thunderous ovation. From then on beautiful, plaintive spirituals, born in slavery, were added to the program.

Over the years the Jubilee Singers became internationally known and loved. They were able to earn enough money to enable Fisk to buy a new site and begin construction of one of the most significant buildings on campus, Jubilee Hall. Today the Fisk University Jubilee Singers still tour at home and abroad. A painting of the early singers hangs in Jubilee Hall.

TENNESSEE STATE MUSEUM is in the lower level of James Polk Cultural Center, 505 Deaderick Street. The museum has several exhibition areas devoted to African-American history, from slavery to the Civil War and the battle of Nashville. The post-Civil War exhibits highlight the struggles of black people during the dark days of Jim Crow. There is also an audio-visual program on black history.

Mon.–Sat. 10–5, Sun. 1–5. Closed holidays. Free.

For further information about Tennessee, contact:

Tennessee Dept of Tourism
PO Box 23170
Nashville, Tennessee 37202
615-741-2158

TEXAS

ABILENE

FORT PHANTOM HILL is 10 miles northeast of Abilene via TX Farm Road 600. In October 1869, 150 black troopers of the 9th Cavalry, with a unit of the 4th Calvary, marched to old Fort Phantom Hill from Fort Concho to search out and destroy the Apaches, Comanches and Kiowas in the area. Instead, about 500 Kiowas and Comanches attacked their camp. After a bitter hand-to-hand engagement, the Indians were forced to flee.

Fort Phantom Hill had been built in 1851 but was abandoned in 1854. Only ruins remain along with the stone commissary, guardhouse and powder magazine. There are interpretative signs. Free.

ALBANY

FORT GRIFFIN STATE HISTORIC PARK, 15 miles north of Albany on U.S. 283 at Clear Fork of the Brazos River, includes the ruins of the 1867 fort. Two troops of the 10th Cavalry were garrisoned at Fort Griffin in 1873–1874 to intercept raiding parties of Comanches who had left the reservation and were attacking along the Texas frontier. In one running battle the Buffalo Soldiers from Fort Griffin killed 11 warriors and recovered 65 stolen horses.

The Fort Griffin State Park features recreational facilities, as well as being the home of a Texas longhorn herd. There are ruins of several old fort buildings, three restored buildings and a visitor center.

Daily 8 a.m.–10 p.m. Admission $2 per car.

AUSTIN

GEORGE WASHINGTON CARVER MUSEUM, at 1165 Angelina Street by the Carver Library, opened in 1980 as the first black local history museum in Texas. The museum features changing exhibits on the black history and culture of Austin and Travis County, along with photos, artifacts, folk craft and art. One section is devoted to George Washington Carver.

Tues.–Wed. 10–6, Thurs. noon–8, Fri.–Sat. noon–5. Free.

DALLAS

MUSEUM OF AFRICAN-AMERICAN LIFE AND CULTURE, in Science Place II Building, 1620 1st Avenue, at Fair Park. Displays of traditional African sculpture and ceremonial objects, as well as exhibits of African-American artistic and historical materials.

Tues.–Sat. 9:30–5:30, Sun. 1–5. Free.

DALLAS MUSEUM OF ART, 1717 N. Harwood, has displays ranging from pre-Columbian to early African artifacts to contemporary works.

Tues.–Sat. 10–5, Thurs. 10–9, Sun. and holidays noon–5. Free.

FORT DAVIS

FORT DAVIS NATIONAL HISTORIC SITE lies at the

northern edge of the town of Fort Davis, near Limpia Canyon, off TX 17 and TX 118. Established in 1854, Fort Davis was a key post in the defense system of western Texas during the Indian Wars. In the course of the Apache Wars, Fort Davis was garrisoned from 1867 to 1881 by black troops of the 24th and 25th Infantry and the 9th and 10th Cavalry. In 1878 alone they covered a record 6,724 miles on scouting expeditions against the Apaches. One of the largest military campaigns undertaken by black troops from Fort Davis was against the Apache Chief Victorio in 1880. Victorio was forced to withdraw to Mexico, where he was killed in 1880.

Fort Davis has been superbly reconstructed to look much as it did during the days of the Indian Wars. There are completely and partially restored and refurnished buildings from enlisted mens' barracks to commissary, staffed with park interpreters in period dress. Each day at 11, 2 and 4, the sounds of an 1875 Dress Retreat Parade are heard throughout the grounds. A visitor center/museum has an entire exhibit area devoted to the Buffalo Soldier and their frontier role.

Daily 8–6 in summer, 8–5 in winter. Closed Jan. 1 and Dec. 25. $3 per car or $1 per person; under age 17 and over age 61 free.

FORT McKAVETT

FORT McKAVETT STATE HISTORIC SITE, on TX Farm Road 864, just south of U.S. 190 (west of Menard), is relatively untouched by time. Although this post, founded in 1852 to protect settlers from Indians, was abandoned in 1883, its ruins have been extensively restored. Interpretative exhibits may be seen in the original hospital building, including photos, dioramas and some 200 artifacts. Sergeant Emanuel Stance of F Troop, 9th Cavalry, became the first black trooper to earn the Medal of Honor while stationed at the fort.

Daily 8–5. Free.

FORT STOCKTON

OLD FORT STOCKTON is located in the historic downtown section of Fort Stockton, on Williams Street between
4th and 5th streets. When the 9th Cavalry arrived here in the
summer of 1867 they found the fort in ruins. During the Civil
War years it had been destroyed by Confederate troops. The
black troopers rebuilt the fort and, although unfamiliar with
the rugged west Texas prairie, they held their own against the
wily Apaches. One of the 9th's most impressive actions during 1868 was running down a band of Apaches who had
raided a wagon train near Fort Stockton and were headed
across the Rio Grande. The Buffalo Soldiers defeated the
Apaches in a running battle which left 25 Apache braves dead
and only two troopers wounded.

Many original buildings of adobe and handhewn limestone
from the fort still stand. Self-guiding tours available from the
Chamber of Commerce at 222 W. Dickinson Street.

Mon.–Fri. 9–noon and 1–5. Free.

FORT WORTH

THE CATTLEMAN'S MUSEUM, 1301 West Seventh
Street, covers the Texas cattle industry from the 1860s to the
present. Video shows, movies, exhibits and talking displays
tell the story of the longhorn cattle drives over the Western,
Goodnight and Chisholm trails, and of the cowboy who
made it all possible. Black cowboys followed the longhorns,
too. As many as 8,000 were engaged in the cattle industry
after the Civil War, some ex-slaves, some free men, and the
museum has exhibits on their life and work.

Mon.–Fri. 8:30–4:30. Closed holidays. Free.

HOUSTON

HOUSTON MUSEUM OF FINE ARTS, 1001 Bissonet Street, includes native arts from Africa and works by African-American artists.

Tues.–Sat. 10–5, Thurs. 10–9, Sun. 12:15–6. Closed holidays. Adults $2, senior citizens and students $1.

LYNDON B. JOHNSON SPACE CENTER is 25 miles southeast of downtown Houston, 3 miles east of I-45 on NASA Rd 1. Lt. Col. Guion (Guy) Bluford, Jr., trained at the Johnson Space Flight Center and became the first black American in space. He flew in the third mission of the space shuttle *Challenger* in 1983 as a mission specialist, conducting scientific experiments and launching satellites in space.

At the visitor center (Bldg. 2), lunar rocks, photos from Mars, movies of space flights and orbital rendezvous may be seen. Exhibits include spacecraft that have been to the moon. Films are shown daily in the auditorium.

Daily 9–4. Self-guided tours originate at Visitor Orientation Center daily except Christmas day. Free.

JACKSBORO

FORT RICHARDSON STATE HISTORIC SITE, 1 mile southwest of Jacksboro off U.S. 281, was built in 1867. The fort was one of the largest military stations in the country, and the northernmost in a chain of U.S. cavalry posts that were used to halt Indian raids. Three companies of the 10th Cavalry were garrisoned at Fort Richardson and served as escorts for General Sherman when he inspected the west Texas forts in 1871. Black troopers helped to arrest three Kiowa Indian chiefs for attacking a wagon train near Jacksboro and transported them to Fort Richardson for trial. Despite the fact that the fort's Buffalo Soldiers provided escorts for civilian mail and supply trains, the troopers were not welcome in the nearby wild frontier town of Jacksboro. The town was southern in its sympathies and had no liking for Yankees, especially black men in Union uniform.

Seven original buildings of the fort still stand, including the enlisted men's barracks which houses a museum of military history.

Museum open Wed.–Sun. 9–5. Adults 50 cents. Recreational facilities and grounds open daily, daylight hours. $2 per car.

SAN ANGELO

FORT CONCHO, established in 1867, is located just east of S. Oakes Street between Avenues C and D. The all-black 24th and 25th infantry regiments, as well as the 9th and 10th Cavalry, all served at Fort Concho at one time or another during their tours of duty in Texas. Colonel Benjamin Grierson and the 10th Cavalry made their headquarters here from 1875 to 1882.

During their tours of duty at Fort Concho, the Buffalo Soldiers not only fought Sioux, Apaches and Comanches, but helped with the first thorough exploration of Texas' Staked Plains.

Fort Concho is the best preserved of Texas' frontier military forts in existence today. The numerous buildings and parade ground have been restored with such authenticity that visitors can almost hear the past echoes of horses' hooves and see the flashing sabers. Exhibits tell the story of the fort and Indian campaigns, with displays on the Buffalo Soldiers garrisoned here.

Tues.–Sat. 10–5, Sun. 1–5. Adults $1.75, senior citizens $1, 6–18 years 75 cents.

SAN ANTONIO

THE ALAMO, the oldest of San Antonio's missions, is located downtown, near the river. When Texas declared independence from Mexico in 1836, the mission became a fortress. During Santa Ana's two week siege of the mission, 187 men fell before the onslaught of the Mexican Army. Two of the best-known defenders of the Alamo were Davy Crockett and James Bowie. Two of the least known were John, an African American who died in the siege, and Joe, the slave of Colonel W. B. Travis, a senior officer at the Alamo.

After his release by General Santa Anna, Joe reported the battle to a contingent of Texas troops in what is believed to have been the first description of the Mexican assault. Joe was later reenslaved but ran away from his new master.

The Alamo and its museums are open Mon.–Sat. 9–5:30; Sun. and holidays 10–5:30. Closed Christmas. Free.

INSTITUTE OF TEXAS CULTURES at HemisFair Plaza is concerned not with historic events but with the people who accomplished them. Twenty-six of the ethnic and cultural groups who helped settle Texas, including African-Americans, are featured in a rich variety of exhibits showing where they came from, what they did, their food and clothing, music and festivals. Multimedia show three times daily in the institute's central dome.

Tues.–Sun. 9–5. Free.

SHEFFIELD

FORT LANCASTER STATE HISTORIC SITE is 9 miles east of Sheffield on U.S. 290, 10 miles south of I-10. Established in 1855 as Camp Lancaster, the fort was positioned as a defense post against Indian attacks along the San Antonio-El Paso Road. K Company of the 9th Cavalry, while on patrol, were bivouacked at old Fort Lancaster in 1867 at Christmastime, and was first tested under fire when 900 Mexicans, Indians and renegade whites attacked the fort. K Company, at full strength, had only 75 men but three hours later they held the field, a tribute to the training of the black troopers, and their skill and courage.

A museum in the visitor center displays maps and artifacts of the fort.

Ruins, picnic area and museum open Wed.–Sun. 8–5. Free.

For further information about Texas, contact:

Texas Travel and Information Division
P.O. Box 5064
Austin, TX 78763-5064
512-462-9191

UTAH

SALT LAKE CITY

BRIGHAM YOUNG PIONEER MONUMENT is located at the southeast corner of Temple Square which is bounded by N. Temple, S. Temple, W. Temple and Main streets. Within the square are memorials and statues and the most famous buildings of the Church of Jesus Christ of Latter-day Saints. On the north face of the Brigham Young Pioneer Monument is a listing of the names and equipment of the pioneers who arrived at the site that was to become Salt Lake City on July 24, 1847.

Three of those early settlers were black men who went west with the first group of Mormons after they were driven out of settlements in the east because of their religious beliefs. Two were slaves, Hark Lay and Oscar Crosby, and the third, Green Flake, was a freeman.

Green Flake also helped bring a second company of Mormon settlers to Utah. This group included 34 black men and women. Green Flake stayed in Utah, owned his own farm, and helped to build the magnificent Salt Lake Temple. The land for the farm was given to Green Flake by Brigham Young as a reward for his services to the church.

Guided tours daily 8 a.m.–10 p.m., May–Sept., rest of year 9–9. Free.

CALVARY BAPTIST CHURCH, at 532 East 700 South,

was founded in the 1890s, and is the oldest African-American Baptist church in Utah. On permanent display inside is an exhibit of historic and contemporary works by African-American artists.

Daily 10–5. Free.

FORT DOUGLAS MILITARY MUSEUM is located on Fort Douglas Army Post, approximately 10 minutes from downtown Salt Lake City. Drive east on 4th South Street, continue as it becomes 5th South, and watch for the sign. Entrance is on Wasatch Drive which separates the fort from the University of Utah campus.

Fort Douglas was built during the Civil War to protect the vital overland mail route. Numerous conflicts flared up between the Mormon pioneers and the non-Mormon troops at the fort. In addition, there were periodic outbreaks of hostility between the army and the Ute Indians. Unlike many other posts, Fort Douglas was not abandoned at the end of the Indian troubles.

The all-black 9th Cavalry Regiment and the 24th Infantry Regiment served at Fort Douglas and there are displays in the museum on the Buffalo Soldiers, along with other exhibits on the military history of Utah. The 24th Infantry Regiment later fought at San Juan Hill in Cuba, during the Spanish-American War. Although it was mistakenly thought that black soldiers were immune to yellow fever, more soldiers in the 24th died from the disease in Cuba than from battle wounds.

Tues.–Fri. 10–4, Sat. 10–12 and 1–4. Closed holidays. A self guided walking tour of the historic fort begins at the museum. Visitors are only allowed to enter the museum. Free.

UNIVERSITY OF UTAH LIBRARY, at 400 South and University streets, has a special collection of research materials on blacks in Utah, including photographs and oral histories. The Special Western Americana Collection contains a videotape about the history of blacks in Utah.

Mon.–Fri. 8–5, Sat. 9–5. Free.

For further information about Utah, contact:

Utah Travel Council
Council Hall/Capitol Hill
Salt Lake City, UT 84114
801-538-1030

VERMONT

BENNINGTON

OLD FIRST CHURCH on Monument Avenue in Old
Bennington Village is one of the most beautiful of New England churches, built in 1805. Vermont was long in the fore-
front of the anti-slavery movement. In 1834 the Vermont
Anti-Slavery Society was formed with dozens of chapters
composed of Quakers and others. Nearly all Vermont newspapers opposed slavery and anti-slavery sermons were common in churches in the states, such as the Congregational Old
First Church. Although black ministers had been outlawed in
the majority of Southern states after the slave revolts of Denmark Vesey in 1822 and Nat Turner in 1831, they still
preached in Vermont. At the Old First Church the Reverend
Lemuel Haynes, a black minister, preached to a white congregation, as did Samuel Ward and Henry Highland Garnet
elsewhere.

Mon.–Sat. 10–noon and 1–4, Sun. 1–4, July 1–Columbus
Day; Sat.–Sun. Memorial Day–June 30. Donation.

BENNINGTON MUSEUM, W. Main Street, has a painting of black minister the Reverend Lemuel Haynes preaching
to a white congregation at the Old First Church in Bennington. In addition, it has copies of William Lloyd Garrison's abolitionist newspapers, *The Liberator* and *The
Journal of the Times*. Both newspapers aroused public opin-
ion against slavery.

Daily 9–5, March–Dec.; Sat.–Sun. 9–5 Jan.–Feb. Closed Thanksgiving. Adults $4, seniors and ages 12–17 $3.

GARRISON MARKER, Old Bennington Common, is located near the site where William Lloyd Garrison founded his first newspaper, *The Journal of the Times*. Garrison, a fiery abolitionist, helped found the American Anti-Slavery Society in 1833, and authored *The Declaration of Sentiments*, which advocated the complete abolition of slavery in the United States. The document was as revolutionary and shocking as the Declaration of Independence had been in its day.

The Anti-Slavery Society had black and white delegates. Three noted blacks who signed the declaration were James G. Barbados, James McCrummell and Robert Purvis. They demonstrated the courage of their convictions even though men and women who spoke out against slavery often had their lives threatened and their homes destroyed. At one time Garrison was set upon by a mob and dragged through Boston on the end of a rope.

BROWNINGTON

THE OLD STONE HOUSE MUSEUM, off Derby-Brownington Village Road, 2½ miles north of Orleans, is a four-story structure that was designed and erected by the Reverend Alexander Twilight. Stone by stone, between 1834–1836, Twilight and his neighbors split and hauled granite blocks until the building reached its full height, a remarkable achievement. Twilight then spent the next two decades instructing the region's school children within its thick walls.

Twilight was an enigmatic character, perhaps a mulatto, rather than black. However, Middlebury College claims him as America's first black college graduate in 1823 although Amherst and Bowdoin colleges both dispute that claim. Twilight was also said to have been the first black legislator, serving in the Vermont legislature in 1836. During 21 years of service, Twilight taught nearly 3,000 students, many of whom went on to successful lives out west.

Now the Old Stone House is a special museum displaying the tools and needlework and crafts, the furniture and art of the region's past. You can still see Alexander Twilight's desk and Bible.

The Old Stone House is part of the Brownington Village Historic District. Open daily 11–5, July–Aug.; Fri.–Tues. 11–5, May 15–June 30 and Sept. 1–Oct. 15. Adults $3, seniors $2, children under 12 $1.

FERRISBURG

ROWLAND T. ROBINSON HOUSE (ROKEBY MUSEUM) U.S. 7. In addition to being the home of a famous writer of Vermont folklore, and of four generations of the Robinson family, the Robinson home was also a very active Underground Railroad station. Fugitive slaves were housed in an upstairs room, entered by a secret stairway and through a long hall which only certain members of the household knew about. From the Robinson home the fugitives were spirited through Vermont and crossed the border at the town of St. Albans, into Canada.

There were a great many Underground Railroad stations in Vermont before the Civil War but Rokeby Museum is the only one open to the public. The house contains one of the most extensive collections of abolitionist memorabilia, periodicals, posters and broadsides, in Vermont. There are also furnishings and personal items spanning the Robinson family's occupancy of the house.

Guided tours at 11, 12:30 and 2, Thurs.–Sun. May–Oct. Adults $2, ages 13–18 and over 55 $1, ages 6–12, 50 cents.

MIDDLEBURY

VERMONT FOLKLIFE CENTER, The Gamaliel Painter House, 2 Court Street, sponsors programs and traveling exhibits designed to celebrate and preserve the powerful traditions and people of Vermont. One of those people is Daisy Turner who is the subject of the videotape, "On My Own," which spans her life from slavery to freedom on a hill farm in Vermont.
Mon.–Fri. 9–5. Donation.

For further information about Vermont, contact:

Vermont Travel Division
134 State St.
Montpelier, VT 05602
802-828-3236

VIRGINIA

ALEXANDRIA

THE ALEXANDRIA BLACK HISTORY RESOURCE CENTER, 638 North Alfred Street (entrance on Wythe Street), interprets the contributions of African Americans to Alexandria's history and culture from 1749 to the present. The black experience is documented with paintings, photographs, books and other memorabilia. The center offers lectures, tours, and activities relating to the history and accomplishments of black Americans.

Tues.–Sat. 10–4. Closed holidays. Free.

APPOMATTOX

APPOMATTOX COURTHOUSE NATIONAL HISTORICAL PARK is 3 miles northeast of Appomattox on VA 24. General Robert E. Lee's formal surrender to General Ulysses S. Grant at Appomattox on April 9, 1865, brought to a close a war that had caused the deaths of 94,000 Confederate soldiers and 360,222 Union soldiers. A total of 178,895 black men served with the Union army in 120 infantry regiments, 12 heavy artillery regiments, 10 light artillery batteries and 7 cavalry regiments. Of that total, 68,178 black men died in the war, either killed in action or from wounds and diseases.

Today Appomattox village has been restored to look as it

did on that fateful April day in 1865. The reconstructed courthouse serves as the visitor center with a museum and audio-visual programs. During the summer months, local inhabitants turn the village into a "living history" area, with black residents playing the roles of free blacks in village life during the Civil War.

Daily 9–5:30 June–Aug., rest of year 8:30–5. Closed federal holidays. Adults $1, seniors and under 17 free.

ARLINGTON

ARLINGTON CEMETERY, *see District of Columbia.*

DR. CHARLES RICHARD DREW'S HOME, 2505 First Street South, was the home from 1920 to 1939 of the noted black physician and teacher who discovered a method of preserving blood plasma. The house is a National Historic Landmark, not open to the public.

CHARLOTTESVILLE

ASH LAWN-HIGHLAND, about 2 miles past Monticello off VA 53 on County Road 795, is an estate once owned by President James Monroe. In addition to the mansion, there is a formal garden and a clapboard slave cabin and overseer's cottage, along with other outbuildings. Monroe was involved in the 1821 founding of the Republic of Liberia in Africa by free black Americans. Liberia was the beginning of an experiment by the American Colonization Society to repatriate former slaves to the home of their ancestors. The capital, Monrovia, was named for President Monroe.

There are guided tours of the main house and demonstrations of cooking and spinning, which would have been performed by women slaves when the Monroes lived at Ash Lawn. Visitors in the summer may see family shows and outdoor evening performances on the estate grounds.

Daily 9–6 March–Oct., rest of year 10–5. Closed Jan. 1, Thanksgiving and Dec. 25. Adults $6, seniors $5.50, ages 6–11 $2.

MONTICELLO, off I-64 (exit 24A) then ½ mile south on VA 20 and 1½ mile east on VA 53. Although it was the genius of Thomas Jefferson that led to the design of his home, Monticello, it was actually built largely by slave labor. Jefferson called slavery "the most unremitting despotism," but he never gave up his own slaves. Today Monticello is one of the most fascinating historic homes in America due, in part, to the many unusual devices invented by Jefferson that may be seen in the house.

One of those inventions is a special kind of music stand. Jefferson had a high regard for the musical talent of the black man. During colonial days it was a common sight to see black musicians entertaining at plantation parties and Monticello was no exception.

Visitors to Monticello are reminded by the tour guides of the vital role black servants played in the life of the plantation. The kitchen and slave quarters may be seen as part of the Mulberry Row exhibit adjacent to the Jefferson Museum.

Daily 8–5 March–Oct., rest of year 9–4:30. Closed Dec. 25. Adults $7, seniors $6, ages 6–11 $2.

THOMAS JEFFERSON VISITORS CENTER on VA 20 just south of exit 24 off I-64 has an exhibit called "Thomas Jefferson at Monticello" that focuses on Jefferson's domestic life, including the role played by his black servants.

Daily 9–5:30 March–Oct., rest of year 9–5. Closed Jan. 1, Thanksgiving and Dec. 25. Free.

FREDERICKSBURG

A brochure on the BLACK HISTORY OF FREDER-ICKSBURG may be received through the Department of

Tourism, 706 Caroline Street, Fredericksburg, VA 22401. *A few of the sites listed are:*

SHILOH OLD SITE BAPTIST CHURCH, 801 Sophia Street. Originally a church with white, slave and free black members, in 1854 it was sold to black Baptists who renamed it the African Baptist Church. After the building was destroyed by a flood in 1886, it was rebuilt and given its present name. Its minister, Lawrence A. Davies, was elected the first black mayor of Fredericksburg in 1976.

SLAVE AUCTION BLOCK, on corner of William and Charles streets, was used for the sale and hire of slaves in the decades before the Civil War. Slave ships arrived at the city dock on Sophia Street. Free blacks also lived in Fredericksburg, especially after the Revolutionary War, and were important to the industry of the area. Some worked as skilled blacksmiths, coopers and cobblers.

The DeBaptiste family of free blacks owned most of the east side of Charles Street in the first half of the 1800s. The family held a secret, illegal school for black youths in their house at the southeast corner of Amelia and Charles Street.

HAMPTON

FORT MONROE is in Hampton, on the peninsula across Hampton Roads from Norfolk. Built in 1819, the fort is shaped like a seven-pointed star and is surrounded by a water-filled moat. This was one of the few military posts not seized by the Confederacy at the outbreak of the Civil War and it became a haven for slaves escaping into Union lines. Union general Benjamin Butler treated the escaped slaves not as returnable property, but as captured "contraband of war." As a result, thousands of slaves became free more than a year before the Emancipation Proclamation. The able-bodied were put to work building roads, erecting fortifications, and as teamsters and foragers. Many of the "contraband" eventually saw combat duty in the Union army.

The Casemate Museum at Fort Monroe, Casemate 20 on Bernard Road, has a permanent exhibit on black history.

Daily 9–5. Closed federal holidays. Free.

HAMPTON UNIVERSITY was founded by General Samuel Armstrong and the Freedmen's Bureau in 1868 for the education of ex-slaves. Many of the beautiful buildings on the campus were constructed by students learning a trade; the magnificent Mansion House, built prior to 1868; the Wigwam, constructed in 1878 as a dormitory for American Indians; and Memorial Church built in 1886. Virginia Hall was "sung up" in 1874 by the Hampton Singers who toured the country much like the Jubilee Singers from Fisk University in Tennessee.

The Emancipation Oak still flourishes on campus. It was under this tree that Mary Peake, a free black woman, first taught children of former slaves in 1861.

Guided tours of the campus are offered.

COLLIS P. HUNTINGTON MEMORIAL LIBRARY at Hampton University has one of the oldest black research libraries in the United States. Its collection includes original slave handbills, pamphlets for and against slavery, and personal papers of Mary McLeod Bethune, George Washington Carver, Booker T. Washington, Martin Luther King, Jr., among many others.

THE HAMPTON UNIVERSITY MUSEUM is reached via Hampton University's County Street, exit off I-64. This museum houses one of the oldest collections of African art in this country, begun in 1868 and numbering about 2,700 pieces. Also at the museum are works by historic and contemporary black artists including one of Henry Ossawa Tanner's early paintings, *The Banjo Lesson,* and an impressive set of murals by Charles White titled *The Contribution of the Negro to American Democracy.*

The collection is particularly strong in works by Harlem Renaissance artists, some a gift from the Harmon Foundation. Most of the major black American artists of the twentieth century are represented.

Mon.–Fri. 8–5, Sat.–Sun. noon–4, Sept.–May; rest of year Mon.–Fri. 8–5. Closed Dec. 22–Jan. 1. Free.

JAMESTOWN

JAMESTOWN SETTLEMENT is next to Jamestown Island, on the Jamestown terminus of the Colonial Parkway, a road that runs from the Yorktown battlefield to Williamsburg to Jamestown. It was on August 20, 1619, at Jamestown colony that blacks first reached America, a year before the Pilgrims landed on Plymouth Rock. On that date in August, twenty black men arrived as indentured servants on a Dutch ship.

Some historians believe that these early black men were treated much like the white indentured servants who were sent to the colonies. After serving their time working on tobacco farms, they bought their freedom and some land of their own. By 1669, however, under the slave laws, black people who arrived at Jamestown were forced to serve in bondage for life. Most of the other Southern colonies also believed that they needed such slave laws, securing their black labor, in order to survive.

Today the recently renovated JAMESTOWN SETTLE-MENT MUSEUM tells the story of the first permanent English colony in America. Through artifacts, murals, colorful artwork, and scenes with life-size figures, visitors can learn about the English settlers and Indians as well as the black slaves who played such an important role in the everyday life of Jamestown.

There is also an excellent living-history program (except in January and February) with costumed interpreters demonstrating colonial life in a replica of Jamestown's original fort. There are also reproductions of the ships that brought the settlers to Jamestown.

Daily 9–5, extended hours June 15–Aug. 15. Closed Jan. 1 and Dec. 25. Adults $6.50, ages 6–12 $3. A combination ticket with the Yorktown Victory Center is available.

MOUNT VERNON

Mount Vernon is at the southern end of the George Washington Memorial Parkway, overlooking the Potomac River, 16 miles south of Alexandria. The home and burial place of President George Washington, Mount Vernon was a working farm which at one time employed 317 slaves. The farm was largely self-sufficient and a wide range of skills were necessary to make sure it ran smoothly. Most of these skills, including those in trades and crafts, such as blacksmiths, carpenters, gardeners, shoemakers, painters, brickmakers, herdsmen and coachmen, were provided by the labor of slaves.

The women slaves worked as house servants or at the Mansion House Farm, usually as spinners and weavers, and lived in the Spinning House Quarters. Wool, flax and cotton were grown on the farm. There were also black millers, coopers and distillers who worked at the mill about a mile from the mansion, and boatmen, who ran Washington's fishing operation.

Unlike some plantation owners, Washington recognized marriages between his slaves, and his personal physician was retained to provide medical treatment for the slaves.

Many of the 90 slaves who worked at the Mansion House Farm lived in the Greenhouse Quarters Complex which, like the Spinning House Quarters and the mansion itself, has been restored. About 50 yards southwest of Washington's tomb is the site of an old Mount Vernon burial ground for slaves. Their names are not recorded. The only person known to have been buried there is William Lee, General Washington's personal servant during the Revolutionary War.

In his will, Washington provided for the freedom of his slaves after Mrs. Washington's death and left detailed instructions for the care and support of the newly freed people.

Daily 9–5 March–Oct., rest of year 9–4. Adults $5, seniors $4, ages 6–11 $2.

NEWPORT NEWS

WAR MEMORIAL MUSEUM OF VIRGINIA, 9285 Warwick Boulevard in Huntington Park, has more than 50,000 military artifacts, covering every conflict America has seen from pre-revolutionary times to Vietnam, the most valuable collection of military memorabilia in the country today.

There is an impressive display on the black role in America's military history, with special emphasis on the all-black 10th Cavalry which served on the western frontier as well as in the Spanish-American War. The museum has educational programs, a military history film collection and a library/ archive which is open by appointment only.

Mon.–Sat. 9–5, Sun. 1–5. Closed Jan. 1, Thanksgiving and Dec. 25. Adults $2, seniors, military and ages 6–16 $1.

PETERSBURG

JOSEPH JENKINS ROBERTS MONUMENT, Halifax and South Sycamore streets, honors the black merchant who left Peterburg to become the first president of the new west African nation of Liberia. Liberia is the oldest republic in Africa and was founded by the American Colonization Society and free blacks in 1817.

PETERSBURG NATIONAL BATTLEFIELD PARK is

two miles east of Petersburg on VA 36. In June 1864 General Grant encircled Petersburg to cut off General Lee's supply lines and force the surrender of the Confederate capital at Richmond. The siege continued for a grim ten months. Among the troops involved were thirty-two black infantry regiments and two black cavalry units. In July a tunnel was dug beneath the Conferate lines and four tons of gunpowder were exploded, creating a huge crater. Federal troops, rushing forward, were trapped in the crater under deadly Confederate artillery fire; but the worst was yet to come.

General Edward Ferrero's all-black 4th Division was ordered forward into the crater. In an orgy of shooting, clubbing and bayoneting, the crater soon became choked with the dead and dying. The losses among the black troops were staggering: 209 killed, 697 wounded, and 421 missing. Altogether the Union had lost 3,798 men killed, wounded or missing in the incident.

Today the Petersburg battlefield is a 1,500-acre park which preserves and interprets the sites involved in the ten months of siege warfare. Many original earthworks remain, as well as many battle points, and there is a reconstruction of the tunnel to the crater in which so many white and black soldiers lost their lives. Exhibits along the way explain one of the most incredible and tragic episodes in the Civil War.

Daily 8 a.m.-dark. Closed Jan. 1 and Dec. 25.

Visitor center is at the park entrance, off VA 36, and contains exhibits on the Petersburg campaign, an audio-visual presentation, and battlefield relics. The four-mile self guiding battlefield tour begins here.

Daily 8–7 mid-June to late Aug., rest of year 8–5. $1 per person and $3 per car.

PORTSMOUTH

VIRGINIA SPORTS HALL OF FAME, 420 High Street.

Black Americans who have been inducted into this Sports
Hall of Fame include tennis player Arthur Ashe, Jr., football
greats Roosevelt Brown, Leroy Keyes, and Earl Faison,
among other noted black Virginia athletes. The hall displays a
collection of photos, plaques, personal equipment and biographical sketches.

Tues.–Sat. 10–5, Sun. 1–5. Free.

RICHMOND

JACKSON WARD, west of the capitol building and on the
north side of Broad Street, is a 22-block area of restored
nineteenth-century homes, and is one of the oldest black
neighborhoods in the United States, dating to the 1700s.
More than 100 of the buildings predate the Civil War. The
nation's first black-owned bank and insurance companies
were chartered here at First and Marshall streets, so that
Jackson Ward has been called the "Wall Street of Black America."

The area has been designated a National Historic Landmark and is the focus of bus and walking tours. Jackson Ward
was the home of some of America's most famous black people. Perhaps best-known was Bill "Bojangles" Robinson, who
was a star of the New York stage and of Hollywood movies,
and Charles Gilpin, the first noted black dramatic actor.
There is a statue of Bojangles at Adams and Leigh strets.

MAGGIE L. WALKER NATIONAL HISTORIC SITE at
110½ East Leigh Street is also in Jackson Ward. Despite being
physically handicapped, black, and female, Maggie L. Walker
founded in 1903 the first bank in the country started by a
woman. She also ran an insurance company, was the editor of
a newspaper, and was a concerned civic leader. The 22-room
red brick home in which she lived from 1904 to 1934 has been
restored with many original furnishings.

Wed.–Sun. 9–5. Closed Jan. 1 and Dec. 25. Free.

TASK FORCE FOR HISTORIC PRESERVATION AND THE MINORITY COMMUNITY is located in Jackson Ward, at 500 N. 3rd Street, and is a cultural center and historic society, with artifacts, oral histories and other documents relating to black life in Virginia and the United States. Mon.–Fri. 9–5. Free.

RICHMOND VISITORS INFORMATION CENTER at 1710 Robin Hood Road, just off I-95 and I-64 at exit 14, provides information and maps of the Jackson Ward area. Information for black heritage sightseeing tours can also be obtained here.

Center open daily 9–7 Memorial Day–Labor Day, rest of year 9–5. Closed Jan. 1, Thanksgiving and Dec. 25.

RICHMOND NATIONAL BATTLEFIELD PARK is 5 miles north of the park visitor center on U.S. 360. Many battles, large and small, took place around Richmond during 1864–1865 as the Union forces fought to gain possession of Richmond and the Confederate forces fought just as desperately to hold on. Many of these battles included black troops.

In July 1864 at Deep Bottom, Virginia, four black regiments withstood an enemy assault which took three hundred lives. Six weeks later at New Market Heights, a brigade of black troops helped take Confederate Fort Harrison. Later, Secretary of War Stanton said of the day's action: "The hardest fighting was done by the black troops." Thirteen Congressional Medals of Honor were awarded to black soldiers after the battle of New Market Heights.

Other battles near Richmond in which black troops engaged were the battle of Chaffin's Farm, with the 8th U.S. Colored Infantry (which had suffered such disastrous losses at Olustee, Florida), and in October, the battle at Darbytown Road, with the black 29th Connecticut Colored Infantry.

Richmond surrendered on April 3, 1865, and the all-black 5th Massachusetts Cavalry were among the first to enter the city.

CHAMBORAZO VISITOR CENTER, 3215 E. Broad

Street, contains exhibits, a slide program and movie, as well as brochures for a self-guiding tour of Richmond battlefield, its forts, breastworks and other landmarks.

Daily 9–5. Closed Jan. 1 and Dec. 25. Free.

FORT HARRISON VISITOR CENTER, in the Fort Harrison unit of the Richmond battlefield, has brochures and exhibits. The Fort Trail begins here.

Daily 9–5 June–Aug. Free.

VALENTINE MUSEUM, 1015 East Clay Street, has many exhibits on Afro-American history, as well as the life and history of Richmond.

Mon.–Sat. 10–5, Sun. 12–5; extended hours Memorial Day–Labor Day. Adults $3.50, seniors $3, students $2.75, ages 7–12 $1.50.

VIRGINIA MUSEUM OF FINE ARTS, 2800 Grove Avenue, one of the largest museums in the South, has excellent holdings of African works among its collection of ancient to contemporary art.

Tues.–Sat. 11–5, Thurs. until 10 p.m., Sun. 1–5. Closed legal holidays. Donation $2.

VIRGINIA UNION COLLEGE, 1500 North Lombardy Street, founded in 18ʿ5, is one of the many church-related colleges established after the Civil War for black students. The college has had many distinguished graduates, including the first black admiral in the U.S. Navy. Some of the historic buildings on campus are built of granite blocks hand-hewn by newly freed black men.

ROANOKE

BOOKER T. WASHINGTON NATIONAL MONU-MENT is 20 miles southeast of Roanoke via VA 116 south to Burnt Chimney, then VA 122 north. The man who was to become the best-known black educator in America was born a slave in 1856 in a cabin on the Burroughs Farm. During the summer, visitors can see the farm much as it appeared and was operated during Washington's boyhood. Costumed interpreters on summer weekends make lye soap, work tobacco, and churn butter, all the chores done on a nineteenth-century farm.

The visitor center has exhibits and a slide show on Washington's life, and provide a ¼-mile self-guiding Plantation Trail tour of the farm. Nature trails and picnic facilities are available.

Daily 8:30–5. Closed Jan. 1, Thanksgiving and Dec. 25. Admission $1, seniors and under 17 free.

HARRISON MUSEUM OF AFRICAN HERITAGE AND CULTURAL CENTER, 523 Harrison Avenue, N.W. (ground floor) has contemporary African-American art, traditional African art, and memorabilia of the Burrell-Harrison School, which was the first public high school for blacks in western Virginia.

The museum presents visual art exhibits, lectures, workshops, recitals, and historic exhibits.

Mon.–Fri. 10–5. Free.

WILLIAMSBURG

Colonial Williamsburg was begun in 1633 and was the capital of Virginia until 1780. When the capital moved to Richmond, Williamsburg became a small, sleepy college town and many of its historic buildings fell to ruin. In 1926, 88 of the historic buildings within the town were carefully and beautifully restored.

In the 1770s, half of the residents of Williamsburg were slaves and free blacks, although little notice was given to that fact by visitors to Williamsburg in the last years. Recently, however, a program has been set underway so that tourists visiting the town today can experience the most comprehensive interpretation of colonial black history in the United

States. Costumed interpreters act out scenes from "The Other Half," the daily colonial life of Williamsburg's black residents. Visitors can see where slaves and free blacks lived, what they ate, and what kind of work they did, as well as observing African-American cultural traditions such as music, dance, storytelling and religion, which helped the African-American cope with the institution of slavery. *Some of the sites to be visited are:*

WYTHE HOUSE, Palace Green, south of Prince George Street, was the home of George Wythe, a lawyer who firmly believed that "the birthright of every human being is freedom." He freed his slaves while he was still alive. Despite Wythe's efforts on behalf of black people, slaves were still regarded as property. They could not, for example, appear in court as a witness against a white man. Ironically, in 1806 when George Wythe was poisoned by his grand nephew, the black servant who witnessed the deed was not allowed to appear in court to testify against the murderer. The grand nephew was acquitted.

BRUSH-EVERARD HOUSE, east side of Palace Green, is more modest then the Wythe home, but this frame house has been carefully restored, complete with brick kitchen, wooden smokehouse, gardens and slave quarters in the scullery or kitchen.

African and eighteenth-century African–American music is performed behind the house in summer.

GOVERNOR'S PALACE faces the Palace Green. It was at this Williamsburg mansion that the talented black musician Si Gilliat played his violin at official state balls in the beautifully decorated ballroom. Candlelight concerts are still given for visitors in the evening at the Governor's Palace. The musicians are dressed in eighteenth-century style, with wigs and satin vests, much the same clothes as Si Gilliat might have worn.

VISITOR CENTER, northeast of the Governor's Palace, provides tickets, introductory film, and information about Williamsburg. Park at the visitor center and use the shuttle buses that leave for the historic area every few minutes. For information about group tours with special emphasis on black life in Williamsburg, contact 1-800-HISTORY.

There are admission tickets of various prices to historic sites within Williamsburg. The basic admission ticket provides admission to 12 exhibition buildings of your choice for $17, ages 6–12 $9.75. The Royal Governor's Pass provides admission to all exhibits, including the Governor's Palace, and can be used for up to 4 consecutive days, adults $21, ages 6–12 $11.25.

CARTER'S GROVE, 8 miles southeast of Williamsburg via U.S. 60 East, was once an estate of 300,000 acres and more than 1,000 slaves. The colonial mansion is furnished with antiques and some period reproductions, with various outbuildings. Of particular interest at this plantation is the recent opening of the slave quarters which marks the first time a major museum has interpreted the challenging issue of slave life on a colonial plantation. The life of a slave on a plantation was often different from that of the slave who lived in a town like Williamsburg. Black, costumed interpreters at Carter's Grove conduct tours through the slave cabins and tell what life was actually like for a house slave at Carter's Grove in colonial days.

Daily 9–5 March–Nov. and throughout the Christmas holiday season. Adults $7.

YORKTOWN

YORKTOWN VICTORY CENTER is on VA 238 near the Colonial Parkway and U.S. 17. At Yorktown on October 19, 1781, Lord Cornwallis surrendered to Washington and Lafayette after a ten-day siege, and the Revolutionary War was ended.

Black soldiers were among those present at the surrender.

One of them, a Rhode Islander named Bristol Rhodes, had lost an arm and a leg in the siege.

Multimedia exhibits and a film chronicle the events from the Boston Tea Party to the 1781 allied victory at Yorktown. In an outdoor encampment, costumed men portray daily life during the Revolutionary War with demonstrations of musketry, field medicine, cooking and crafts. Picnic facilities are available.

Daily 9–5, extended hours June 15–Aug. 15. Closed Jan. 1 and Dec. 25. Adults $5, ages 6–12 $2.50.

For further information about Virginia, contact:

Virginia Division of Tourism
1021 East Cary St.
Richmond, VA 23219
804-786-4484

Colonial Williamsburg Foundation
Box C
Williamsburg, VA 23187
804-229-1000

WASHINGTON

CENTRALIA

In 1850 George Washington, born in slavery but adopted by a white family, headed west with a wagon train to the Oregon Territory with his foster parents. Washington settled on a homestead along the Chehalis River. There he prospered and eventually founded a town called Centerville, now called Centralia (exit 82 off I-5). He built streets, churches and a public park, and sold lots at low prices to encourage new citizens. During the Panic of 1873, Washington, although he was then 76 years old, helped save his town by buying and shipping in food from other cities and providing jobs for the unemployed.

There are other towns in the West that were built by black men and women, towns like Boley, Oklahoma, and Nicodemus, Kansas, but perhaps no other owes so much to the strength and good will of one man alone.

George Washington is buried in Centralia Cemetery, not far from George Washington Park, at Pearl and Harrison streets.

TIMBERLINE LIBRARY, 110 South Silver Street, in front of George Washington Park, has material on the life of black pioneer George Washington. Between the library and the park is a plaque noting the accomplishments of unheralded black pioneers of the northwest.

Mon.–Thurs. 10 a.m. –9 p.m., Fri. Sat. 9–5. Free.

CHEHALIS

LEWIS COUNTY HISTORICAL MUSEUM, 599
Northwest Front Street, has an exhibit on the life of black
pioneer George Washington.
Tues.–Sat. 9–5. Free.

ILWACO

LEWIS AND CLARK INTERPRETIVE CENTER is in
Fort Canby State Park, 3 miles southwest off U.S. 101 at the
tip of Cape Disappointment. The center traces the 2½-year,
8,000-mile trek led by Lewis and Clark from St. Louis to the
Pacific Ocean. The exhibits portray medical treatment, foods,
entertainment, discipline and Indian contributions toward the
trip's success, with emphasis on the human aspects of the
expedition. Clark's black slave York, who accompanied the
expedition, is featured in many different ways in the center.
Multimedia presentation depicts the highlights of the journey.
Daily 9–5, May 7–Sept. 30. Free.

SEATTLE

DOUGLASS-TRUTH LIBRARY, 2300 East Yerler Way, is
one of the few libraries that has collected materials on the
little-known history of black pioneers in the Pacific Northwest. Because of its great distance from the South, there were
relatively few black immigrants to the northwest, but those
that did arrive discovered a freer life than they had known and
often encouraged family members to join them. Although
some black pioneers homesteaded, others contributed to the
growth of such cities as Seattle and Tacoma.
Mon.–Wed. 1–9, Thurs. 10–9, Sat. 10–6. Free.
MOUNT ZION BAPTIST CHURCH, 1634 19th Ave-
nue, had a black congregation as early as 1890. In 1975 the

congregation built a new church which is unique throughout the country for its remarkable architecture, using Afro-centric designs. Twelve unfinished wood beams support the building, representing the unfinished nature of African-American history. African religious themes may be seen in carvings around the pulpit. Eighteen stained glass windows portray important black historical and religious figures, from Nat Turner to Prince Hall, Sojourner Truth to Martin Luther King, Jr., and include one of Washington's own black pioneers, George W. Bush of Tumwater.

Mon.–Sat. 9–5. Sunday services 8 and 10:45.

SEATTLE ART MUSEUM, located in the center of Volunteer Park (may be entered at E. Galer and 15th Avenue E. or E. Prospect and 14th Avenue E.), has more than 40 acres of formal gardens. The Seattle Art Museum houses the world-famous Katherine White collection of African art.

Tues.–Sat. 10–5, Thurs. to 9, Sun. and holidays noon–5. Closed Thanksgiving and Dec. 25. Adults 42, ages 6–18 and over 61 $1. Free on Thurs.

TUMWATER

SIMMONS PARTY MEMORIAL, in Tumwater Falls Historical Park at the foot of Grant Street, is dedicated to those pioneers who endured the hazards of the Oregon Trail to start a new life in Puget Sound in 1845. Among the pioneers whose names are inscribed on the monument is George W. Bush.

Bush was a free black and a prosperous Missouri cattle trader who joined Michael Simmons and other white families in a wagon train west to Oregon in 1844 when Missouri banned free blacks from settling in the state. Having earlier explored the western wilderness with a French trader, Bush was welcomed as a guide. However, when the train reached Oregon, they learned that here, too, free blacks had been banned. The Simmons party took a vote and decided to go north with George Bush into what was then considered British territory and therefore had no restrictive black laws.

George Bush and his son, William Owen Bush, developed one of the most valuable farms in the territory, near the present city of Tumwater. During a near famine in the winter of 1852, Bush, rather than sell his wheat to speculators, distributed it among the hungry. Such was the respect with which Bush was held by the community that when his claim to the farm was threatened because he was black, his neighbors successfully petitioned Congress to confirm it in 1854.

A permanent display and a great deal of documentary information about George W. Bush may be found at the HENDERSON HOUSE MUSEUM, Tumwater Historic District, 602 DesChutes Way.

Mon.–Sat. 9–5, Summer; Mon.–Fri. 10–4, Winter. Donation.

For further information about Washington, contact:

Tourism Development Division
101 General Administration Building, AX-13
Olympia, WA 98504-0613
206-586-2088 or 1-800-544-1800

WEST VIRGINIA

CHARLESTON

BOOKER T. WASHINGTON MEMORIAL STATUE is located on the grounds of the state capitol on Kanawha Boulevard E., facing the Kanawha River. Washington is one of West Virginia's most famous citizens, having spent his boyhood in Malden, West Virginia. For his great achievements in advancing the status of the black race, Washington was elected to the Hall of Fame for Great Americans. A crusader for black education, he transformed Tuskegee Institute, Alabama, into a world-famous center for vocational training, the first black institution of its kind in the U.S.

Capitol is open Mon.–Sat. 8:30–4:30. Free.

WEST VIRGINIA STATE MUSEUM is in the Cultural Center in the Capitol Complex at Greenbrier and Washington streets. Located on the lower level of the Cultural Center, the museum traces West Virginia history from Indian migration to the early 1900s, including exhibits dealing with slavery, the exploits of the militant abolitionist John Brown and the Civil War in the state. The Cultural Center often offers black musical and cultural events and includes a library and theater.

Mon.–Fri. 9–8, Sat.–Sun. 1–5. Free.

CLIFFTOP

CAMP WASHINGTON-CARVER is on WV 1, adjacent to Babcock State Park. Named for the famous black leaders, the camp was built originally as a "Negro 4-H Camp" in 1937 to instruct young people in rural areas in agricultural skills and is on the National Register of Historic Places. Now operated by the West Virginia Department of Culture and History, it is home to an African-American Heritage Arts Camp which each summer provides workshops for students in literature, dance, music, visual arts and theater, striving to preserve and nurture the black cultural heritage.

Open from May–Sept. Contact Camp Washington-Carver, Route 1, Box 5, Clifftop, West Virginia 25831, for schedule of events.

OLD STONE HOUSE (TYREE TAVERN) is located 2 miles south of junction of U.S. 60 and WV 41. Built in 1824, this solid stone building served as a tavern and stagecoach way station to many famous pre-Civil War visitors such as Andrew Jackson, Henry Clay and Thomas Hart Benton. The tavern was also a site for slave auctions although slavery was practically non-existent in western Virginia. West Virginia split from Virginia at the beginning of the Civil War and joined the Union as a separate state in 1863. Furnished with rustic antiques, the Old Stone House is open to the public.

Daily 10–2 Jan.–Nov., 10–4 Dec. Free.

HARPER'S FERRY

HARPER'S FERRY NATIONAL HISTORICAL PARK covers 2,500 acres and is located at the confluence of the Potomac and Shenandoah rivers and at the junction of Maryland, Virginia and West Virginia. The important federal arsenal and armory at Harper's Ferry were the targets of abolitionist John Brown in October 1859. Accompanied by

18 of his 21-man army (5 of whom were black) Brown captured the arsenal. He had hoped that slaves would rise to join him in his raid and that he would then arm them from the arsenal. However, he and his men, after considerable bloodshed, were forced to withdraw to the engine house of the armory complex and use it as their fort. Unable to withstand the attack of Colonel Robert E. Lee and a force of 90 marines, Brown and the survivors of his army were compelled to surrender.

Ten of John Brown's men died at the fort, including two of his sons and two black men, Lewis Leary and Dangerfield Newby. Brown and six of his followers were tried for treason, convicted and hanged at Charles Town. One of those hanged was John Copeland, a black student from Oberlin College. Copeland wrote a friend before his death on the gallows, "I am not terrified by the gallows, which I see staring me in the face, and upon which I am soon to stand and suffer death for doing what George Washington was made a hero for doing."

Black history and the role played by blacks in the raid on Harper's Ferry is a dominant theme of the Harper's Ferry National Historical Park. *Some of the many historic buildings and sites that have been restored here are:*

JOHN BROWN MONUMENT which stands by the B & O Railroad and marks the original site of the firehouse where Brown and his men made their stand.

JOHN BROWN STORY MUSEUM, on Shenandoah Street, is located in the old brick armory firehouse where John Brown was captured. The National Park Service has an exhibit and film on John Brown's raid and a profile of each man involved in the raid.

Daily 8–5. Free

JOHN BROWN WAX MUSEUM on High Street portrays John Brown's violent exploits and scenes from his daring raid on Harper's Ferry with life-size tableaux and the latest technology of sound and animation.

Daily 9–5 April–Dec.; Sat.–Sun. 10–5 Feb.–March. Adults $2, ages 12–18 $1.50, ages 6–11, 75 cents.

VISITOR CENTER on Shenandoah Street is housed in five restored buildings and includes a museum. An exhibit in the museum tells of Storer College, one of the first schools established for freed slaves after the Civil War. Frederick Douglass was among the first trustees of the college. In 1906 W. E. B. DuBois held the second meeting of the Niagara Movement at Storer College, leading to the establishment of the NAACP.

There is also an orientation film on Harper's Ferry, and maps for walking tours of the town's historic sites are offered free of charge.

Living History programs are presented throughout the town.

Daily 8–6. Closed Dec. 25 and Jan. 1. Free.

Harper's Ferry National Historical Park is also a popular recreation area with hiking trails, fishing, canoeing and rafting trips. Park is open daily. Closed Dec. 25. Admission is $5 for each car, $2 for individuals.

KIMBALL

KIMBALL WAR MEMORIAL was built for black World War I War veterans in the 1920s. 370,000 black Americans served with the United States forces in World War I, a war that was supposed to make the world safe for democracy, although harsh Jim Crow laws were then in effect in America. Black men and women found little democracy or safety in either North or South at that time.

LEWISBURG

JOHN WESLEY METHODIST CHURCH, East Foster Street, was built in 1820, with a gallery in which the black congregation sat. After the Civil War, the church was taken over by five slaves and it is still a functioning black church today.

OLD STONE CHURCH is on Church Street, 2 blocks southwest of U.S. 60 and U.S. 219. The center of the town of Lewisburg has been designated a National Historic District, having more than sixty eighteenth- and nineteenth-century buildings of historic and architectural interest. The Old Stone Church was built of native stone in 1796. The original slave balcony can be seen inside with its beautiful hand-carved woodwork. It was because they were forced to sit separately from the white congregation that blacks were soon forming and building their own churches wherever possible.

Daily 9–4. Free.

MALDEN

AFRICAN ZION BAPTIST CHURCH at 4100 Malden Drive, founded in 1863 by ex-slaves, is regarded as the mother church for black Baptists in West Virginia. The present church was built in 1872 and remains largely unaltered. BOOKER T. WASHINGTON regularly attended this church when he lived in Malden as a boy. Malden was an industrial center and the young Washington, who was born a slave in 1856, was employed at the Malden Salt Works. Taken in by the Ruffner family, Washington was encouraged to attend Hampton Institute in Virginia, then came back to Malden to teach before returning once more to Hampton. There are a number of sites associated with Washington in the Malden Historic District, including a park named in his honor.

For further information about West Virginia, contact:

Division of Tourism
State Capitol Complex Bldg. 6
Room 564
2101 Washington St. E.
Charleston, West Virginia 25305
1-800-225-5982

WISCONSIN

GREEN BAY

GREEN BAY PACKER HALL OF FAME, 855 Lombardi Avenue, opposite Lambeau Field in the Brown County Veterans Memorial Arena. The newly renovated Hall of Fame tells the story of the Green Bay Packers from their beginnings in 1919 to the present when the team has become synonymous with the word football. Among the Packer Hall of Famers are such famous black players as Herb Adderley, Willie Davis and Willie Wood.

The story of the Packers is told in fascinating video productions, displays of uniforms, equipment, awards, photographs and memorabilia. Visitors can test their knowledge of Packer lore with electronic quiz games and a hands-on display on passing and place kicking.

Daily 9–6 July–Aug., rest of year 10–5. Closed Dec. 25. Adults $5, seniors $4, children 6–15 $3, children 5 and under free.

JANESVILLE

THE TALLMAN HOUSE, 440 N. Jackson Street (on U.S. 14 Business, 2 blocks northeast of junction with U.S. 51), was built by William Tallman, a successful land speculator and ardent abolitionist. Abraham Lincoln was a guest in his lavish, twenty-six room house in 1859. The house also sheltered some not-so-famous guests—escaped slaves.

When it was safe for slaves to come into the house, a lantern signal would be given at a window on the second floor. A fugitive would be hidden in the basement or the servants' bedrooms in the back wing. One of the bedrooms had a steep staircase concealed in a closet. If an alarm was raised, the fugitive would climb up the staircase to a small room in the attic, until it was safe to move on. Sometimes the escaped slave's next stop was the Milton Inn in Milton, Wisconsin.

The Tallman House, completely furnished, is now open to the public. There is a visitor center and museum of local history housed in the former barn.

Tours on the hour Tues.–Sun. 11–4, June–Aug.; Sat.–Sun. only in May and Sept. Adults $3, seniors $2.50, ages 5–18 $1.50.

MADISON

THE STATE HISTORICAL SOCIETY OF WISCONSIN, 816 State Street, has one of the most important collections of documents in the field of civil rights, as well as materials on slavery and black participation in the Civil War. The collection is open to the public.

Mon.–Sat. 8–5. Free.

MILTON

MILTON HOUSE MUSEUM, 18 S. Janesville Street, was built in 1844 as an inn and was connected to a log cabin by an underground tunnel. Before the Civil War, the Milton Inn served as a station on the Underground Railroad. The basement entrance to the tunnel was hidden behind sacks of grain. When pursuers appeared at the inn, the slaves would escape through the tunnel. At the other end, a small trapdoor opened from the floor of the log cabin leading to the tunnel below. There were no steps. The slaves had to use a rope to climb out.

The Milton Inn, log cabin, and underground passageway have been presrved as historic landmarks, along with a restored general store and livery stable.

Tues.–Sun. 11–4, June 1–Labor Day. Adults $3, ages 5–18 $1.75.

MILWAUKEE

AMERICA'S BLACK HOLOCAUST MUSEUM, 2479 Martin Luther King Drive, is a very new museum, patterned after the Jewish Holocaust Museum. Through books on slavery and racism, paintings, photographs of lynchings of black people, and various artifacts ranging from slavery's African beginnings to the Reconstruction period after the Civil War, the museum shows how Africans endured their own form of holocaust in America during and after their days of slavery.

Mon.–Sat. 9–5. Sundays by appointment. Closed some holidays. Adults $1.50, children under 12, 75 cents.

MILWAUKEE ART MUSEUM, 750 N. Lincoln Memorial Drive, in its collection of nineteenth- and twentieth–century art, also has a small collection of paintings by black American artists, including works by Henry Ossawa Tanner and contemporary sculpture by Richard Hunt.

Tues.–Wed. and Fri.–Sat. 10–5, Thurs. noon–9, Sun. noon–5. Closed holidays. Adults $3, seniors and students $1.50, under 12 free with an adult.

MILWAUKEE PUBLIC MUSEUM at 800 W. Wells Street, has exhibits on natural history as well as the cultural development of different civilizations. Visitors can enter various environmental exhibits, a tropical rain forest, dinosaur swamps, and sites in Africa, Asia and Middle America. Particularly outstanding are the collections of American Indian and African artifacts.

Tues.–Sun. 9–5, Mon. noon–9. Adults $4, ages 4–17 $2.

WAUKESHA

LYMAN GOODNOW'S GRAVE, Prairie Home Cemetery. There were many reasons why a slave sought freedom. Sixteen-year-old Caroline Quarrels made her break for freedom after her mistress, in a fit of temper, cut off Caroline's long, shining black hair. Caroline fled from Missouri, pursued by slave catchers when her mistress put up a reward of $300 for Caroline's return.

Underground conductors passed Caroline along from one station to another. At Waukesha, Wisconsin, an abolitionist stronghold, Lyman Goodnow escorted Caroline the last 600 miles by night to safety in Detroit.

Today there is a marker in Cutler Park honoring Lyman Goodnow, who conducted the first slave through Wisconsin to Canada.

THE WAUKESHA COUNTY MUSEUM, 101 W. Main Street, has a good deal of research material dealing with the Underground Railroad which was very active throughout Wisconsin before the Civil War. The abolitionist newspaper, the *American Freeman*, was published in Waukesha between 1844 and 1848.

Tues.–Sat. 9–4:30, Sun. 1–5. Closed holidays. Free.

For further information about Wisconsin, contact:

Department of Tourism
123 West Washington Ave.
Madison, WI 53707
1-800-432-8747

WYOMING

BUFFALO

JIM GATCHELL MEMORIAL MUSEUM, 100 Fort Street, houses some 10,000 artifacts of Indians, settlers and soldiers, including extensive coverage on the Johnson County Cattle War of 1892. The conflict was between big cattlemen trying to drive out the farmers, or "nesters," coming into the territory. The United States Army finally had to step in to restore order, using Buffalo Soldiers of the 9th Cavalry Regiment.
Daily 9–9, June 1–Sept. 6. Closed July 4. Free.

FORT LARAMIE

FORT LARAMIE NATIONAL HISTORIC SITE is 3 miles southwest of the town of Fort Laramie. Like Fort Douglas in Utah, Fort Laramie, built in 1834, was an important outpost on the westward trek. All the major emigrant trails came together at this point and followed the same route west. There are a number of trails running into Fort Laramie and a number branch off from South Pass later, but for a 250-mile stretch, "everyone went westering together," white and black.
Some went west as slaves, such as Alvin Coffey, who earned enough money in the gold fields of California to buy his

family's freedom. Others were free blacks, like wagon guide
Green Flake, who led one of the Mormon caravans to Utah,
and black farmers George Bush and George Washington who
left the midwest to seek a new free life in the Northwest.

There is a museum among the restored historic buildings at
Fort Laramie with artifacts illustrating the civilian, military
and Indian history of the northern plains and the trail west.
From June through mid-August there are living history demonstrations of military and civilian life at the fort in the 1870s.

Daily 8–7 June 1–Labor Day, rest of year 8–4:30. Closed
holidays. Adults $1.

LANDER

THE FORT WASHAKIE BLOCKHOUSE is located at
the Windriver Indian Reservation, WY 287, 18 miles northwest of Lander. From 1880 through 1890, black troops of the
9th and 10th Cavalry regiments served at the fort. The 9th,
while stationed there, rescued a unit of infantry from Fort
Steele, which was being attacked by a Ute war party. They
drove off the Indians and went on to construct Fort Du-
schesne in Utah.

Daily April–June, 9–5. Free.

RAWLINS

OLD FORT STEELE is 15 miles east of town off I-80.
Only ruins remain of this fort, built in 1868 to protect railroad workers and settlers. Rawlins in its early days was a wild
frontier town and often vigilante justice prevailed. The black
9th Cavalry Regiment was among those garrisoned at Fort
Steele.

Open daily. Free.

For further information about Wyoming, contact:

Wyoming Div. of Tourism
I-25 at College Drive
Cheyenne, WY 82002
1-800-225-5996